Nietzsche's *Human, All Too Human*

Edinburgh Critical Guides to Nietzsche
Series editors: Keith Ansell-Pearson and Daniel Conway

Guides you through the writings of Friedrich Nietzsche (1844–1900), one of modernity's most independent, original and seminal minds

The Edinburgh Critical Guides to Nietzsche series brings Nietzsche's writings to life for students, teachers and scholars alike, with each text benefitting from its own dedicated book. Every guide features new research and reflects the most recent developments in Nietzsche scholarship. The authors unlock each work's intricate structure, explore its specific mode of presentation and explain its seminal importance. Whether you are working in contemporary philosophy, political theory, religious studies, psychology, psychoanalysis or literary theory, these guides will help you to fully appreciate Nietzsche's enduring significance for contemporary thought.

Books in the series
Nietzsche's *The Birth of Tragedy from the Spirit of Music*, Tracy B. Strong and Babette Babich
Nietzsche's *Philosophy in the Tragic Age of the Greeks*, Sean Kirkland
Nietzsche's *Unfashionable Observations*, Jeffrey Church
Nietzsche's *Human, All Too Human*, Ruth Abbey
Nietzsche's *Dawn*, Katrina Mitcheson
Nietzsche's *The Gay Science*, Robert Miner
Nietzsche's *Thus Spoke Zarathustra*, Charles Bambach
Nietzsche's *Beyond Good and Evil*, Daniel Conway
Nietzsche's *On the Genealogy of Morality*, Robert Guay
Nietzsche's *The Case of Wagner and Nietzsche Contra Wagner*, Ryan Harvey and Aaron Ridley
Nietzsche's *Twilight of the Idols*, Vanessa Lemm
Nietzsche's *The Anti-Christ*, Paul Bishop
Nietzsche's *Ecce Homo*, Matthew Meyer
Nietzsche's *Late Notebooks*, Alan Schrift

Visit our website at edinburghuniversitypress.com/series-edinburgh-critical-guides-to-nietzsche to find out more

Nietzsche's *Human, All Too Human*

A Critical Introduction and Guide

Ruth Abbey

EDINBURGH
University Press

Edinburgh University Press is one of the leading university presses in the UK. We publish academic books and journals in our selected subject areas across the humanities and social sciences, combining cutting-edge scholarship with high editorial and production values to produce academic works of lasting importance. For more information visit our website: edinburghuniversitypress.com

© Ruth Abbey, 2020

Edinburgh University Press Ltd
The Tun – Holyrood Road
12(2f) Jackson's Entry
Edinburgh EH8 8PJ

Typeset in 11/13 Bembo by
IDSUK (DataConnection) Ltd, and
printed and bound by CPI Group (UK) Ltd,
Croydon, CR0 4YY

A CIP record for this book is available from the British Library

ISBN 978 1 4744 3081 4 (hardback)
ISBN 978 1 4744 3083 8 (webready PDF)
ISBN 978 1 4744 3082 1 (paperback)
ISBN 978 1 4744 3084 5 (epub)

The right of Ruth Abbey to be identified as the author of this work has been asserted in accordance with the Copyright, Designs and Patents Act 1988, and the Copyright and Related Rights Regulations 2003 (SI No. 2498).

Contents

Acknowledgements — viii
Chronology — ix
Abbreviations — xii

Introduction — 1
   Style — 3
   Enlightenment — 6
   Epistemology-plus — 13
   Structure — 14
   Chapter summary — 16

1. Of First and Last Things — 21
   Historical philosophy — 21
   Epistemology-plus — 25
   Impediments to truth — 28
   Free spirits — 32
   Conclusion — 34

2. On the History of the Moral Sensations — 36
   The origins of morality — 37
   Psychology — 42
   The historical and the psychological — 46
   The ego and its own — 47
   Regarding others — 50
   Free will — 53

3. The Religious Life	58
A scientific view of religion	58
Christianity	61
Paragons of Christianity	65
Beyond Christianity	65
4. From the Souls of Artists and Writers	69
Who and what?	69
Art and science	71
The genius	73
5. Signs of Higher and Lower Culture	80
Conservatism and change	81
Free spirits	83
Ingenious	85
Contours of higher culture	88
6. The Human in Society	98
The French moralists	99
Amour-propre	101
Unsocial sociability	104
Friendship	107
7. Woman and Child	110
The female intellect	111
Courtship and marriage	115
Parenthood	120
Free spirits	123
Rée on women	125
8. A Glance at the State	129
Democracy and equality	130
Religion and politics	136
Socialism and nationalism	139
Revolution	142
Politics and culture	144
9. Conclusion to HAH: Alone with Oneself	149
10. *Mixed Opinions and Maxims*	157
Of first and last things	158
On the history of the moral sensations	163
The religious life	167

From the souls of artists and writers	171
Woman and child	183
A glance at the state	186
Conclusion	189
11. *The Wanderer and his Shadow*	190
The protagonists	191
Care of the self	195
Free will	200
Equality	206
Punishment	208
Art	210
Politics	216
Etcetera	221
Glossary of Key Terms	225
Guide to Further Reading on *Human, All Too Human*	229
Bibliography	231
Index	237

Acknowledgements

First and foremost I thank Keith Ansell-Pearson and Dan Conway for inviting me to write this book. Gratitude is owed also to the two anonymous reviewers of the preliminary proposal for their encouragement and insightful suggestions for how to improve. Anna Gallagher heroically read the draft of the MS, carefully noting my errors and making suggestions from her invaluable perspective. The book is better for her contribution.

Thanks are also due to Melissa Anderson, Erica Brown, Paul Keyser, Mary Jean Kraybill, Sarah Lauzen, Blake Levinson, Michele Lowrie, Ainat Margalit, Katharine Mershon, Sophie Phillips, Theresa Ricke-Kiley, Fran Spaltro and Susanne Wengle. Thanks too to my family and friends in Australia – Lisa Abbey, Chris Abbey, Marilyn Abbey, Bec Abbey, Hayden Abbey, Jo Crawford, Melinda Freyer, Cecily Hunter and Catherine Kovesi. You might not even know it, but each of you in your own way helped me through the difficult time that coincided with the writing of this book.

My beloved feline friends, Spunkee and Renee, also lit my way, and tiny orphan Scottie was present for the penultimate phase. My last book included a dedication to the homeless cats of Hyde Park Cats. Still they come, as sweet and inspiring as ever. I work for the day when there won't be any homeless feline dedicatees for any of my books.

Chronology

1844	Nietzsche is born on 15 October in the small village of Röcken in the Prussian province of Saxony, the son and grandson of Protestant clergymen.
1849	Nietzsche's father dies.
1858–64	He attends the Gymnasium Schlpforta, one of the most famous boarding schools in Germany.
1864	Begins study at the University of Bonn in theology and classical philology.
1865	Transfers to Leipzig University, following his philology professor F. W. Ritschl. He first reads Schopenhauer's *The World as Will and Representation*.
1866	First reads Lange's *History of Materialism*.
1868	Meets Richard Wagner for the first time.
1869	With the support of Ritschl, Nietzsche appointed Extraordinary Professor of Classical Philology at the University of Basel without yet earning his doctorate. Begins frequent visits to the Wagners at Tribschen, on Lake Lucerne.
1870	Volunteers as a medical orderly in the Franco-Prussian War, but contracts severe illnesses and returns to Basel within two months.
1872	Publishes his first book, *The Birth of Tragedy Out of the Spirit of Music*, which is sharply criticised by other philologists.

1873–74	Publishes the first three *Unfashionable Observations*, which mark Nietzsche's increased movement away from his philological training. Relationship with Wagner begins to sour.
1876	Publication of the final *Observation*, 'Richard Wagner in Bayreuth', timed to coincide with the Bayreuth Festival. Nietzsche attends the Festival and is disgusted by it.
1878	Volume 1 of *Human, All Too Human* appears, beginning what scholars consider to be Nietzsche's middle period, influenced by Voltaire. Friendship with Wagner ends.
1879	Publishes volume 2, part 1 of *Human, All Too Human: Assorted Opinions and Maxims*. Health problems force Nietzsche to resign from Basel (with a pension), and he spends the next ten years in Swiss and Italian boarding houses.
1880	Volume 2, part 2 of *Human, All Too Human: The Wanderer and his Shadow* appears.
1881	Publication of *Dawn: Thoughts on the Presumptions of Morality*.
1882	Publishes *The Gay Science*, books 1–4. In April travels to Rome, meets Lou Salomé, and proposes marriage to her. She declines and the relationship ends badly.
1883	Writes and publishes the first and second parts of *Thus Spoke Zarathustra: A Book for All and None*. Wagner dies.
1884	Completion of third part of *Zarathustra*. Breaks with his sister Elizabeth over her fiancé's anti-Semitism.
1885	Final part of *Zarathustra* circulated privately.
1886	Publishes *Beyond Good and Evil: Prelude to a Philosophy of the Future*. New publisher reissues *Birth of Tragedy* and *Human, All Too Human*, with new prefaces by Nietzsche.
1887	Publishes *On the Genealogy of Morality: A Polemic*. Also reissues *Daybreak* and publishes expanded edition of *The Gay Science*.

1888	Publishes *The Case of Wagner* and writes his final four short books: *Twilight of the Idols*, *The Antichrist*, *Ecce Homo* and *Nietzsche contra Wagner*.
1889	Suffers a physical and mental collapse in Turin and never recovers. After being briefly institutionalised, he spends the remaining years of his life in his mother's and sister's care.
1894	Elizabeth founds the Nietzsche Archive, which is eventually moved to Weimar.
1900	Dies on 25 August in Weimar.

Abbreviations

BGE	*Beyond Good and Evil*, Nietzsche 2002
BT	*The Birth of Tragedy*, Nietzsche 1999
D	*Dawn: Thoughts on the Presumptions of Morality*, Nietzsche 2011
EH	*Ecce Homo*, in Nietzsche 2005
GM	*On the Genealogy of Morality*, Nietzsche 1994
GS	*The Gay Science*, Nietzsche 2001
HAH	*Human, All Too Human*, Nietzsche 1995
MOM	*Mixed Opinions and Maxims*, in Nietzsche 2013
WS	*The Wanderer and his Shadow*, in Nietzsche 2013

Introduction

> However far human beings may reach with their knowledge, however objective they may seem to themselves to be: in the end, they still carry away nothing but their own biography. (HAH 513)

Peruse any biography of Nietzsche and you will readily see what a turbulent time in his life it was when he was working on *Human, All Too Human*.[1] Starting around the middle of 1876, several significant changes were either underway or intensifying. Among the most important was his gradual disentanglement from his formerly close relationship with Richard and Cosima Wagner. Nietzsche was finding his erstwhile mentor's religious tendencies, nationalism and prodigious egotism increasingly insufferable. Having been an early enthusiast for the philosophy of Arthur Schopenhauer, Nietzsche was also rethinking the value of his philosophy. These two major developments are themselves connected, because admiration for Schopenhauer was one of the things that united Nietzsche to Wagner.[2] After the incredible speed with which he had entered the profession, Nietzsche was having significant doubts about his propensity for an academic

---

[1] Unless noted, Hayman (1980), Hollingdale (1999) and Young (2010) provide the bases for the biographical information used here. For a very detailed account of this time in Nietzsche's life, see D'Iorio (2016).
[2] As Ronald Hayman says, 'If the inevitable breach with Wagner had not come so soon, it might have taken Nietzsche longer to emancipate himself from Schopenhauer and the tradition of idealism' (1980: 190).

career.[3] His health was poor: he suffered from blinding headaches and debilitating gastrointestinal problems on a recurring basis. At a few points his health was so bad that he felt close to death. He moved from place to place in search of a conducive climate and affordable accommodation (Handwerk 2013: 557). But during this period he was also meeting new friends or consolidating relatively new friendships, principal among them Malwida von Meysenbug[4] and Paul Rée.[5] At this point Nietzsche also imagined himself as a candidate for marriage and so was prospecting for a suitable wife.[6]

In addition to all this turmoil in his personal life, this was a period of immense intellectual transition and fermentation for Nietzsche. As Richard Schacht remarks, HAH is 'very much the product of a mind in transition, moving in many different directions and in many different ways' (1996: xi).[7] This was also a very productive time in Nietzsche's scholarly life. The work originally titled *Human, All Too Human* was published in early 1878. *Mixed Opinions and Maxims* appeared in 1879 and *The Wanderer and his Shadow* in 1880. HAH also marks the beginning of what is often called Nietzsche's middle period (which ends with the conclusion of Book IV of *The Gay Science*). This periodisation comes

---

[3] He resigned from his teaching position at Basel by letter on 2 May 1879, citing chronic ill health with no prospects for full recovery. The university's governing body approved his request on 14 June that year, effective 30 June. They awarded him an annual pension for six years (Levy 1985: 119–21; cf. Handwerk 2013: 556).

[4] Nietzsche met von Meysenbug through Wagner's circle in the early 1870s (Hollingdale 1999: 88).

[5] Hollingdale records that Rée was a non-student auditor of Nietzsche's 1873 lecture series on the pre-Platonic philosophers (1999: 90).

[6] He had proposed, by letter, to Mathilde Trampedach on 11 April 1876. Four days later he withdrew his offer, again by letter, realising, no doubt with some assistance from her rejection, how hasty and inappropriate it was (Leidecker 1959: 67–8; cf. Hollingdale 1999: 95). Before that month was out, however, Nietzsche was writing to Elisabeth outlining the help that von Meysenbug was giving him in finding a wife (Hollingdale 1999: 109). As Hollingdale says, 'it is at odds with received opinion about Nietzsche, and yet it is true, that for much of his life he was on the look-out for a wife' (1999: 95). Although it was probably less true for the later years of his life, it was certainly true at this time. As Hollingdale also points out, Nietzsche was experiencing the 'all my friends are getting married' syndrome between 1874 and 1877 (1999: 95).

[7] Ansell-Pearson (2018: 24) also quotes this.

INTRODUCTION 3

from one of the first interpretive works about Nietzsche – Lou Salomé's *Friedrich Nietzsche in seinen Werken* – published in 1894. Indeed, Salomé originated the idea that three distinct periods can be discerned in Nietzsche's corpus.[8] Whatever one thinks about this periodisation, and however much similarity or difference one finds among the five works of the middle period, it cannot be denied that HAH instigates some important changes that differentiate it from Nietzsche's previous works.[9] Some of these innovations become, moreover, permanent features of his work. These include his self-representation as a psychologist,[10] his genealogical excavations of morality,[11] and his appeal to fellow good Europeans to overcome the parochialism and antagonism of nationalism. With this he sloughs off the preoccupation with national greatness that characterised *The Birth of Tragedy*.

Style

At a very basic level, the text of HAH looks different from the four long essays that comprise the *Untimely Meditations*, marked as it is by breaks between pieces of writing of different lengths and peppered as it is with aphorisms (Hill 2007: 37; Franco 2011: 13).[12] As Thomas Brobjer says, with the advent of HAH Nietzsche 'went from writing essays to writing aphorisms' (2008a: 62). Brobjer suggests that this reflects Rée's influence, for Rée's own collection of aphorisms, *Psychological Observations* [*Psychologische Beobachtungen*], had been published in 1877. In addition to writing aphorisms, Rée

---

[8] On the scholarly neglect of the middle period, see Abbey (2000) and Ansell-Pearson (2018). For information on some recent scholarship on these works, see Abbey (2014).
[9] See Acharya (2015) for an argument about continuity between the earlier works and HAH, at least on the issue of the role of science and its relationship to culture. He detects a shift in emphasis rather than a radical break.
[10] See, for example, BGE, Chapter 9, 269.
[11] Cf. Hayman (1980: 199), Morrison (2003) and Young (2010: 249).
[12] I don't agree with Franco's claim that each numbered paragraph has its own discrete argument. In some cases the passages need to be read together to fully grasp their point. As Franco himself says shortly after, the aphorisms 'are not simply isolated or disconnected insights' (2011: 15). And it is not the case, as Franco says (2011: 13), that each passage has its own title. Some remain untitled.

also wrote about their importance.¹³ Yet while many commentators call HAH aphoristic, the first real aphorism does not appear until section 66, nearly halfway through chapter 2. Aphorisms dot the work from then on until the first sustained run of them appears at the start of chapter 6. The practice of opening the chapter with a string of aphorisms is repeated in chapters 7 and 9, with the latter containing the largest number of genuine aphorisms in HAH. Yet the aphorism turns out to be just one of many styles deployed in HAH. Nietzsche also uses numbered and titled passages, most of which are paragraph-length while some occupy a page or more.¹⁴ What HAH really inaugurates is, therefore, Nietzsche's stylistic diversity: that 'most manifold art of style' upon which he prides himself in *Ecce Homo*¹⁵ starts here. This stylistic diversity is further enhanced when WS stages brief dialogues – between the Wanderer and his Shadow, Pyrrho and the old man (WS 213) and unnamed speakers (WS 71, 90).¹⁶

One reason for the stylistic diversity that begins with HAH is that while the aphorism is well suited to fine-grained analyses of personality and to the communication of specificity, this form cannot serve all of Nietzsche's scholarly purposes. It is, for example, singularly inhospitable to the times when his analysis takes a broad trajectory in moral observation and speculation. Reborn in a limited arena – the salon – the aphorism cannot bear the historical perspective that attracts Nietzsche and that he insists is essential to

---

[13] Other possible influences include Lichtenberg (Brobjer 2008a: 63), Schopenhauer, La Rochefoucauld and Chamfort. Handwerk also points to the similarities with Schopenhauer (Nietzsche 1995: 378). But Brobjer believes that Rée's influence is the strongest (2008a: 41, 64).

[14] Of the three works considered here, MOM is the most aphoristic, with around three items appearing on average on each page. HAH and WS have closer to two items per page, on average.

[15] 'Why I Write Such Excellent Books', Section 4.

[16] What Carol Diethe says about GM applies also to HAH: 'Nietzsche is often referred to as an "aphoristic" writer, but this falls short of capturing the sheer variety of forms and styles he adopted. In fact, the number of genuine aphorisms in his works is relatively small; instead, most of what are called Nietzsche's "aphorisms" are more substantial paragraphs which exhibit a unified train of thought (frequently encapsulated in a paragraph heading indicating the subject matter), and it is from these building blocks that the other, larger structures are built in more or less extended sequences' (Nietzsche 2007: xv).

the advancement of knowledge. His longer purview often requires lengthier argument and illustration (or allusion and assertion) than the aphorism can sustain. This explains why, when he wants to emphasise the history of moral designations or exemplify an alternative ethic, he typically reverts to the longer paragraph form, which can occupy two or more pages and which might be better called an essayette or reflection than an aphorism (cf. Nietzsche 1995: 377).[17]

But the topic itself is not determinative of the genre: many issues are approached via a multitude of styles such that Nietzsche will discuss them in an aphorism and a paragraph and a longer passage. As we learn from Robin Small, this too is characteristic of Rée's work, for while the aphorism can deliver short sharp psychological observations to great effect and with great efficiency, it is not useful for the sort of extended and historical analysis Rée moved towards in his next book, *The Origin of the Moral Sensations* (Small 2005: 56, 58). So both thinkers should be seen as including aphorisms in their repertoire but not confining themselves to this vehicle in any strict sense (cf. Small 2005: 59). Nietzsche's adoption of the mixed genre mode is just one of several ways in which his burgeoning friendship with Rée marks his work at this time.

Thanks to Small we have a detailed and highly informative study of their philosophical friendship. Both advocate a historical approach to knowledge, both admire the natural sciences as a paradigm for knowledge, and both strive to make the study of morality more scientific. But it would be too simplistic to say that Nietzsche fell under Rée's spell during these years, as some of HAH's first readers, confused by this seemingly sudden shift in Nietzsche's style, did (Hollingdale 1999: 90; Young 2010: 274). As Small indicates, the changes in Nietzsche's interests and approaches had been preparing themselves for some time (2005: xviii, xx, 57). His friendship with Rée mobilised, rather than caused, those changes, as Brobjer also suggests: 'The changes in Nietzsche's thinking, and the psychological crisis, seem to have begun before he met Rée,

---

[17] Nicholas Martin calls them 'discursive miniatures' (2008: 88). Cohen offers many interesting remarks about Nietzsche's style in HAH (2010: ch. 6).

but the reading and friendship with him clearly reinforced and probably radicalised the changes' (Brobjer 2008a: 62; cf. 41; see also Cohen 2010: 52–3; Hollingdale 1999: 90–1).

Enlightenment

Nietzsche's middle period is sometimes also called his positivist or enlightenment phase. And within that, Keith Ansell-Pearson conveys that HAH 'is typically construed as . . . being his most positivistic text in which the scientific interpretation of the world is privileged and guides the inquiry into religion, metaphysics, art and culture' (2018: 17).[18] While HAH does repeatedly express admiration for science's methods and procedures, and for the values and characteristics of its practitioners, and while Nietzsche is relentlessly critical of metaphysics, it is an exaggeration to call the work positivist in any robust sense. This is especially the case if Young is correct to claim that positivism is 'the assumption that the world is, and is *only*, the way natural science says it is' (2006: 86, emphasis original). We need to keep in mind that what Nietzsche means by science is the careful, dispassionate quest for knowledge, the possibility of seeing the world as it really is, without wishful thinking or the need for imputing meaning to it. As Small points out, 'When Nietzsche refers to science (*Wissenschaft*) . . . he is invoking a concept of disciplined inquiry which applies to classical philology as much as to the investigation of natural phenomena' (2005: 9).

This point about what science connotes for Nietzsche finds illustration in HAH 8 where he analogises science to philology, claiming that 'It requires a great deal of understanding to apply the same sort of more rigorous exegesis to nature that philologists have created for all books: with the intention of simply understanding what the writing means to say, not to scent or in fact to presuppose a double meaning.'[19] Likewise in HAH 266 he writes that one of the benefits of exposing Gymnasia students to the

---

[18] Cohen sees Nietzsche as embracing 'his own form of positivism' in HAH (1999: 104), but seems to equate positivism with enthusiasm for science.
[19] I modify Handwerk's translation but follow Hollingdale's by including the *jetzt* (now) from Nietzsche's text.

INTRODUCTION   7

classics is that they hear 'concepts, technical terms, methods and allusions' that are unfamiliar from everyday life. 'If the students only listen, their intellects will involuntarily be preformed along the lines of a scientific way of seeing things' (HAH 266). We find it illustrated again when a few passages later Nietzsche talks about reading rather than listening. He congratulates philologists for their art of careful reading and trying to decipher what an author is saying. 'All of science attained continuity and steadiness only when the art of reading correctly . . . reached its peak' (HAH 270). These passages all demonstrate that HAH's invocations of science should not be conflated with unadulterated praise for the natural sciences, and cast doubt on the aptness of the positivist moniker for this work. As Gianni Vattimo says, 'while idealizing science as a model of method, [HAH] does not attribute the sole legitimate and valid knowledge of the world to the positive sciences' (2000: 149).[20]

The term enlightenment seems more a propos than positivist for these writings and, unlike the latter,[21] this is a term that Nietzsche applied to his own work at this time.[22] Nietzsche frequently appeals favourably to the Enlightenment, he associates it with the growth of scientific knowledge, and he situates himself as part of the Enlightenment. But his relationship to the Enlightenment is nuanced. Consider his suggestion that Schopenhauer's thought was something of a throwback: 'the whole medieval Christian way of viewing the world and perceiving humanity could . . . celebrate its resurrection in Schopenhauer's teaching' (HAH 26). Yet this throwback has proven to be a boon for knowledge by fostering a

---

[20] Although Vattimo devotes a chapter of his book to each of D and GS, he makes only passing reference to HAH. See also Jessica Berry's helpful remarks on Nietzsche's views on science in HAH (2015: 107–10).

[21] As Magnus and Higgins note, Nietzsche was going to use the term positivist to describe HAH retrospectively, but abandoned that version of the preface (1996: 61 n. 21).

[22] Franco calls his book on the middle period *Nietzsche's Enlightenment*, but nowhere does he define what he means, nor what he thinks Nietzsche means, by enlightenment beyond saying that Nietzsche 'imparts his own distinctive meaning' to this term (2011: x). Vinod Acharya cautions against portraying Nietzsche as an Enlightenment thinker at this time, but overlooks the fact that Nietzsche employs this term himself. Acharya also charges me with this mistake of considering Nietzsche as an Enlightenment thinker (2015: 27 n. 25), while failing to mention Franco's title.

better understanding of Christianity than was available elsewhere in Nietzsche's time because of the influence of Enlightenment rationalism. By taking an overly rationalist approach, the Enlightenment lost sight of some of religion's power and the reasons for its influence. Schopenhauer offered a valuable corrective to the Enlightenment view, enabling one to understand Christianity's appeal. So what looks like a criticism of Schopenhauer for holding on to an obsolete view turns out to be beneficial to human knowledge. While Schopenhauerean philosophy is evidence that 'the scientific spirit is not yet strong enough', this weakness turns out to be salutary. This explains this section's title: 'Reaction as progress'. This claim – that the period of the Enlightenment did not understand religion, and that Schopenhauer supplied a more useful interpretation (more useful, that is, to those who really want to understand religion rather than simply endorse it) – is repeated in HAH 110.

But whereas Schopenhauer inadvertently advanced enlightenment, Nietzsche portrays himself as consciously picking up the baton to carry the Enlightenment forward.

> Only after this great success of justice, only after we have corrected in so essential a point the way of viewing history that the Age of Enlightenment brought with it, can we once more bear the flag of the Enlightenment farther – the flag with the three names: Petrarch, Erasmus, Voltaire. We have made reaction into progress. (HAH 26)[23]

This identification of Voltaire as an Enlightenment thinker in whose footsteps Nietzsche follows reminds us that HAH's first publication included a dedication on the 100th anniversary of Voltaire's death.[24] Although he removed this from later editions of the text, his enthusiasm for Voltaire persists across the rest of his work (Garrard 2008: 606–7). The idea that in HAH Nietzsche is seeking to revive the qualities of the Enlightenment

---

[23] See HAH 219 for a variation on this theme.
[24] Martin (2008) underlines this element of Nietzsche's thinking and offers an illuminating account of the appeal Voltaire held for him. Cf. Rethy (1976: 289).

also appears in his contrast between Voltaire's 'moderate nature' and Rousseau's 'passionate follies and half-lies' (HAH 463). He picks up the Voltairean catch-cry, *Ecrasez l'infâme*,[25] which was originally directed at the Catholic Church, its religious intolerance and its alliance with the French state. Redirecting it to Rousseau and the 'optimistic spirit of revolution' (HAH 463), he charges that their optimism wrongly trusted in both the natural goodness of humans and the Revolution's ability to unleash and restore this goodness. This naïve, optimistic, Rousseauean spirit of the revolution 'has for a long time frightened off the spirit of enlightenment and of progressive development: let us look to see – everyone within himself – whether it is possible to call it back again!'

In WS Nietzsche notes again how the Enlightenment became entangled with the French Revolution, with dire consequences. These were not, in Nietzsche's estimation, natural allies, for left to its own devices, the focus of the Enlightenment would have been to change particular individuals and to gradually affect 'the customs and institutions of peoples as well' (WS 221). However, the Enlightenment got bound up with the Revolution and assumed some of its violence and ferocity. The challenge for those who want to keep the flame of enlightenment alive is to extricate it from the mentality of the French Revolution and restore to it its individual focus and the possibility of gradual social change. As Nietzsche says, 'He who grasps this will also know out of what compound it has to be extracted, of what impurity it has to be cleansed, so as then to continue the work of the Enlightenment in himself, and to strangle the Revolution at birth, to make it not happen' (WS 221). So once again we see that he situates himself as both legatee and vehicle of enlightenment.[26] Although WS 189 does not refer specifically to the Enlightenment, it does describe the great task ahead of humanity – that of 'preparing the earth for

---

[25] Meaning 'crush/destroy the infamous'. Nietzsche's original text omitted the circumflex from *l'infâme*.

[26] Garrard (2008: 596) underlines how unusual it is to separate the Enlightenment from the French Revolution in this way, and observes that in his later writings, Nietzsche changes position to enunciate a continuity thesis between the two.

a growth in the greatest and happiest fertility' as being 'a task of reason, and for reason' (WS 189).

Along with Voltaire, Descartes also played a role in the very first edition of HAH, which, in lieu of a preface, included a passage from Part 3 of the *Discourse on Method*. The passage describes Descartes' decision 'to employ my entire life in cultivating my reason and to advance myself as far as I could in the knowledge of the truth . . .'[27] It also recounts the philosopher's contentment at making this choice. Nietzsche expunged the passage from the book's subsequent edition, along with its dedication to Voltaire. But it is interesting to note that in this work's first inception, Nietzsche praised this famous seventeenth-century French philosopher, scientist and rationalist.[28]

Although he does sometimes refer to the Enlightenment as a period or epoch (HAH 110), by 'enlightenment' Nietzsche also means a longer, ongoing process that has been present, and either advanced or retarded, across the centuries of Western civilisation (cf. Garrard 2008: 596–7). For one example of how he understands the historical process of enlightenment, consider his claim that during the Middle Ages

> the Jewish freethinkers, scholars and physicians . . . held fast to the banner of enlightenment and spiritual independence . . . it is not least thanks to their efforts that a more natural, rational and . . . unmythical explanation of the world could once again emerge triumphant and that the ring of culture that now unites us with the enlightenment of Greek and Roman antiquity remained unbroken. (HAH 475)

Petrarch from the fourteenth century and Erasmus who lived from the mid-fifteenth to mid-sixteenth century would not normally be classified as part of the Enlightenment. But this again reflects the dual meaning Nietzsche gives to enlightenment – as

---

[27] The passage is included in Gary Handwerk's translation of *Human, All Too Human* (1995). The page on which it appears has no number. Handwerk comments briefly on it in the second volume (2013: 564).
[28] See Rethy (1976) for a fuller discussion of this.

a particular historical epoch and as a process that has ebbed and flowed across the course of Western history. He considers the Renaissance to have been an enlightened phase in Western history because of its great respect for of scientific thinking (cf. HAH 237. HAH 219 offers a variation on this theme.) As Nietzsche's just-cited call 'to continue the work of the Enlightenment in oneself' hints, enlightenment is also viewed as a personal project, a quality and process that individuals can and should cultivate within themselves. So Nietzsche thinks of enlightenment in a dual sense – as an undulating historical process and as a personal project, rather than simply a particular era. In this there are parallels with Immanuel Kant's essay 'What is Enlightenment?' (1784). Although there is no direct evidence that Nietzsche was familiar with this essay,[29] it is striking to see the convergences in their thinking about what enlightenment requires. At this time, Nietzsche could only applaud Kant's definition of enlightenment as

> man's emergence from his self-imposed immaturity. Immaturity is the inability to use one's understanding without guidance from another. This immaturity is self-imposed when its cause lies . . . in lack of resolve and courage to use it without guidance from another. *Sapere Aude!* [dare to know] 'Have courage to use your own understanding!' – that is the motto of enlightenment. (Kant 2019)

As Kant soon adds, laziness joins cowardice as an explanation for immaturity:

> It is so easy to be immature. If I have a book to serve as my understanding, a pastor to serve as my conscience, a physician to determine my diet for me . . . I need not exert myself at all. I need not think, if only I can pay: others will readily undertake the irksome work for me. (Kant 2019)

---

[29] Brobjer numbers Kant among Nietzsche's major philosophical influences. He reports that Nietzsche read Kant's third critique but also read a lot about Kant by commentators (2008a: 36–9). It is possible that he encountered the ideas in this essay in the secondary literature or that the parallels between their views are just coincidental.

The Nietzschean elements here are manifest – the emphasis on intellectual independence and on the personal qualities that are necessary accompaniments to this – courage and vigour. Indeed, Nietzsche's portraits of the scientific person (or spirit or soul) in HAH repeatedly emphasise the intellectual virtues needed for this sort of heroism.[30]

But whatever the idiosyncrasies in Nietzsche's conception of it, HAH, MOM and WS show him to be more receptive to the Enlightenment tradition than he is typically taken to be. Nietzsche's praise for the Enlightenment is real but nuanced and somewhat idiosyncratic.[31] Brobjer, an astute and sensitive reader of Nietzsche's corpus, captures some of what was happening to Nietzsche's thought at this time in this way:

> During 1875 and 1876, Nietzsche went through an intellectual and emotional crisis and changed fundamental aspects of his Weltanschauung, including breaking with Schopenhauer, Kant, and Wagner. Nietzsche then exchanged his earlier enthusiasm for metaphysics, idealism, pessimism, art and aesthetics for a position that was sceptical and free-spirited, placed science above art, and praised the Enlightenment. (2008a: 61)

But even our brief discussion thus far shows the fragility of Brobjer's account. Schopenhauer has not been completely broken with and in some ways Kant is embraced.

---

[30] On this point my reading departs from Garrard's who sees Nietzsche as defining the Enlightenment as a purely French phenomenon and excluding German thinkers. He imputes to Nietzsche the view that Kant was an enemy of the Enlightenment at this time (Garrard 2008: 600, 603). Although he does not refer to HAH, David Owen (2003) has made this point about the convergences between Kant and Nietzsche's views and concludes that Nietzsche's philosophy expresses a ruthless and relentless commitment to Kant's maxim of enlightenment: *Sapere Aude!* See also Ansell-Pearson (2018: 48, 57).

[31] Ansell-Pearson (2018) portrays Nietzsche as adducing an ethos of Epicurean enlightenment in his middle writings. But as chapter 2 of his book testifies, he also recognises more modern influences on Nietzsche's enlightenment stance.

Epistemology-plus

Keith Ansell-Pearson and Duncan Large observe that HAH 'is remarkably different in tone and outlook from his previous published work. Wagner was repulsed by Nietzsche's new philosophical outlook, and even Nietzsche's closest friends wondered how it was possible for someone to discard their soul and don a completely different one in its place' (2006: xxiv; cf. Small 2005: 31–3; Cohen 2010: 250 n. 5; Young 2010: 273–4). While HAH indisputably inaugurates some important changes in Nietzsche's work of the kind noted above, this introduction and guide proposes and practises a reading of this work that is more attentive to its turbulent nature. Throughout these writings we find Nietzsche's thought to be in constant debate with itself; R. J. Hollingdale refers to 'his dialectical skill in experimenting with points of view' (1999: 112). Seen through this prism, this is not the work of someone who has 'discarded one soul and donned another': the reality is more complicated – and more interesting!

As part of its project of making this turbulence visible, this introduction and guide will show that throughout HAH Nietzsche repeatedly returns to the dilemma of how to live with the knowledge generated by science. His enthusiasm for science, though genuine, is far from unbridled and does not completely eclipse his previous enthusiasms. And while he does endorse the scientific approach as the best path to true knowledge, he does not shy away from the dangers and debilitations that seeking and finding such knowledge generate. Those who read him as a wholehearted enthusiast for science or positivism in this work neglect Nietzsche's own concern with the existential shadow that science casts. I cannot, therefore, agree with Young's claim that HAH 'adopts and inhabits' the stance of the scientific person (1992: 59) as a complete picture of what is happening in this work. Rather than being a poster boy for modern science, Nietzsche is better read as conducting an honest, searching and troubled conversation with himself about the implications of treading the scientific path to knowledge. Young is closer to the mark when he says that 'Given that his fundamental concerns lie always with life, "trying on for size" means asking how positivism stands with regard to the possibility of a healthy humanity' (2006: 61). As this suggests, Nietzsche's assessment of knowledge is, moreover, never purely epistemological; he also repeatedly attends to the ethical, experiential and aesthetic dimensions of knowing. This applies both to his critique of metaphysics and to his promotion of scientific knowledge in its stead. In both cases he asks, in addition to the truth value that this approach yields, what sort of character traits does the pursuit of this form of knowledge require? What will it feel like to pursue and acquire this sort of knowledge? Will a sense of beauty or satisfaction be engendered by this quest? I call this cluster of concerns his 'epistemology-plus' perspective and we will encounter this perspective in chapter after chapter of HAH.

Structure

Although originally published separately in quick succession, HAH, MOM and WS were eventually amalgamated, with the second and third works forming Volume II of HAH. Gary Handwerk reports that Nietzsche's new publisher suggested this fusion in 1886 (2013: 561).[32] In its two-volume form, HAH represents the longest publication in Nietzsche's corpus. When these three writings were combined into a two-volume work, Nietzsche appended a Preface to each volume. In recognition of this publication history, this introduction and guide treats the three original works separately, so that the title HAH applies only to the work with nine chapters and 638 numbered sections published originally under that title. Separate chapters are devoted to *Mixed Opinions and Maxims* and *The Wanderer and his Shadow* respectively.[33] The Prefaces, having been added so much later, are not treated here as part of the original writings.

---

[32] Hayman reports that one thousand copies of HAH were printed but only 120 sold (1980: 213; cf. Nietsche 1995: 374).
[33] Cf. Cohen (2010) who confines himself largely to HAH, discussing 'The Problem of Volume II' separately. Young's analysis of Nietzsche's views on art at this time separates HAH from MOM from WS (1992: 58). However, when discussing Nietzsche's views on religion a decade later, Young reverses course to treat 'the three works as the unity Nietzsche presented them as being in 1886' (2006: 6).

My decision not to discuss the 1886 Prefaces is atypical, for most scholars who comment on HAH do appeal to the Prefaces to help make sense of the work. Yet with this introduction and guide, I take myself to be giving an overview of how Nietzsche was thinking at this time. For that reason a discussion of the 1886 Prefaces does not belong here. In my view, moreover, the Prefaces are part of the rewriting of his history that Nietzsche engaged in and what they shed light on is what he was thinking after, but not during, the writing of HAH, MOM and WS. On the few occasions when I do refer to the works after HAH, it is always a reading forward (something that starts in HAH is continued) rather than reading backward, which is what drawing on the Prefaces to explain HAH does.

The parts of this introduction and guide that deal with HAH are, moreover, organised according to its own chapter divisions. Nietzsche elected to create chapters so we should assume, a priori, that this has some theoretical or thematic import. Two issues can be discerned with regard to his division of the work into chapters. One is to what extent the sections within each chapter relate to one another in any specific way – is there intra-chapter cohesion? The other is about whether and how each chapter within HAH relates to the others. On this later question, Paul Franco claims that 'The chapters stand alongside one another without any clear indication as to how they are to be integrated into a single, coherent argument' (2011: 15). This does not, however, prevent him from structuring his chapter about HAH around Nietzsche's first five chapters of that book, which suggests that the chapter divisions and their order do carry some relevance after all. Franco later says that chapter 3 of HAH 'forms a bridge between the preceding chapter on morality and the ensuing chapters on art and culture' (2011: 35), which indicates again that the chapters do not exist in splendid isolation from one another. What is also odd about Franco's approach is that although he insists on treating HAH, MOM and WS as a unity, he arranges his chapter devoted to all three around the chapter order of HAH alone.

Laurence Lampert, by contrast, imputes considerable integrity to HAH's chapter structure, arguing that this work 'treats philosophy in a single chapter' (chapter 1) (2017: 159) while chapters

2, 3 and 4 treat morality, religion and art respectively (2017: 171). Although it is basically correct, Lampert's approach strikes me as overly schematic – the distribution of Nietzsche's ideas across the work is not so highly disciplined as this. Indeed, the whole work can be read as a meditation on what a philosophy of the future should look like, and the issues of morality, religion and art thread themselves through the work as a whole. Nietzsche brings out, moreover, how metaphysical thinking has been influenced by religion, and art by metaphysics and religion, so these topics cannot be strictly separated in his way of handling them.

By moving through the material chapter by chapter and taking each chapter sequentially, this introduction and guide facilitates the exploration of both of the above questions. It proceeds as if the chapters might have some meaning and integrity as organisational units and explores them sequentially to see if the order in which they appear has any significance. Only after running that test can we decide whether the way Nietzsche organises his material has any salience. It is also important to recall that Nietzsche gave each of HAH's chapters a title, which further suggests that there may be some order, structure and purpose underlying the book's design. The approach adopted here is akin to that of Jonathan Cohen in his very fine study of HAH (2010).[34] But unlike Cohen's book, this introduction and guide devotes a chapter to each of HAH's chapters and one to MOM and to WS each. Although this introduction and guide proceeds sequentially, it does not claim to offer a comprehensive account of these three works. It picks up on the main themes and concerns of each chapter rather than providing commentary on each section.[35]

Chapter summary

Chapter 1 of HAH insists that traditional forms of knowledge such as metaphysics and religion are no longer viable, advocating instead a historical approach to knowledge which Nietzsche

---

[34] See in particular chapter 6 of Cohen (2010) and its reflections on structure and style.
[35] In this way it contrasts with Monika Langer's 2010 study of *The Gay Science* which comments assiduously on every passage.

presents as a type of science. The scientific style of thinking championed in HAH contents itself with small, unpretentious truths, and encourages a corresponding modesty and humility in its practitioners. This chapter also contains HAH's first reference to the volume's dedicated addressees – free spirits. Considerations of the epistemology-plus perspective that I impute to Nietzsche are woven throughout this chapter.

Chapter 2 looks at how morality originated and asks how compatible Nietzsche's remarks on this topic are with one another, as well as what evidence he provides for these claims. It then probes his self-presentation as a psychologist which begins in HAH and carries over into his following works. I draw attention to some of the signs of Rée's influence on Nietzsche at this time as well as to the presence of the epistemology-plus aspect of his thinking. Two strands of moral analysis can be found in HAH. On the one hand, Nietzsche practises psychological observation of the sort inspired by the French moralists which aims for perspicuous encounters with the depths and complexity of the human psyche. But on the other we have Nietzsche tracing the evolution of moral evaluations over time, and for that he typically needs longer passages that make more detailed exposition possible. The chapter goes on to discuss Nietzsche's views on egoism, fellow feeling and free will.

Chapter 3 outlines HAH's treatment of religion. Nietzsche believes that religion as a general phenomenon has no truth value, and that religious claims have no metaphysical validity. This chapter reviews his arguments against religion in general and Christianity in particular, touching upon the similarities between his approach and that of a German philosopher from a previous generation, Ludwig Feuerbach. It brings out Nietzsche's scientific and psychological stance towards Christianity and concludes by discussing whether he thinks that Christianity will ultimately disappear.

In chapter 4, Nietzsche looks into the souls of artists and writers. My discussion begins by cataloguing exactly who and what Nietzsche has in mind when he speaks of the arts, artists and writers. He ventures a scientific approach to art and reveals the close affinity between art, religion and traditional metaphysics. He tries to deflate myths about the artistic process. The chapter then segues into his account of the artistic genius. It concludes by reflecting on what Nietzsche thinks the future holds for art.

Nietzsche is clear that the present is an interregnum and the future could go in more or less positive directions. Chapter 5 explores what the signs of a higher culture are for him, as well as what role the free spirit might play in bringing such a culture into being. Although vital forces for progressive change, free spirits also face myriad obstacles to realising this potential.

Chapter 6 begins by noting the relatively heavy use of the aphoristic form in 'The Human in Society'. It also observes the wide range of topics canvassed there, and connects the use of the aphorism, as traditionally conceived, with Nietzsche's more disjointed approach to his subject matter. But despite this, some common concerns unite chapter 6's contents. One is the preoccupation with how one appears to others and the competition for status that this gives rise to. Rousseau's concept of *amour-propre* is invoked as a way of making sense of this. I go on to propose that we use Nietzsche's own account of the complementary dynamic between benevolence and malice suggested in chapter 2 as a way of arranging some of this chapter's fascinating insights into human motivation. This chapter concludes with an overview of Nietzsche's observations about friendship.

Chapter 7 starts with Nietzsche's views on women and, following a developmental model, moves from girls as students to intellects to unmarried women to wives and finally to women as mothers. It then considers Nietzsche's remarks on men in some of these roles. It moves thence to look at his remarks on familial relations from the child's perspective. It considers why Nietzsche rules marriage and family life out for free spirits and concludes by briefly comparing his views on this range of topics – gender, love, romance, sexuality and the family – with those of Rée.

Chapter 8 of HAH contains the most sustained discussion of explicitly political subjects of all of Nietzsche's works. Its passages treat democracy, political parties, political actors, the modern quest for equality, civil religion, socialism, revolution and war as well as the state. Its major unifying thread comes from Nietzsche's reflections on the rise of democracy and egalitarianism in modern Western societies and the superannuation of older, more hierarchical, more elitist and exclusionary forms of politics. This issue, in turn, connects with some of the other questions already raised in HAH such as what a higher culture of the future might look like, how it can be prepared for, and what role free spirits might play in paving its way. Nietzsche does not see free spirits as being political actors but as operating instead in the cultural sphere. Indeed, as we shall see, he posits a zero-sum relationship between political power and cultural elevation.

Chapter 9 represents the conclusion to HAH as Nietzsche originally conceived and published it. 'Alone with Oneself' offers the most miscellaneous collection of ideas in any chapter of HAH, and many of its aphorisms do not obviously relate to the chapter's title. It also contains the largest number of genuine aphorisms in HAH, MOM or WS. I focus therefore on the way in which Nietzsche chose to conclude HAH by emphasising convictions as impediments to truth and to the free spirit's quest for knowledge. I also bring out the presence of his epistemology-plus perspective in his handling of these issues.

Chapter 10 is devoted to the 408 sections that make up *Mixed Opinions and Maxims*, published in 1879 as an addendum to HAH. Nietzsche offers this collection of opinions and aphorisms without any chapter structure or guidance about how they might be related to or separated from one another. Yet I propose that there is more cohesion than initially meets the eye. Indeed, on closer inspection we find that most of MOM's contents can be assimilated to the chapter titles of HAH: MOM introduces nothing new in terms of topics and even cleaves closely to the chapter structure of the earlier work. The major topics explored are epistemology, morality, religion, art, gender and politics. This is not to deny, however, that some of the topics familiar from HAH are treated differently in MOM: art provides one example of this. Chapter 10 tracks MOM's major ideas and concerns as they appear in the text chronologically, unless there is a strong thematic connection between earlier and later passages.

Chapter 11 is devoted to *The Wanderer and his Shadow*, published in 1880. It begins by examining who or what the eponymous Wanderer and his Shadow represent. It goes on to identify and describe what I call an ethic of care of the self in this work, and to consider whether Nietzsche forwards a new understanding of philosophy in WS. His continuing critique of free will is outlined and his views on equality, punishment, aesthetics, politics, gender, religion and pity are laid out. Although Nietzsche has changed his mind about some things by the time he gets to this work, such as what the purpose of philosophy is and the value of war, Handwerk is basically correct to claim that these two later works 'are not in any strong sense a step forward philosophically for Nietzsche' (2013: 561; cf. 568–9).

By the time we get to the end of these three works, we might be in a position to consider what the title phrase, *Human, All Too Human*, means, given that Nietzsche went on to use this as the title for the two-volume work. According to Handwerk, the phrase first appears in a notebook from September 1876 (Nietzsche 1995: 367). It is then used in HAH 35, which equates 'reflection upon what is human, all too human' with 'psychological observation'. Young proposes that the title conveys Nietzsche's reply to the philosophical tradition that has insisted that things such as 'religion, art and morality' require a metaphysical explanation. Nietzsche is showing in these works that, on the contrary, they can be explained as purely human phenomena (2010: 243, 249). Ansell-Pearson takes a similar approach, suggesting that Nietzsche takes 'the sublime inventions of human nature' such as art, religion and morality and shows them to be strictly human (2018: 24; cf. 28). Magnus and Higgins take the ordinary humans referred to by this phrase to contrast with the image of the free spirit that Nietzsche introduces in these works (1996: 31). In this sense, the designation 'all too human' suggests a type of underachiever compared to what some humans are capable of.

At the close of his commentary on these three works, Handwerk proposes a less deflationary or disappointed connotation for the refrain human, all too human, with Nietzsche encouraging his readers to see humans as neither animals nor deities, but 'of a kind unlike anything that has inhabited the earth before them . . . quite remarkable and rich with potential' (2013: 584). I incline towards this more hopeful and prospective reading, with the 'human, all too human' conveying not so much disappointment as a call to future possibilities. We do not yet know, according to Nietzsche, what the fully and only human is capable of. His work sends out the challenge to make that which is all-too-human a cause of great future celebration.

1
Of First and Last Things[1]

This chapter begins with the first big question that Nietzsche grapples with in HAH, that is, what form of knowledge is best. He insists that traditional types of knowledge such as metaphysics and religion are no longer viable, advocating instead a historical approach to knowledge which he presents as a type of science. The scientific style of thinking championed in HAH contents itself with small, unpretentious truths, and encourages a corresponding modesty and humility in its practitioners. HAH's first chapter also contains its first reference to the volume's dedicated addressees – free spirits – and so this chapter closes with some reflections on that topic. Considerations of the epistemology-plus perspective that I impute to Nietzsche are also woven throughout this chapter.[2]

Historical philosophy

If the first big question that Nietzsche grapples with is what form of knowledge is best, this of course raises the question – best for what? At first glance the answer is obvious; the question is asking what form of knowledge is best for arriving at the truth. But even in his so-called enlightenment phase, Nietzsche expresses ambivalence about both the possibility and the value of uncovering truth. Finding the truth might not be possible because human life has been so mired in error, deception and fiction. Language

---

[1] I follow Hollingdale rather than Handwerk by deleting 'the' before 'First'.
[2] Chapter 6 of Lampert (2017) also offers an overview of chapter 1 of HAH.

itself is a conspirator in this thicket, for words generalise by necessity and thus mislead us about the singular and changing nature of things. But even were it possible, finding the truth might not be desirable. If the truth is grim or unsalutary, uncovering it could make life chronically miserable and even stifle one's desire to go on living. Or it might be that the process of uncovering this truth is dull, technical and laborious, drawing few to it. Either or both of these scenarios – the truth is impossible to find; the truth is undesirable to know – would throw the worth of the quest for truth into sharp doubt.

Nietzsche is adamant that traditional metaphysics and religion are no longer viable forms of knowledge. Metaphysical philosophies like those of Plato, Kant and Schopenhauer, which posit a fundamental truth – the existence of the forms, or the thing in itself, or the will – and then task philosophy with getting to that underlying truth, are no longer tenable in Nietzsche's view. He likens the idea that there is a more real world than the one we live in and know via the senses to dreaming (HAH 5).[3] With metaphysics, however, the fabricated world does not disappear when we wake up. Fictional material dominates the way we understand and evaluate ourselves and our world. But even if the metaphysical world were real, humans could never know it and so for all practical purposes, it might as well not exist. As he says, 'we could assert nothing at all about the metaphysical world except its otherness, an otherness inaccessible to and inconceivable for us; it would be a thing with negative characteristics' (HAH 9).

The sort of metaphysical philosophy that Nietzsche rejects privileges that which is unchanging and enduring over that which becomes and develops. We get a good sense of how traditional philosophy prioritises permanence from this work's opening words, which observe that philosophy's key questions have remained unchanged for two millennia (HAH 1). Philosophers have thus

---

[3] HAH 12 makes some very strange claims about dreams and earlier stages of human development. It is hard to interpret and assess what Nietzsche is saying, as he gives no leads as to where he is getting these ideas from other than what 'travelers' report about 'savages'. This allusion recurs in HAH 13. The point of these claims seems to be to discredit metaphysics by aligning it with dreaming, and then making a blurred boundary between dreams and wakefulness a feature of more primitive cultures. His wider polemical point seems to be that metaphysical thinking is characteristic of lower cultures.

refused to see that humans change over time, as does their capacity for knowledge.[4] As Nietzsche says in the next section outlining the 'Original failing of philosophers':

> A lack of historical sensibility is the original failing of all philosophers; many even inadvertently take the most recent shape of human beings, as it emerged under the imprint of specific religious or even political events, as the fixed form from which we must proceed. They do not want to learn that humanity has come to be, that even the faculty of cognition has also come to be . . . the philosopher sees 'instincts' in present-day humanity and assumes that these belong to the unchangeable facts of humanity and can therefore provide a key to understanding the world generally; all teleology is built upon speaking of the human being of the last four millennia as something eternal . . . (HAH 2)[5]

Insisting instead that 'everything . . . has come to be', Nietzsche repudiates any belief in eternal facts or absolute truths (HAH 2, 16), and posits a historical approach to knowledge as a superior alternative to metaphysical approaches. This 'historical philosophy' he recommends can, in turn, 'no longer be thought of as separate from natural science' (HAH 1). Such an approach does not assume either that real things do not change or that things that do not change are more real than those that do. Scientific approaches see and accept becoming, in nature, in humans, in societies, cultures and moralities. As this indicates, Nietzsche is not pitting science against philosophy in any implacable sense: rather, he is urging philosophers to become less metaphysical and more scientific and thus more historical in their thinking.[6]

---

[4] A passage in chapter 5 declaring that Schopenhauer 'denies development' indicates that he has Schopenhauer in mind here too.
[5] Later in this passage Nietzsche refers to primeval times in which everything essential to human development occurred. He does not tell us what those essentials are, nor when primeval times were, beyond saying that they predate the four thousand years of human history we are familiar with. Nor does he tell us how he knows about primeval times.
[6] For a different view, see Acharya, who contends that HAH's 'general project . . . is to uphold science and safeguard it from subjection to philosophical questions' (2015: 23).

As well as acknowledging change and becoming, the sort of scientific thinking that Nietzsche advocates contents itself with small, unpretentious truths, and encourages a corresponding modesty and humility in its practitioners (HAH 2, 3, 6). Metaphysical philosophy enchants precisely because it is more like art and religion than it is like science or history: creative and imaginative, it conjures symbols and images (HAH 3). A scientific approach to knowledge can, by contrast, seem initially to be dull, sedulous and pedantic. Yet this emphasis on what is small and unpretentious need not doom a scientific approach to trading only in isolated or potentially trivial points of information: it can, on the contrary, move incrementally towards a fuller picture of nature or the person. But it does so with a caution and rigour that is alien to high-flying, undisciplined metaphysical speculation (HAH 16, 22).

The grand and exciting consequences that scientific inquiry could have appear when Nietzsche imagines the sort of large-scale improvements that could be ushered in were the scientific approach to knowledge applied to society. Passage 24, 'Possibility of progress', declares that from now on, progress can be based on a willed, conscious decision by individuals to move their culture and society forward. Its expansive vision embraces 'better conditions for the emergence of people, for their nourishment, upbringing, instruction; [people] can manage the earth in economic terms as a whole, weigh the powers of humanity generally against one another and put them to work . . . progress is possible'.[7] As he explains in the next section, a concern with universal progress need not demand universalisation of methods. He questions Kant's assumption that truly moral action is that which can be replicated by all others, suggesting instead that sometimes the most beneficial course requires a division of labour, with different groups or collectivities doing different things that ultimately redound to the benefit of all.[8] Nietzsche presents the challenge

---

[7] Nietzsche's faith in progress as expressed here already distances him from Rée, who thought that there was no progress in human affairs (Small 2005: xv).
[8] He could have in mind here something like the Ricardian doctrine of comparative advantage. But his further point, that this is a challenge for great minds of the next century, suggests that he didn't have a well-worked-out position in mind but was, instead, more invested in criticising Kant.

of devising the best means for advancing human progress as the enormous task facing the great minds (or spirits – he calls them *der grossen Geister*) of the twentieth century (HAH 25). Part of what is going on behind the scenes here as Nietzsche ruminates on matters of epistemology is his shifting personal alignments and allegiances. As indicated in the Introduction, while writing HAH Nietzsche was disentangling himself from his previously close relationship with Richard and Cosima Wagner and forging a new relationship with Paul Rée. Although not named, Wagner is associated with the trilogy of religion, metaphysics and art that are all subject to strenuous critique in HAH. Wagner's religion was Christianity, his metaphysics was Schopenhauerean, and music was his art. The privileged place that Schopenhauer afforded music as an expression of the world as will meant, moreover, that Wagner's own art and his Schopenhauerean metaphysics were intimately connected. By criticising art, religion and metaphysics as a trinity, Nietzsche is therefore also impugning what Wagner stands for and what Nietzsche himself was once closely allied with. Rée, by contrast with Wagner, strove for a scientific approach to morality and introduced Nietzsche to English thinkers such as Herbert Spencer and Charles Darwin, who insisted on a historical approach to human culture and society. I am not proposing that we reduce Nietzsche's intellectual positions to personal relationships nor suggesting that the intellectual position is always the dependent variable – he might, after all, have been drawn to different people at different times because of their intellectual positions. But awareness of his changing personal alignments can help to shed some light on the twists and turns in his thinking.

Epistemology-plus

Yet as also indicated in the Introduction, Nietzsche's position on knowledge is never purely epistemological; he also attends to the ethical, experiential and aesthetic dimensions of knowing. This applies as much to his critique of metaphysics as to his promotion of scientific knowledge in its stead. In both cases he asks, in addition to the truth value that the approach yields, what sort of character traits does the pursuit of this form of knowledge require? What will it feel like to seek and perhaps acquire this sort of knowledge? Will a sense of beauty or satisfaction be engendered by such a quest? What I label his 'epistemology-plus' perspective surfaces in chapter 1 when, fully cognisant of the ethical, experiential and aesthetic appeals of traditional metaphysics, he looks for a way to identify and move people beyond their meretricious charms. But as we shall see, he does not always think that such a shift will be possible or even desirable.

When it comes to answering these 'epistemology-plus' questions about the scientific approach he is promulgating, Nietzsche's answers do not, at first at least, sound so promising. The truths of science are 'modest, simple, sober, apparently even discouraging' while those of metaphysics are 'beautiful, splendid, intoxicating, perhaps even enrapturing' (HAH 3). He wonders whether the demise of religion with its gaze towards the eternal and the subsequent refocusing of attention towards change, becoming and small, unpretentious truths will deter people from looking to the long term and from forging enduring institutions. He ponders whether the sort of scientific approach to knowledge that he advocates can inspire individuals to think beyond themselves and their immediate needs and interests (HAH 22). This is an especially pressing question given his belief that most people are already inclined towards self-absorption (HAH 33). He hopes that ultimately science can instill this sense of investment in the future: 'the sum of incontestable truths . . . that have outlasted all the storms of scepticism and all disintegration, can in time become so great (in the dietetics of health, for example) that it prompts people to undertake "eternal works"' (HAH 22). But this must be a hope rather than a prediction because it is still too soon to say how things will look when or if science displaces metaphysics.

At the halfway point of chapter 1, the passage entitled 'Metaphysical explanations' (HAH 17) suggests that scientific knowledge can provide not just inspiration for the future in the way that metaphysics has, but also that it can supply the same personal comforts and consolations as metaphysics. Nietzsche starts by explaining why a (supposedly generic) young person values metaphysical explanations. Their attraction lies in the sense they give to things that had seemed undesirable or repellent. If, moreover, the young person feels dissatisfied with himself, metaphysics can offer the comforting knowledge that he is not responsible for those elements of the self that disturb or distress him. The young person is thus drawn to metaphysical inquiry for reasons extraneous to the love of knowledge and the clear-eyed quest to understand the world. With time the youth comes to realise, just as Nietzsche is doing, that science is a better path to knowledge. It can, fortunately, also provide the same personal reassurances as metaphysics had: 'physical and historical explanations induce at least as much of a feeling of irresponsibility, and . . . the interest in life and its problems is perhaps kindled even more strongly in this way' (HAH 17). This passage suggests that science and metaphysics are equally placed when it comes to the existential aspects of the epistemology-plus challenge, while science appears to have the upper hand when it comes to truth value. This unusual passage is surely primarily autobiographical, indicating that it is not remiss to read Nietzsche's intellectual struggles in this work as also partly personal tussles.

But this line of interpretation – that the new scientific form of knowledge Nietzsche is advocating has an ethos and an aesthetic to accompany it, and that he is trying to think through this bundle of goods – is somewhat at odds with other remarks he makes about science. At one point he suggests that science cares only for the truth. In the individual fields of science, 'one seeks knowledge and nothing further – whatever may come of it' (HAH 6). If that is so, why does Nietzsche feel compelled to present its truths in a certain way or to depict the whole enterprise as higher than metaphysics? Similarly, HAH 7 says that science and philosophy parted company when Socrates and his legatees inquired after the happiness that philosophy brings. Science, presumably, does not share this concern and so can pursue knowledge unencumbered by questions about the non-epistemological payoffs. And yet throughout chapter 1, Nietzsche ruminates repeatedly on the non-epistemological consequences of a scientific approach to knowledge. Along with working hard to devalue the metaphysical, he wants to educate and persuade his readers about the value and appeal of a historical and scientific approach to philosophy.

In order to encourage his readers to follow him in rejecting metaphysics and pursuing the scientific path to knowledge instead, Nietzsche has to persuade them not just that the results will be truer but also that a superior sensibility will accompany this. There must be a transvaluation of values such that 'what has been laboriously acquired, what is certain, enduring, and hence rich in consequences for all further knowledge, is . . . something higher; to hold onto it is manly and shows valor, simplicity, temperance' (HAH 3). Indeed, the title of HAH's first chapter, 'Of first and last things' [*Von den ersten und letzten Dingen*] could be alluding to a line in three of the New Testament gospels, where Jesus predicts that in heaven, many who are first on earth will be last, while those who are last will be first.[9] What the New Testament remarks suggest is that eternity could witness a dramatic reversal of the social hierarchy that prevails on earth, with the implication that this overturning would produce a more just ordering. The hierarchy whose overturning Nietzsche is prophesying and helping to bring about is not a social but an intellectual one, for he is reflecting on the tendency to value religious and metaphysical beliefs over the smaller, more modest and less pretentious truths that the natural sciences, and inquiries modelled after them, can reveal. So the things that are currently first for philosophers – religious and metaphysical matters – shall become last, while those that are deemed less important – engagement with empirical matters – shall come first. In this case it is interesting to see him repurposing rather than rejecting a religious trope to describe and prescribe a process that will superannuate religion.

Impediments to truth

In addition to wavering between a disregard for the consequences of truth and a deep concern for the non-epistemological effects of scientific knowledge, another tension Nietzsche faces in his newfound enthusiasm for science is that even if science is more honest than metaphysics, he continues to insist that all knowledge involves falsification at some very basic levels. Consider, for example, his passage 'Language as a supposed science', which attacks the idea that the name given to something reveals anything about its reality or essence. Instead Nietzsche

---

[9] See Matthew 19:30; Mark 10:31; Luke 13:30.

suggests that all naming is arbitrary labelling. A scientific approach could, presumably, accommodate this nominalist insistence on the arbitrariness of all signs, but Nietzsche goes beyond that to say that scientific approaches such as logic and mathematics are also founded on falsehoods. Logic posits identity – between different things or within the same thing over time – and identity is false according to Nietzsche (cf. HAH 18). Identity is false because all things are individual and thus not completely identical with any other, and because in order for something to stay the same, change has to be denied. Mathematics posits straight lines and real circles which are also fabrications (HAH 11). Number itself is a fiction, assuming as it does that there are multiples of the same thing rather than myriad particular things, which takes us back to Nietzsche's critique of identity (HAH 19). These ideas echo those from Nietzsche's 1873 essay, 'On Truth and Lying in an Extra-Moral Sense', but when he penned those earlier arguments, famously calling truth 'a mobile army of metaphors', he was not trying to valorise any notion of rigorous and rewarding science.[10] Carrying these ideas over to a phase in which he advocates the pursuit of scientific knowledge creates some challenges that he does not always acknowledge, let alone resolve.

One possible way of reconciling this apparent tension between the claim that language, logic and mathematics are all founded on fictions and HAH's valorisation of scientific approaches to knowledge is to say that the cause of truth gains by identifying the falsehoods that abound in any quest for reliable knowledge. But if those falsehoods turn out to be fundamental, legion or both, how can science continue as anything more than a critical endeavour that identifies and knocks down fallacies? And if its contribution is exclusively or even primarily critical in this way, how can it provide the foundations for a better future? If we go back to the epistemology-plus challenge, what sort of character, experience and aesthetic would this primarily critical pursuit foster?

---

[10] Maudemarie Clark discusses the differences between Nietzsche's positions in these two texts and, referring to HAH 10, argues that HAH's focus is not the thing-in-itself. Its concern is the way the world known through common sense 'fails to correspond to the world disclosed by science' (1990: 96; cf. 97). See also Lampert (2017: 163–4) on the connection between this passage and Nietzsche's unpublished essay.

It is interesting to note in this context the slide from truth to history that occurs in HAH 16. There Nietzsche suggests that science culminates in 'a genetic history of thought'. Such a science will recognise that human history has proceeded on the basis of myriad 'errors and fantasies' that can never be fully expunged. Science can thus reveal error as necessary to human knowledge and development, but it cannot liberate us wholly from such error:

> Rigorous science can really free us only to a small extent from this world of representation – which would not be all that desirable, anyway – insofar as it essentially cannot break the force of age-old habits of sensation: but it can quite gradually . . . elucidate the history of the genesis of that world as representation – and lift us at least momentarily above the whole process. (HAH 16)

Here Nietzsche doubts not just the possibility but even the desirability of humans being wholly freed of deception. The world as we can know it must to some extent be our representation, and that representation necessarily involves some falsification. The extent to which a historical or scientific sensibility informs us about humans' enmirement in deception, falsification and fabrication is also evident in the passage 'A few rungs back'. Even though Nietzsche insists there that traditional metaphysics and religion are no longer viable, he urges that we appreciate the good things those errors have facilitated. Describing the condition of someone (such as himself) who has overcome religion and metaphysics, he insists that instead of stopping at self-congratulation for attaining these intellectual heights, such a person needs to look back and acknowledge the valuable things that those wrong beliefs made possible (HAH 20).

Echoes of this same view appear later in the chapter where Nietzsche announces that

> Error has made human beings deep, delicate, inventive enough to put forth such blossoms as the religions and arts. Pure knowledge would not be in a position to do so.

Anyone who disclosed to us the essence of the world would cause us all the most unpleasant disillusionment . . . the world as representation (as error) . . . is so rich in meaning, deep, and wonderful, bearing happiness and unhappiness in its lap. (HAH 29)

Towards the end of chapter 1 he explains why 'being illogical is necessary for human beings' and from this necessity 'arises much that is good' (HAH 31). The belief that human life is deeply imbricated in deception returns again when he says that being illogical 'is so firmly fixed in the passions, in language, in art and religion, and generally in everything that lends value to life that we cannot remove it without thereby doing irremediable damage to these beautiful things' (HAH 31). So here art and religion are posed against truth, but they are esteemed as beautiful things that too much logic would damage. Indeed, only the naïve would believe that humans could ever become purely logical creatures, and he points out that even getting closer to this goal would incur major costs. He continues in this vein in 'Being unjust necessary' (HAH 32) and 'Error about life necessary for life' (HAH 33). Once again, the gain for truth and science seems to come in perceiving how inevitable error and deception are. Even basic responses such as pleasure and pain or attraction and aversion are submerged in error, for the subject experiencing these reactions does not hold to fixed standards of pleasure and pain. Because Nietzsche sees humans as being in constant flux, as we change so must our assessments of pleasure and pain (HAH 32).[11] When attention is paid to these passages in the very first chapter of HAH, it becomes impossible to receive Nietzsche at this time as an unapologetic advocate for any conventional notion of positivism with its faith in observable data and reliance on experience. Nietzsche is, instead, conducting an honest, searching and troubled conversation about the requirements and consequences of treading the scientific path to knowledge.

---

[11] To further illustrate the fact that pleasure and pain are not in any way fixed categories in Nietzsche's approach to the psyche, chapter 3 mentions the ways in which religion can encourage people to find pleasure in pain (HAH 108).

Free spirits

In all these sets of reflections Nietzsche is suggesting that even if it were possible, exposure to the unvarnished truth would be undesirable. Once again we witness him evaluating scientific knowledge from the epistemology-plus perspective. He is very explicit about this at the start of chapter 1's closing passage, asking 'But won't our philosophy thus turn into tragedy? Won't truth become inimical to life, to better things? . . . [could] we consciously remain in untruth?' (HAH 34). He responds to these pressing questions by making temperament decisive; what matters is how one lives with such knowledge, and that, in itself, is not a purely epistemological problem. For that reason, chapter 1 culminates with a portrait of the sort of personality Nietzsche envisages as the scientific person *par excellence*. The last thing in this chapter on first and last things is a profile of the new philosopher. Such a figure sees religion and metaphysics for the beautiful illusions they are, and can live unaided by them without descending into despair at life's meanness or meaninglessness. Although believing in and working for the improvement of humanity, his learning also lends a certain distance and detachment from this world. He relishes that 'free, fearless hovering over people, customs, laws and the traditional evaluations of things'. The knowledge such a person is committed to acquiring simplifies his temperament and cleanses him of the push and pull of clashing desires (HAH 34). Although Nietzsche has not yet deployed this phrase, there is also a joy in this person's wisdom. Such 'a secure, mild, and basically cheerful soul' is neither offended to be part of, nor aspiring to rise above, nature (HAH 34). As we shall see, this becomes something of a pattern in HAH: chapters 2, 3, 8 and 9 also conclude with vignettes of the person pursuing the sort of scientific knowledge Nietzsche advocates. There he considers the ramifications of particular doctrines and intellectual positions for the character, temperament and outlook of those holding them.

HAH's first chapter also contains its first reference to the volume's dedicated addressees – free spirits (HAH 30). Nietzsche refers to the free spirit [*Der Freigeist*] in the second part of a passage which warns of the mistakes that a critic of traditional philosophy might make. It would be unwise for such a critic to simply reverse or negate standard views. Take, for instance, the view, which Nietzsche traces to ancient Greek thinkers influenced by Socrates, that if a belief brings happiness, it must be true (HAH 7). In rejecting this equation, the free spirit should not fall into the obverse error of holding that if a belief causes pain, it must be correct. Free spirits must practise a more radical scepticism about, and more thorough revision of, the foundations of philosophical thinking. It reinforces this work's emphasis on the scientific thinker's modesty and humility that HAH's first substantive reference to free spirits comes in the context of the errors they might incur. Whatever their talents and qualities, free spirits can remain in thrall to the metaphysical tradition even as they think they are escaping it. This warning against errors to which critics are heir also shows that Nietzsche knows what a battle he is facing in attempting to lessen the sway of traditional habits of thinking.

Even though he does not say this expressly, it is possible and perhaps even probable that the philosopher's profile with which Nietzsche concludes this chapter is a sketch of the free spirit. The free spirit terminology is introduced, as indicated above, in HAH 30. It is immediately followed by a passage entitled 'Being illogical necessary' (HAH 31) and then by one entitled 'Being unjust necessary' (HAH 32) and then by 'Error about life necessary for life' (HAH 33). After all these necessities, the next reference to freedom comes right at the end of the passage and the chapter. As cited above, the person of knowledge hovers over the concerns of others in a free and fearless way. He shares the joy of this state of detached engagement but, Nietzsche suspects, this might be all he has to offer others. Any freedom he knows is quite different from the freedom experienced by the person of action. This chapter's cryptic closing remarks leave us wondering how this attitude of individual detachment from worldly concerns is compatible with the free spirit being an agent of change and progress in the way that some of chapter 1's other remarks imply will be the case with the new, higher, scientific culture. If this is a sketch of the free spirit, it is left unclear how that person interacts with the free person of action. But then we have to remind ourselves that we are just at the start of this book, which itself is a new start for Nietzsche.

Conclusion

This summary of HAH's opening chapter gives the lie to the commonplace that Nietzsche held truth to be unattainable, for he sometimes maintains that truth can and should be pursued and he prescribes ways in which this should be done. The sort of truth whose pursuit he commends are the more provisional, falsifiable truths of science rather than the permanent, unconditional truths sought by traditional philosophers, but he repeatedly portrays it as a form of truth nonetheless. Yet while chapter 1 is in part an encomium to the scientific or historical model of knowledge so that Nietzsche can recruit more scholars to his cause, he remains repeatedly cognisant of the continuing appeal of religion and metaphysics, and asks some hard questions about what might be lost should science come to enjoy the cultural pre-eminence that religion and metaphysics have hitherto exercised. The epistemology-plus perspective adduced here leads me to reject Brobjer's interpretation of the middle writings as too schematic. Of Nietzsche's work, he contends that

> One fundamental tension is the dichotomy between his affirmation, on the one hand, of life, health, and creativity . . . and on the other hand, of honesty, intellectual integrity, skepticism, of having the courage to see the world as it is, and thus of truth, knowledge, scholarship, and science . . . for the middle Nietzsche (1876–82) it [the center of gravity] is on the second side . . . (2004: 301)

As we can see on the basis of chapter 1 of HAH alone, Nietzsche remains persistently concerned with both sets of issues during one of the first years of Brobjer's periodisation. There is no such centre of gravity in HAH; instead we witness Nietzsche weighing the pros and cons of honesty and intellectual integrity and courage.

This synopsis of chapter 1 also gives the lie to those who emphasise the disjointed and discontinuous nature of Nietzsche's writings, for a number of key themes are raised and pursued coherently and consistently throughout this first chapter. Nietzsche's answers to these questions might not be coherent and consistent, but as I emphasised in the Introduction, this was a period of immense intellectual transition and fermentation for him. HAH is best understood as Nietzsche trying on and turning over a range of possible positions. But whatever else we say about chapter 1, Hayman is correct to observe that Nietzsche 'moves away from his declared objective of concentrating on small, inconspicuous truths' (1980: 200).

2
On the History of the Moral Sensations

Chapter 2 puts into practice what chapter 1 emphasised – that is, that in order to become scientific and thus more truthful, philosophy must become historical. This turn to history means inquiring into 'the origin and history of the so-called moral sensations . . . the older philosophy is not at all familiar with these problems' (HAH 37). Nietzsche spends a great deal of time in this chapter emphasising that moral valuations have a history; they have not remained, and will not remain, the same over time and across societies. As he insists in passage 42, 'the rank ordering of good things is not something settled and identical for all time; if someone prefers revenge to justice, he is moral according to the standard of an earlier culture, immoral according to the present one' (cf. HAH 101).

This chapter looks at Nietzsche's remarks about how morality originated and asks how compatible they are with one another as well as what evidence he provides for his claims. It then probes his self-presentation as a psychologist which begins in HAH and carries over into his subsequent works.[1] I draw attention to some of the signs of Rée's influence on Nietzsche at this time as well as to the presence of the epistemology-plus aspect of his thinking. I point out that chapter 2 blends two strands of moral analysis. On the one hand, psychological observation of the sort inspired

---

[1] See, for just one example, GM III, 19.

by the French moralists aims for perspicuous encounters with the depths and complexity of the human psyche. But on the other, Nietzsche traces the evolution of moral evaluations over time and for that he typically needs longer passages that host more detailed exposition. The chapter goes on to discuss Nietzsche's views on egoism, fellow feeling and free will.

The origins of morality

Nietzsche elaborates on this idea of moral valuations having a history in HAH 45, 'Dual prehistory of good and evil'. This important passage goes beyond insisting that they have a history to asserting what that history is, how it is that moral valuations come about. Here he grounds them in power, declaring that the concepts of good and evil first derived from powerful and weak groups within the same society. Those who were powerful, noble and masterful considered themselves to be good, while the weak, base and slavish were deemed by them to be evil. Nietzsche makes it clear that these evaluations emanate from the strong, or those who constitute 'the ruling tribes and castes' [*der herrschenden Stämme und Kasten*]. So the powerful portions of society effectively deem being powerful to be the same as being good, and lack of power is determined by them to be evil. As Nietzsche puts it,

> Whoever has the power to requite,[2] good with good, evil with evil, and who really also engages in requital and is therefore grateful and vengeful [*dankbar und rachsüchtig*], is called good; whoever is powerless and cannot engage in requital is considered bad. (HAH 45)

By this logic, a strong and powerful enemy is not evil, for strength and power are attributes of the good.

Of course, one problem with this way of formulating his point appears when Nietzsche claims that powerful people saw themselves as good because they were able 'to requite, good with good,

---

[2] I follow Hollingdale and the German original by including a comma after 'requite', which Handwerk omits. It does not change the meaning of Nietzsche's point though.

evil with evil' [*Gutes mit Gutem, Böses mit Bösem*] (HAH 45). This presupposes definitions of good and evil that do not rely on the power to requite and thus runs contrary to his claim that goodness derived originally from that very power. I think he would need to say that they were able to requite like for like and then make that power of requital good. But this vulnerability in the way he expresses his argument here simply suggests that Nietzsche is trying out a brand new mode of analysis of morality that needs some fine tuning. And this mode of analysis goes on to become central to his later characterisation of master and slave moralities.

HAH 45's association of revenge with gratitude echoes the previous paragraph 'Gratitude and revenge' [*Dankbarkeit und Rache*] (HAH 44). There Nietzsche declares gratitude to be 'a milder form of revenge'. His logic seems to be that if someone does something kind or generous for a powerful person, the powerful person responds with gratitude. This becomes an exercise of reciprocity or exchange which suggests that the giver and the receiver are on somewhat equal terms; they have penetrated each other's 'sphere', as Nietzsche puts it. In this moral topography, gratitude becomes an expression of power rather than weakness. This section also contains Nietzsche's argument that designations of goodness originally derived from power: 'every society of good people, which originally meant powerful people, puts gratitude among the first duties' (HAH 44). In a later passage he effectively reveals that his model for this is the ancient Greeks, for whom 'taking revenge belongs to good moral behaviour' (HAH 96).[3]

Yet despite their convergence on revenge being seen as moral by those powerful enough to enact it, this passage's larger point about the source of morality is quite different from that of HAH 44 and 45. Nietzsche begins this later passage by declaring that the designation 'good' originally applied to people who simply

---

[3] Nietzsche's term is *guten Sitte*, which Handwerk translates as 'good moral behavior'. Hollingdale renders this 'part of good custom', which reflects the fact that *Sitte* can mean custom, habit, manners or morals. So a potential rendering of this line is 'when exacting revenge was part of good manners'. The overall point remains the same – that some cultures have valorised revenge because it betokened power. And of course, Nietzsche's larger point here is that morality began as custom, so the ambiguity of the German term helps him to make his point. Indeed, Hollingdale entitles this passage 'Custom and what is in accordance with it'.

followed their society's customs and conventions (HAH 96). By this logic, the greater the ease with which one conformed, the better the person, but the sine qua non of goodness is to act in accordance with custom whatever one's motivation or comfort level. The term evil was, conversely, applied to those who flouted society's conventions. These customs and conventions themselves arose in order to preserve the society, so the good person is one who contributes to that society's self-reproduction over time, while the evil one resists and disrupts it. Shortly after, in HAH 99, Nietzsche claims that what underpins custom is coercion (*der Zwang*). People are forcibly brought together into some sort of collectivity – a state or society – which will punish those who deviate, presumably from what the group needs for its self-preservation. In order to avoid pain, most individuals comply and over time that compliance becomes normalised, valorised and even comfortable.

Of course, the content of what is customary can change over time and from one society to another, but even here Nietzsche notes that one commonality across societies has been the belief that harming one's neighbour is especially problematic, and so this harm has come to be equated with evil. So notwithstanding his earlier insistence on a thoroughgoing historicising of morality, here Nietzsche's meta-point posits a universal phenomenon: 'to be moral, to follow custom, to be ethical, means showing obedience to long-established law or tradition' (HAH 96). His proximate target seems to be the belief, prevalent in his time and subscribed to by both Schopenhauer and Rée, that the essence of moral behaviour is unegotistical action. His point is that when we take a longer and wider view, we find that the essence of moral behaviour has been to conform to custom and convention and to thereby preserve society, not to act unegotistically. Seen thus, the current Christian-inspired emphasis on unegotistical action is much more recent and more local. So in this move Nietzsche historicises a key component of current morality to destabilise it, but he does so by making universal rather than historicist claims about morality.

This grounding of morality in custom is, of course, a different origin story for the designations of good and evil from that provided in HAH 44–5, which, as we saw above, accentuated strength and weakness respectively. Fifty passages apart, Nietzsche makes no effort that I can discern to reconcile these two accounts. Nor can they easily be made compatible, because following a society's customs and conventions (HAH 96) is quite different from being powerful and noble (HAH 45), just as resisting a society's conventions is not proof of weakness. One consequence of the disjointed way in which Nietzsche presents material in HAH could be that most readers do not stop to ask how or whether these divergent and perhaps even contradictory accounts of the origins of the meaning of good and evil can be made to cohere.[4]

It must also be noted that while Nietzsche repeatedly claims to be offering a historical account, he actually supplies very little in the way of historical evidence. It could be that he is relying on historical accounts provided by others to support his claims about the origins of moral valuations, but he provides no guidance as to what these accounts are nor whence they come.[5] This is history by assertion rather than demonstration. Had he provided more historical evidence for his claims, it might have helped us to decide which account of morality's origins was more persuasive or even to perceive a way to combine them.

This attention to the fact, if not always the detail, of history and the link between the origins of morality and power is evident in a number of chapter 2's passages. In HAH 92's account of the origin of justice, Nietzsche contends that justice only comes into being when there are adversaries of relatively equal power who realise that continuing to fight would simply damage and then exhaust both, precisely because of the power parity between

---

[4] In response to Brobjer's claim that these two passages represent divergent accounts of morality, Iain Morrison tries to reconcile them by reference to a passage in MOM (89) which argues that the good of community preservation is promoted by masters but they do not subordinate themselves to it (2003: 664–6). But even if Morrison is correct to reconcile these accounts, it is by reference to a later work. It means that Nietzsche initially published HAH with the contradiction unresolved, and, indeed, not even identified as far as I can see.

[5] Lampert points out that Nietzsche was reading works of paleoanthropology by such authors as John Lubbock, Edward Tylor and Walter Bagehot (2017: 162, 164, 184). But my point remains that Nietzsche never cites the sources for the grand claims he makes about human history.

them. They agree to give up arms and negotiate a truce which they call just. Justice thus originates in power and a calculation by the powerful about what best serves their self-preservation. It has, despite those origins, come over time to be associated with the unegotistical and the disinterested, so once again Nietzsche adopts a historical perspective to dislodge the permanence of a contemporary understanding of morality. This passage on justice's origin in parity of power does at least invoke Thucydides on the Peloponnesian War and the Melian Dialogue (HAH 92), but that is the closest Nietzsche comes in these sections to supplying evidence to back up his claims about the past.

The foundational link between morality and power is posited again in HAH 93 where Nietzsche asserts that rights are accorded to weaker parties by stronger ones and then only because the stronger party has some interest in protecting and preserving the weaker. In all of these instances, Nietzsche returns to what he claims are the roots of moral designations to show that they began with forces that are quite different from, and perhaps even contrary to, the things they are associated with now. Moral valuations that are currently surrounded by an aura of loftiness, abstraction and impartiality began in pragmatic exchanges based on power and interests in self- or other-preservation.

Whatever problems might accompany them, it can be helpful to consider what Nietzsche's purpose is in crafting these origin stories. By showing that when it comes to moral valuations, the outcome (customary morality/justice/rights) is far removed from the provenance (coercion/power/self-preservation/need), he sets his historical perspective in contrast to traditional metaphysics. The latter sees only frozen and isolated essences, whereas his more scientific approach to the moral life emphasises how a force can mutate into its opposite. This rationale for his historical accounts thus transports us back to the beginning of HAH where Nietzsche complains that traditional philosophy has no way of explaining how something can arise from its opposite. Examples he gives of such mutations include 'disinterested contemplation from wilful desire, living for others from egoism' (HAH 1). Traditional philosophy has denied 'that one emerged from the other and assume[d] that more highly valued things has a miraculous origin immediately out of the core and essence of the "thing in itself"' (HAH 1). His historical approach to philosophy is superior because it can permit such transformations. But permitting them and proving them are different steps, and I would suggest that Nietzsche provides more permission than proof.

At the end of the very first passage in HAH, Nietzsche also observes that 'Humanity loves to put from its mind questions concerning origins and beginnings . . .' This same point appears as he concludes the passage on the source of justice, where he muses 'How scarcely moral the world would seem without forgetfulness. A poet could say that God posted forgetfulness as the doorkeeper at the threshold to the temple of human worth' (HAH 92). This reveals another purpose for his historical accounts of morality, which is deflationary. What appears now to be lofty and impartial has much more banal origins, and even origins that would appear distasteful by the standards of that moral value. So Nietzsche is trying to embarrass contemporary morality and puncture its pride and pretensions by reminding it of a past that it would prefer to keep hidden.

As Rüdiger Safranski helpfully suggests, for a neo-Heraclitean like Nietzsche who holds that everything is in flux, returning to the origin of some phenomenon does not provide the key to unlocking its meaning. As Safranski explains in his chapter on HAH,

> For Nietzsche . . . the antimetaphysical, 'scientific' principle is based in a refusal to regard the originary, primary, and fundamental as higher, more valuable, and richer . . . Metaphysics places a high value on lofty origins, whereas science . . . works from the assumption that the originary is nothing but a contingency and inertness from which more subtle, complex, meaningful structures can be developed . . . Meaning, significance, and truth do not lie at the beginning or the end. Reality is everything that is in flux. (2002: 171)

Psychology

Chapter 2 also ushers in a significant feature of Nietzsche's work that persists for the rest of his oeuvre: his self-image as a psychologist committed to the unblinking examination of the human psyche, especially as it pertains to moral life. As Iain Morrison puts it, in HAH 'Nietzsche's approach to morality . . . involves an attempt to see moral beliefs as the product of human psychology, rather than as a set of metaphysical "truths" that are somehow given to, or discoverable by, us' (2003: 657). In this chapter's opening passage, Nietzsche equates psychological observation [*die psychologische Beobachtung*] with reflection on the human, all too human (HAH 35), implying that a book ostensibly devoted to this topic must pay considerable and careful attention to the psyche. This same connection between close psychological observation and all too human things is drawn in HAH 37.

In referring to 'psychological observation', Nietzsche echoes the title of Rée's collection of aphorisms, *Psychological Observations* [*Psychologische Beobachtungen*], published in 1875.[6] Indeed, this chapter's title, 'On the History of the Moral Sensations' [*Zur Geschichte der moralischen Empfindungen*], alludes to a work published by Rée in 1877, *The Origins of the Moral Sensations* [*Der Ursprung der moralischen Empfindungen*] which Nietzsche cites in HAH 37 (and HAH 133). It is also amazing to see the amount of overlap between the concerns of Rée's second book and Nietzsche's. As this chapter alone will indicate, Nietzsche echoes Rée's interest in the origin of the concepts of good and evil, the question of free will and responsibility for our actions, and the origins of justice.[7]

Chapter 2's important opening passage enumerates the benefits of psychological observation, and in doing so illustrates the epistemology-plus approach to knowledge attributed to Nietzsche in Chapter 1. Although Nietzsche believes in the truths that psychological observation can yield, the advantages he starts with are psychological rather than epistemological. The practice

---

[6] Brobjer (2008a: 62) recounts that Nietzsche read 'with great enthusiasm' Rée's anonymously published *Psychological Observations* in the year in which it appeared. Young explains that when Nietzsche wrote to congratulate Rée on the work, the latter replied that he also admired Nietzsche's work. They subsequently become firm friends for a limited period at least (Young 2010: 213).

[7] I do not venture any comparison of their views. Valuable work on that topic has been done by Small (2005) and by Donnellan (1982). The only exception to this comes in Chapter 7 where I compare their views on gender, love and marriage because this has not, to my knowledge, been conducted by others.

of psychological observation affords relief from the burdens of living because when one is on the hunt for insights into the human psyche, any situation, no matter how awkward or dull, can turn a profit. The pursuit of psychological insights affords comforts in even 'the thorniest and most disagreeable stretches of one's own life' (HAH 35). The rewards that such observation brings have, however, been forgotten as Nietzsche laments that he lives in an age inept and inexperienced at generating psychological insights. Not only do his contemporaries fail to engage in psychological observation, they are not even aware of earlier experts in this art, such as the seventeenth-century French moralist La Rochefoucauld. Rare is it to find anyone who has read this 'great master of the psychological maxim' (HAH 35), and even rarer to find someone who reads without reviling him. Contemporary audiences can therefore have very little understanding of how difficult aphorisms are to compose. Those who have never attempted this craft – i.e. the vast majority – fail to appreciate the challenge. Nietzsche's interest in the French moralists was reignited by his relationship with Rée, so this is, of course, indirect praise for Rée as a rare individual who reads and appreciates the French moralists and who attempts to write aphorisms himself. As someone who is joining Rée in this practice, Nietzsche is also praising himself while at the same time presenting himself and Rée as untimely thinkers.[8]

But in the interests of balance, Nietzsche weighs the disadvantages of psychological observation in the chapter's second passage (HAH 36). The major one is that psychological insight can corrode belief in human goodness. Disabusing humans of their faith in benign human nature can diminish their happiness and can even reduce the amount of goodness in the world by making people mutually mistrustful. A suspicious approach to human motivation can, in this way, become a self-fulfilling prophecy.

---

[8] Young neglects this aspect of HAH when he declares it to be, among 'all of Nietzsche's other published works . . . unique in its abandonment of the . . . stance of the outsider alienated from his time and culture' (1992: 59). HAH 616 also encourages an untimely estrangement from the present.

So there is a definite trade-off between illusion, happiness, trust in one's fellows and 'philanthropy' [*Menschenfreundlichkeit*] on the one hand, versus truth and 'the spirit of science' [*Geiste der Wissenschaft*] on the other (HAH 36). Rée stands alongside La Rochefoucauld as 'skillful marksmen who again and again hit the bullseye . . . of human nature' (HAH 36). But on this dimension of psychological observation, it is not clear that Nietzsche wants to align himself wholly with these two predecessors. Even though these marksmen's 'skill evokes amazement' (HAH 36), Nietzsche worries that these 'masters of psychical examination' implant 'a sense of suspicion and reductionism into the souls of humans'. Here he is viewing the archery team from the concerned perspective of the philanthropist. This distancing also shows again that despite Rée's powerful influence on him during HAH, they are not of the same mind on all matters. And this passage also illustrates what I am calling Nietzsche's epistemology-plus position, because once more he worries not just about the truth of certain ideas but also about how those holding such ideas will live, feel and experience these beliefs. The disadvantages of psychological observation he enumerates are not epistemological but psychological, social and ethical.

But whatever their risks, Nietzsche ultimately insists on the timeliness of such untimely reflections, urging that close psychological observation is now essential. Psychological observation à la La Rochefoucauld and Rée frees people of the errors and misjudgements of previous doctrines, based as they were on false psychological premises, such as the belief in unegoistic action (HAH 37).[9] Nietzsche's own use of the aphorism starts in this chapter (HAH 66) and it is especially suitable for those occasions when he wants to demonstrate the value of psychological observation. Short, sharp sentences that penetrate the heart and puncture the pride provide ideal vehicles for insights into human psychology. Consider, for example, passage 87, entitled 'Luke

---

[9] Elgat (2015) explains clearly how this is a reaction against and rejection of Schopenhauer's view of morality.

18:14 improved', which declares 'He who humbles himself wants to be exalted.' Yet whatever its value, Nietzsche also evinces some discomfort with the unscientific origins of psychological observation. Reborn in the salon, it was indulged in for motives other than pure intellectual probity. The sort of psychological scrutiny engaged in by the French moralists nonetheless yielded numerous valuable insights about human motivation and offers prototypes of the sort of scientific thinking that Nietzsche champions in chapter 1, which starts with small, unpretentious truths (HAH 3). But those beginnings should now be built upon by cold and bold thinkers such as Rée (HAH 37) and, presumably, Nietzsche himself. So although La Rochefoucauld's legacy is largely dormant in contemporary Europe, Nietzsche believes that he and Rée are in the process of reviving it, firm in the conviction that the present and the future need these unfashionable insights into the realities and complexities of human motivation, 'fruitful and frightful' [*fruchtbar und furchtbar*] though they be.

The historical and the psychological

But what La Rochefoucauld and his legatees bring to the study of morality is different from what Nietzsche is also emphasising in this chapter, which, as noted above, is the need for a historical approach. The French moralists accentuate the mystery and complexity of the psyche, but that is not exactly the same as Nietzsche's insistence on acknowledging large-scale moral change or continuity over time. Indeed, the use of the aphorism in the moralist tradition to deliver pithy statements about morality could encourage a sort of smug essentialism which mistakes the particular and the local for the universal, which is the opposite of what Nietzsche is trying to achieve with his historical approach. So chapter 2 hosts these two disparate strands of moral analysis running concurrently. On the one hand, psychological observation aims for perspicuous encounters with the depths and complexity of the human psyche and produces small, unpretentious (but not for that insignificant) truths about the self. But on the other we have Nietzsche tracing the evolution of moral evaluations over time[10] and for that he typically needs longer passages that make more detailed exposition possible. Not only do these strands run concurrently, but Nietzsche intersperses them, just as he mixes aphorisms with longer passages. It is interesting to note that Rée does not do this. His *Psychological Observations* comprises mostly aphorisms, with a much smaller ratio of paragraphs to aphorisms than HAH. And the few longer passages that appear there are rarely longer than a paragraph. A three-page analysis of vanity appears separately at the end of the work and is called an essay. His other work that influenced Nietzsche at this time, *The Origins of the Moral Sensations*, is a series of short essays. Rée does not, as Nietzsche does, present his ideas in a continuously mixed mode.

The ego and its own

One thing that unites these two strands – the historical and the moralist analyses of moral life – is, however, their tendency to deflate, for like Nietzsche's historical excursions, the insights of the French moralist tradition often show moral valuations and beliefs to be not as lofty or pristine as they seem. Both approaches are powered by what we could now call a hermeneutic of suspicion. One of the ways in which the French moralist tradition tries to puncture and deflate morality is by showing that many moral actions that appear to be other-regarding are, in fact, self-regarding and self-rewarding. This exposé of the egoism that underlies much moral action no doubt appealed greatly to Nietzsche at this time, for he holds the belief in unegotistical actions to be one of the great errors of the philosophical and religious tradition. Early in chapter 2 he complains of 'how a false ethics is constructed on the basis of an erroneous analysis of the so-called unegotistical

---

[10] As Handwerk puts it 'Both the language and the intellectual perspectives of the French moralists were deeply shaped by their own metaphysical nature . . . Even as Nietzsche drew upon their concerns and adopted features of their style, he began working out a historical perspective on psychological causality . . . [he placed] psychological observations within a historical trajectory' (Nietzsche 1995: 369).

actions' (HAH 37). As indicated above, he wants to show that many actions that appear disinterested or altruistic actually have some form of self-interest at their base. He does not want to be judgmental about this, however; he is not suggesting that such self-motivated actions are wrong (cf. Donnellan 1979: 306). As he announces in HAH 101, 'Egoism is not evil'. It is, on the contrary, wholly normal for humans to pursue what they perceive as pleasure and avoid what they perceive as pain. Human action is best understood as pre-moral and based on interests, desires and perceptions of pleasure and pain. 'There are no sins in the metaphysical sense; but . . . no virtues either' (HAH 56; cf. HAH 101, 102, 107). Different societies and cultures have coated these impulses with different moral valuations, but at base, human action is what Nietzsche calls innocent, or morally neutral.

One of the ways in which Nietzsche throws into doubt the supposed separation between egotistical and unegotistical actions that underlies the traditional view is by multiplying the ego or the self. In the very next passage to the one just cited, he criticises the idea of unegotistical actions and suggests that it is simplistic to see the agent as a unified self acting on behalf of or in the benefit of another. Rather, the agent is multiple, with one strand of the self wanting to act in one way and another in another. What looks like unegotistical action can be explained as the triumph of one strand over another. Hence the title of this passage: 'Morality as self-division of human beings' (HAH 57). Thus what the ego or the self is, and what emanates from the ego, is not immediately clear or self-evident.

And because the ego is not a single, unified structure, developing an ego, and acting upon it, is more of a project than a given.[11] Thus in the passage entitled 'Morality of the mature individual', Nietzsche suggests that people need to become more egoistic, more self-concerned, and more attentive to the personal. The other-regarding ethos that has dominated moral thinking has

---

[11] This seems to be Nietzsche's point in a passage from chapter 9 entitled 'Greatness means: giving direction'. There he writes that 'with all who are great in spirit. All that matters is that a single one provides the direction that the many tributaries must follow' (HAH 521). Assuming, of course, that the tributaries are inner strands of the self and not external forces.

eclipsed the importance of self-regard. Yet self-regard need not translate into selfishness; he imagines that when people pay more attention to themselves, they could become more helpful to their fellow humans and contribute more to the general welfare. As he says

> To make of oneself a whole person, and in all that one does, to keep an eye upon one's own highest welfare – that gets us further than those sympathetic movements and actions for the sake of others ... we all still suffer from having far too little consideration for what is personal in us; it has been badly developed ... Even now we want to work for our fellow human beings, but only so far as we find our own greatest advantage in this work, no more, no less. (HAH 95)

As this makes clear, the mature individual Nietzsche envisages here does want to work for his or her fellow human beings and so cannot be considered selfish or indifferent to the well-being of others. Although he does not marshal it for this purpose, this passage illustrates well Bernard Reginster's insistence that Nietzsche is not 'suggesting that the genuine altruist may have no self interested motives alongside altruistic ones ... the fact that an action follows from self-interested motives in addition to other-regarding ones does not necessarily undermine its altruistic value' (2000: 180).[12]

As this suggests, while Nietzsche is expressing scepticism about the equation of moral actions with unegotistical ones, it would be a mistake to read him as swinging to the opposite extreme and claiming that all action is necessarily entirely egotistical.[13] To dispute the claim that to count as moral, actions must be unegotistical

---

[12] Reginster provides a close reading of Nietzsche's views on egoism which draws on some of the passages from HAH as well as from his wider oeuvre.

[13] Yet I take this to be what Morrison is claiming when he says that 'The essence of Nietzsche's early view on moral action is that all actions are egoistically motivated and that moral judgments are false in the sense that they operate on the faulty assumption that unegositic action is a possibility' (2003: 660). Young likewise says that in HAH, under the influence of Rée, Nietzsche 'affirms the (false) doctrine of psychological egoism, specifically psychological hedonism' (2006: 66). I take Nietzsche's position to be more nuanced than this. For a valuable account of his position, see Elgat (2015).

is not the same as saying that unegotistial actions are impossible. Consider, for example, the passage 'Sympathy stronger than suffering' (HAH 46), which contends that a person can suffer greatly when their friend does something disgraceful. The sympathetic sufferer is more pained by their friend's guilt than they would be if the disgrace and the guilt were their own. One of the reasons for this increased suffering is that 'our love for him is stronger than his love for himself'. Nietzsche concludes that 'the unegotistical element in us . . . is more strongly affected by his guilt than the unegotistical element in him'. Although he clarifies that the term unegotistical 'is never to be understood too strictly, but only in an attenuated way', this passage conveys a genuine faith in the possibility of unegoistical love and concern, at least between friends.

Regarding others

This question about the nature and possibility of fellow feeling resurfaces a few passages later in HAH's fascinating discussion of benevolence. Benevolence means 'those expressions of friendly sentiment in social interaction, that smile of the eyes, that shaking of the hands, that comfortable pleasure with which almost all human interactions are intertwined' (HAH 49). So this is not the potent, intimate bond of sympathy that can make us suffer more on another's behalf than they suffer themselves, but a micro expression of sociability among acquaintances. But although each particular expression of benevolence is small, due to their regularity and pervasiveness they add up to exercise an important impact on social life. These small, frequent, iterated and effective human bonds should command more attention than they do; indeed, they also fall into the category of modest, unpretentious truths to which his new science should attend and which it should value. Nietzsche describes these things – 'good naturedness, friendliness, politeness of the heart' – as frequent manifestations of the unegotistical drive. His portrayal of benevolent sociability seems utterly sincere; he does not suggest that benevolence is a self-rewarding attitude and he gestures towards no obvious payoff to the self from appearing benevolent to others. He somewhat confusingly qualifies this by saying that 'there is not actually much that is unegotistical in them' (HAH 49) without explaining what they do consist in, if not the unegotistical. But however much there is in them that is unegotistical, there is something that illustrates that he is not suggesting that unegotistical action or motivation is impossible.

But not all social interaction is benign. It is intriguing to see that in the very next passage, Nietzsche portrays malice as the counterpoint to benevolence. In his own twist on the Kantian notion of unsocial sociability, malice is a micro expression of unsociability among acquaintances; like benevolence, it is frequent and pervasive. As Nietzsche depicts it, 'In social conversation, three-quarters of all questions are asked and three-quarters of all answers are given in order to give a little bit of pain to the interlocutor' (HAH 50). Indeed, he says that benevolence is the 'ever-ready remedy' to malice.

This passage about the complementary dynamic between benevolence and malice starts, however, as a reflection on pity, which is another form of fellow feeling. HAH 50 begins by endorsing La Rochefoucauld's views on this topic as expressed in his 'Self Portrait'. The moralist distinguishes between those who are capable of reason and others, recommending that pity be the province of the latter. Not driven by reason, this group needs emotions such as pity to spur them to help others. For the rational, pity is not only redundant but risky because it 'enfeebles the soul' (HAH 50). Although those who are protective of their soul's welfare should take care not to experience pity, they should nonetheless feign it when appropriate, because inferior types will be consoled by shows of pity in their direction and for their benefit. 'One should, to be sure, manifest pity, but take care not to possess it' (HAH 50).

Although HAH 50 basically endorses the view expressed in La Rochefoucauld's 'Self-Portrait', Nietzsche also accuses the moralist of being insufficiently suspicious of pity-seekers' motives. Recall that this is part of the very same chapter where Nietzsche has worried that masters of psychical examination such as La Rochefoucauld implant 'a sense of suspicion and reductionism into the souls of humans'. Unlike the overly trusting moralist, Nietzsche suggests that what spurs people to seek pity is not their being sufficiently stupid to be consoled by this so much as their thirst for power. They want to hurt those who have not been similarly disadvantaged or made wretched by inciting them to feel sorry for the sufferer. The ability to cause distress in unafflicted people affirms that the pitied are not wholly devoid of strength and power. Making oneself an object of pity becomes a (minor) triumph rather than a further diminution of the self. Hence Nietzsche's conclusion that 'the thirst for pity is thus a thirst for self-enjoyment, and that at the expense of one's fellow men; it displays man in the whole ruthlessness of his own dear self: but not precisely in his "stupidity" as Larochefoucauld thinks' (HAH 50). But none of this suggests that pity cannot be unegotistical action. The charge of egoism is directed here at pity-seekers, not pity-showers. A display of pity is encouraged because it can make its recipients feel comforted, and that desire to do some good to those who are suffering seems in itself to be unegotistical.[14]

In myriad ways then, chapter 2 complicates what it means to feel for others. A fascinating passage towards its end associates fellow feeling with proximity; we have to learn that others suffer and how, and we do this by getting closer to them. A lot of what might look like egoism or indifference is actually ignorance born of distance; people are too far removed from one another to comprehend their suffering. Nietzsche runs through a number of things that can make it hard to understand others and thus appreciate that and how they suffer, including historical distance, species difference, the gap between the person giving the orders to harm and the person executing them (executing the orders that is, although it can be an order to execute). As the passage concludes, 'That another being suffers must be learned; and it can never be fully learned' (HAH 101). We are more likely to be moved by, or try to prevent or mitigate, the suffering of one who is close to us. But as Nietzsche points out, proximity can be acquired; it is not a given. Or at least degrees of it can be learned, even if we can never fully comprehend the suffering of

---

[14] For a fuller discussion of Nietzsche's relationship to La Rochefoucauld, see Abbey (2015).

another. So once again, Nietzsche is not implying that unegotistical actions are impossible but only that they should not be presumed to be automatic.

Free will

Along with its simplistic faith in unegotistical actions, another major flaw in traditional philosophy that Nietzsche holds his historical approach to uncover is the belief in free will. This belief enables us to impute responsibility to individuals for their actions, and to praise or blame them accordingly. Asserting this belief to be one of the fundamental errors of this tradition in chapter 1 (HAH 18), he elaborates on this claim in chapter 2. Indeed, having spent the first four sections of chapter 2 weighing some of the pros and cons of his own approach to psychology, Nietzsche launches into an attack on the idea of free will. He writes about 'The history of those sensations that we use in order to attribute responsibility to someone, that is, of the so-called moral sensations' (HAH 39). By linking the issue of free will to chapter 2's title in this way, Nietzsche accords it a central place in this chapter's efforts. This same connection between 'the history of moral sensations' and the doctrine of free will and the accountability it imputes is also made about a third of the way through the passage. There Nietzsche identifies Schopenhauer with the belief in free will and the accountability to which it gives rise, but it is, of course, much more pervasive throughout Western culture, being also a central plank of Christianity.

HAH 39 declares that the belief in free will develops through four phases. The first way of evaluating actions morally is via their consequences; actions with beneficial consequences are called good and those with harmful consequences evil. (Of course, this raises the question of how to deem something beneficial or harmful, but Nietzsche does not broach this here.) The labels good and evil then shift from the consequences to the actions that brought them about. From there these labels migrate to the motives of the actor who performed the action. And from there good and evil are applied to the individuals as a whole who harboured those motivations. The move in moral valuation thus goes from 1) consequences to 2) actions to 3) motives and to 4) persons and, at this journey's destination, persons come to be held responsible for their actions and their consequences (HAH 39). The feeling of free will is, Nietzsche says, 'a quite variable thing': it differs from person to person and from culture to culture and 'is perhaps present only during a relatively short period of world history' (HAH 39). He thus reiterates that humans have not always thought about their actions as the product of free will, and thus historicises and relativises this doctrine. But he adds that even if people feel like the free agents of their action, this does not mean that they are (cf. HAH 106), so merely feeling free is not decisive here.[15] Part of Nietzsche's wider purpose in HAH is to point out that moral action is far more complicated than people have given it credit for, and so against this backdrop, the belief in free will appears naive. Many forces and influences affect actions: to assume that action is just the outcome of individual choice is too simplistic. And if action is overdetermined in this way, the individual cannot bear sole responsibility for it.

Yet there are also moments in the text when Nietzsche moves beyond complicating any simplistic notion of free will to rejecting it entirely, and swinging to the opposite extreme to claim that there is no freedom at all in human action. In HAH 106, for example, he conjures the image of an omniscient mind who could see that all human action was pre-prescribed. This knowledge, currently unavailable to human minds, allows human agents to harbour the delusion of free will, but it is a delusion. This same idea of determinism is mentioned in the very next passage which attributes all action to 'nature and necessity' (HAH 107). However, this moment of what might be a version of Laplacean determinism is not something that Nietzsche sustains, and not something that he can sustain if the cohort of future figures he hopes to summon are to be thought of as free spirits, for these figures must exercise freedom in some form or forms.[16]

---

[15] Other passages condemning the belief in free will as erroneous include HAH 102.

[16] Thanks to Keith Ansell-Pearson for alerting me to the possible link with Laplace in HAH 106. For other arguments as to why Nietzsche cannot maintain determinism as a fully fledged alternative to free will, see Abbey (2000: 24–33).

Nietzsche also approaches the question of free will from what I have been calling the epistemology-plus perspective. He comments briefly, and perhaps ironically, in HAH 91 that the belief in noble and magnanimous actions – either one's own or others', he does not specify – lends a certain enjoyment to life. This 'would fade if the belief in complete irresponsibility were to gain the upper hand'. However, just eight sections later, he identifies the less attractive responses that the belief in free will provokes: 'hatred, vengefulness, malice, an entire degradation of the imagination' (HAH 99). We do not react in these ways to animal action because free will is imputed to humans only. Thus, as indicated above, we congratulate or censure humans for their actions because we believe them to have been chosen. But Nietzsche's longest reflection in this chapter on what the ethical, social and existential consequences of abandoning the belief in free will might be comes in the chapter's closing passage. Like chapter 1, chapter 2 culminates in a portrait of what the person who adopts and absorbs Nietzsche's scientific approach to philosophy would, or perhaps should, be like.

Beginning with a variation on his remarks in HAH 91, Nietzsche indicates that losing the belief that humans are responsible for their actions can be very hard for those who locate human nobility in the capacity for free will. This realisation that actions are not the product of free will disorients all ethical evaluations – how or where are praise and blame to be allocated henceforth? Nietzsche suggests that actions can be admired for their aesthetic value – as beautiful, strong and full – but not their ethical value. As this chapter's final passage progresses, Nietzsche bundles together the insights about morality contained in HAH so far: the erosion of the belief in free will; the awareness that moral evaluations are changing and unstable; the realisation that good and its supposed opposite are not diametrically opposed but intimately related and differ at most in degree rather than kind; the insistence that people are motivated primarily by the desire for pleasure and aversion to pain; and the realisation that moral valuations are immersed in error. All of these insights into the true character of morality 'can cause profound pain' [*kann tiefe Schmerzen machen*] (HAH 107), although *Schmerzen* here might be better translated as grief, given the imagery of rebirth that appears in the passage. Such grief will, to be precise, be engendered in only a small minority of people, according to Nietzsche. But he encourages the new person of knowledge to look beyond the difficulties occasioned by these truths about morality to see them as presaging a different and better future. He hopes that the reaction of 'sorrow' [*Traurigkeit*] can be transformed, depicting a possible future state and the uncertainty that precedes it in a manner that is richly poetic, thick with metaphor and religious imagery. The butterfly wants to break out but is confused by an 'unknown light', a 'kingdom of freedom'. For those able to see it, 'the sun of a new gospel' pierces the metaphorical twilight and fog of this time of uncertainty (HAH 107). If this is Nietzsche advocating a new science, he is a poet of that science.[17]

The new person of knowledge who might result from this period of transition and uncertainty will take a particular stance towards this new understanding of morality: 'comprehending, not loving, not hating, overlooking' (HAH 107). This echoes the profile of the new philosopher, and perhaps free spirit, that closed chapter 1, where we got a sense of distance and detachment from this world which is not tantamount to a stance of disengagement. This same image of detachment also appears in HAH 56, which outlines some of the key elements of his new understanding of morality. Any belief that humans are fundamentally evil or fundamentally good needs to be abandoned. These premises are useful as heuristic devices, and, because they have been so influential up until now, they help us understand ourselves. But they are false in Nietzsche's estimation and must be transcended. The person who comes to understand morality in this new way 'easily arrives at peace of soul'. Such a person has knowledge as the 'single goal that fully governs him' and this focused quest for understanding helps to regulate the desires. Just as chapter 1 advanced the idea that the knowledge being sought would simplify the temperament and cleanse the knower of the push and pull of clashing desires, so here, being governed by this

---

[17] Lampert (2017: 178–80) also discusses these passages.

single goal makes the person 'cool' and calms 'all the savagery in his disposition' (HAH 56). This correct understanding of morality also liberates the person from all manner of old, 'tormenting conceptions' such as ideas of sinfulness and Hell. At the close of chapter 2 Nietzsche makes it clear that the evolution of the person who can exhibit the right attitude towards this new knowledge about morality and the self will be a long, slow process, and could take 'some thousands of years' (HAH 107). Nonetheless, he seeks to reassure his readers that the turmoil he is stirring up in their understandings of moral life will have a salutary outcome: current 'human beings who are unwise, unjust, conscious of their guilt' will be superseded by 'a wise, innocent human being (one conscious of his innocence)' (HAH 107). At one point his attempt to assure his readers that this time of turmoil will have a positive outcome is so great that he describes this type of person as the 'single goal' towards which 'everything is streaming' (HAH 107). It is interesting to see the terminology of the single goal recur here, for in the passage just discussed, true knowledge about morality is that goal, whereas here the goal is the person who harbours that knowledge and can productively inhabit it. These two uses of the phrase are not contradictory of course, especially because in the earlier use in HAH 56, Nietzsche's interest is not just the knowledge itself but how having it affects the knower. So in all these ways we witness the presence of what I am calling the epistemology-plus perspective in chapter 2.[18]

---

[18] But this is not to suggest that Nietzsche adheres to it consistently in this chapter either. In HAH 38, for example, he lapses back into one of the views he occasionally expresses in chapter 1 which is the opposite of the epistemology-plus position. He characterises science as caring only for the truth, and not for the consequences of its findings.

3
The Religious Life[1]

Chapter 3 makes Nietzsche's belief that religion as a general phenomenon has no truth value, and that religious claims have no metaphysical validity, abundantly clear. He does not believe that God, gods or the divine exist in any real sense. As he says in this chapter's second passage, 'we cannot believe those dogmas of religion and metaphysics if we have the strict method of truth in our hearts and heads' (HAH 109). Chapter 2 made a similar but more specific claim, that 'the awakening sciences . . . have point by point rejected Christianity' (HAH 68). This chapter reviews Nietzsche's arguments against religion in general and Christianity in particular, touching upon the similarities between his approach and that of Ludwig Feuerbach, a German philosopher of the previous generation. It brings out Nietzsche's scientific and psychological stance towards Christianity and concludes by discussing whether Nietzsche thinks that Christianity will ultimately disappear.

A scientific view of religion

False beliefs in the existence of a reality beyond the human and the natural worlds have real effects, but claims about gods, God, Jesus as his son, original sin, Hell or Heaven have no metaphysical

---

[1] Chapter 3's title 'The Religious Life' illustrates my previous chapter's point about the close proximity between Rée's concerns and those of Nietzsche. The former's *Psychological Observations* includes a section 'On Religious Things'.

status or credibility for Nietzsche. Religion of any variety is a human projection. In this way he follows the anthropological account of religion laid out by Ludwig Feuerbach in his 1841 work, *The Essence of Christianity*. Feuerbach explains religion as humans projecting their own best qualities into the transcendent realm. Religions tell us nothing true about this realm, but they do reflect aspects of the people and societies that create them. As Feuerbach puts it in that work's Introduction, 'The essential determinations he [the human] attributes to those other individuals must always be determinations emanating from his own being – determinations in which he in truth only projects himself, which only represent his self-objectifications' (Feuerbach 1972).[2]

In addition to portraying religion as a purely human artefact, Nietzsche also presents it as anachronistic. In section 111 he contends that a religious understanding of nature has been superseded by a scientific one, and that because of this 'we see the gates to a religious life closed to us once and for all'. This, of course, only makes sense if religion is seen primarily as an attempt to understand nature and its mysteries, in the way that Nietzsche suggests towards the end of this long passage. If we conceive of religion as doing something more or different than providing an account of the natural world, then the advancement of natural science need not displace religion.[3] Yet whereas a scientific view of nature is typically seen to be at odds with a Romantic one,[4] the first part of

---

[2] According to Brobjer, Nietzsche had been familiar with his ideas in *The Essence of Christianity* since 1860 (2008a: 44, 134, 247). Jörg Salaquarda also identifies Feuerbach as an important influence on Nietzsche's thinking about religion (1996: 95). Although not mentioned often, Feuerbach's name starts appearing in Nietzsche's writings, including his letters and notebooks, in 1870. References to his work continue until 1889 according to *Nietzsche Source* (http://www.nietzschesource.org). Although most of Nietzsche's references to him appear in notebooks, he is mentioned in GM. Eugene Kamenka sees Nietzsche as one of Feuerbach's legatees (1970: viii).

[3] As Young observes, 'it is not entirely clear what the relevance of this passage is to the refutation of "all extant religions"' (2006: 63). Jeffrey Church, however, contends that this understanding of religion as an attempt to explain and master an alien nature derives from David Hume, Feuerbach and David Strauss (2019) and that Nietzsche was familiar with it from his attack on Strauss in the first *Untimely Meditation*.

[4] See, for example, Taylor (1989).

this passage fuses them in a fascinating way. Nietzsche writes that as science has revealed nature's laws and regularities, so

> with Goethe we all recognize in nature the great means for soothing the modern soul, we hear the ticking of this largest of clocks with a yearning for peace, for being at home and in stillness, as if we could drink in this regularity and thereby come to enjoy ourselves for the first time. (HAH 111)

In this way, a scientific understanding of nature can be fused with its Romantic function, which is to soothe the soul and enable the individual to feel at home.

Nietzsche adopts a more conventional Enlightenment posture towards Christianity as outdated two sections later in the passage entitled 'Christianity as anachronism'. There he writes mockingly of beliefs in Jesus as the Son of God, of drinking his blood, and so forth. He concludes with the rhetorical question, 'Are we supposed to believe that something like that is still believed?' (HAH 113). The idea that religion and science are mutually exclusive also informs section 128, which suggests that the goal of modern science is to improve the material conditions of life by reducing pain and increasing longevity. He characterises this as creating 'a sort of eternal bliss' and thus as offering something that has typically been religion's preserve. This is a humorous rendering of an idea that appears in the first section of chapter 3 when Nietzsche predicts that as religion loosens its grip on the social imagination, so people will turn their energies to improving their living conditions. In a quasi-Marxist vein he suggests that whereas in the past religion sought to console people for life's sufferings, in future those sufferings can be reduced through action taken to relieve them, leaving less of a function for religion.

'For every religion has been born out of fear and need' (HAH 110). Having rejected religion's claims to truth, Nietzsche sets out to offer a psychological account of religious belief. This both complements the Feuerbachian anthropological account and is in keeping with his own self-image as a psychologist. Nietzsche's psychological approach to religion operates on two dimensions: he considers both those aspects of the human psyche that give rise to religion (HAH 132, 135) as well as the psychological traits that religion fosters. That religions encourage certain self-interpretations and understandings of sensations and experiences in their followers is evident when he writes that 'Religion and art (metaphysical philosophy too) endeavour to bring about a change in sensibility, in part by changing our judgment about experiences' (HAH 108). Just as humans produce religions, so religions produce humans. But different religions produce different types of humans, and most of Nietzsche's gaze is trained upon the kind of person formed by Christianity.[5]

Christianity

As Julian Young points out, HAH 'contains Nietzsche's first sustained critique of Christianity' (2006: 62) and thus ushers in a feature of his work that made him (in)famous. Indeed, notwithstanding its generic title, chapter 3 is mostly concerned with Christianity rather than religion in general.[6] It does, occasionally, acknowledge other religions – Nietzsche contrasts Hellenic religion with Christianity (HAH 111, 141), for example, and concedes that Indian saints might not fit the profile he sketches of Christian saints (HAH 144). And some of the things he says about Christianity do apply to religion more generally, such as his rejection of its truth value and its status as a human projection. But, for the most part, the religion whose life he has in his sights here is Christianity. And he does not like what he sees. As he puts it, 'it was the fault of the mirror if their nature appeared to them so gloomy and hateful, and that mirror was their work, the very imperfect work of human imagination and judgment' (HAH 133). So while all religions falsify and fabricate, Christianity

---

[5] Cf. Young's point that 'Though Nietzsche places a great deal of methodological emphasis on the *origins* – historical and psychological – of Christian belief, his main effort . . . concerns not origins but rather the unhealthy *consequences* of such belief' (2006: 65, emphasis original).

[6] And Christianity is not, of course, a single thing but an internally heterogeneous tradition. See Salaquarda (1996: 95–8) for the claim that it is essentially Schopenhauer's view of Christianity that Nietzsche engages.

does so in especially harmful directions. As Franco observes, 'Nietzsche here, for the first time in his published writings, identifies [Christianity] as a major factor in the barbarization of modern culture' (2011: 35).

A helpful entrée into Nietzsche's critique of the sort of person Christianity produces appears in 'The destiny of Christianity'. According to this aphorism 'Christianity came into being in order to unburden the heart; but it first had to burden the heart in order to be able to unburden it afterward. In consequence, it will perish' (HAH 119).[7] By Nietzsche's reckoning, Christianity oppresses the human heart in manifold ways. It tells people that they are sinful from the start, it makes them feel intrinsically and persistently unworthy, it renders many natural inclinations, such as eating and sex, suspect and shameful, and it locates release and redemption from this condition outside them. It loudly proclaims 'the complete unworthiness, sinfulness, and contemptibility of humanity' (HAH 117). Another passage explains that Christianity aims not to make people as moral as possible but to make them feel as bad about themselves as possible; construing natural proclivities as sinful in particular has this effect (HAH 141).[8]

To make matters worse, Christians are encouraged to compare themselves with and seek to emulate their God, but that is bound to be a losing proposition, as God is all good and is perfect. '[I]t is from gazing into this shining mirror that his [the Christian's] own nature appears to him so gloomy, so unusually deformed' (HAH 132; cf. 133). One of the particular ways in which Christian doctrine makes humans feel bad about themselves is by depicting God as the paragon of unegotistical action and exhorting humans to emulate this (HAH 132). As we saw in Chapter 2, Nietzsche thinks that unegotistical action in its pure form is impossible, or at the very least extremely rare. He reiterates that view here, declaring that 'Never has any human being done something solely for others and without any personal motive' (HAH 133). He then

---

[7] This point is echoed in an aphorism from chapter 9 which asserts that 'There are people who want to make other people's lives harder for no other reason than to offer them afterward their recipes for making life easier, for example, their Christianity' (HAH 555).
[8] See also Franco's discussion of some of the major themes of this chapter (2011: 35–8).

proceeds to a deconstruction of the whole concept of unegotistical action, enlisting the views of La Rochefoucauld and Rée as part of this critique. He points out that even if it were possible, unegotistical action is not a universalisable good, for in order for one person to act for others, there must be others willing to accept this person acting on their behalf and thus deriving some personal benefit from it. And once again he questions why it is that morality is so closely associated with unegotistical action and motivation.

Nietzsche thus goes beyond Feuerbach, for whom religion represented a projection of human qualities on to God. As Feuerbach sees it,

> The consciousness of God is the self-consciousness of man; the knowledge of God is the self-knowledge of man. Man's notion of himself is his notion of God, just as his notion of God is his notion of himself – the two are identical. What is God to man, that is man's own spirit, man's own soul; what is man's spirit, soul, and heart – that is his God. God is the manifestation of man's inner nature, his expressed self; religion is the solemn unveiling of man's hidden treasures, the avowal of his innermost thoughts, the open confession of the secrets of his love. (Feuerbach 1972)

In Nietzsche's hands, this perspective shows up as way too benign, at least in the case of Christianity. What is perverse about Christianity that Feuerbach misses is that it projects the worst possible view of humans – they are original and continuing sinners, abject failures, redeemable only by grace. The God of Christianity also represents things that humans could never achieve, such as unegotistical action and motivation. From Nietzsche's perspective, God is not 'the manifestation of man's inner nature' but an impossibility who functions to make already debased humans feel even worse about themselves, while at the same time offering to redeem them. Christians are also informed that this perfect omnipotent entity would be sitting in judgement on them, and this belief invokes fear as well as shame for their own imperfect natures (HAH 132). In contrast to Feuerbach's depiction then, for Nietzsche, Christians' notion of themselves is not identical with their notion of God: rather, Christians portray themselves as inferior slaves to God their master.

One of the things that enables Nietzsche to determine how harmful Christianity is to people's self-perceptions is his immersion in ancient Greek religion from his years as a philologist. Although it is also a human construct, Greek religion projects a much more salutary and affirmative view of the gods and their relations to humans. This becomes clear in passage 114, 'The non-Greek element in Christianity', which reports that

> The Greeks did not see the Homeric gods above them as masters and themselves beneath as slaves, as did the Jews. They saw, as it were, only the mirror image of the most successful specimens of their own caste, hence an ideal, not an antithesis of their own being . . . A human being thinks nobly of himself when he gives himself such gods and puts himself in a relationship like that of the lesser nobility to the higher . . .[9]

The foil that ancient Greek views provide to Christianity also appears in two places in section 141. Nietzsche contrasts Christianity's demonisation of eros and procreation with the view of the pre-Socratic philosopher Empedocles who 'knows nothing at all shameful, diabolical, sinful about erotic things'. Later in that long passage he describes how 'in the world of antiquity an immeasurable force of spirit and ingenuity was expended in order to increase the joy in life by means of festive cults'. Christianity, by contrast, blackens everything, which is why Nietzsche dubs it here a 'pessimistic religion'. Of course, he is not simply juxtaposing ancient and Christian outlooks; he further believes that Christianity defeated the ancient view and thus spread its misery far and wide across Western civilisation.[10]

---

[9] Although Nietzsche does not yet portray Christianity as a slave religion, this passage contains a germ of that later argument.

[10] In chapter 2 he criticises those who 'believe that the triumph of Christianity over Greek philosophy is proof of the greater truth of the former . . . it was only the case that the coarser and more violent force triumphed over the more spiritual and delicate one' (HAH 68). As this chapter has indicated, all religions are false for Nietzsche so what matters in evaluating them is the mirror of humans they hold up.

Paragons of Christianity

The last third of chapter 3 comprises an in-depth examination of the most extreme form of Christianity by delving into the psyche of saints and ascetics.[11] As we saw in Chapter 2 of this introduction and guide, Nietzsche complicates the idea of the self in HAH 57, insisting that it is simplistic to see the agent as unified. Rather, the agent is a multiple self, with one side of that self wanting to act in one way and another in another. What looks like unegotistical action can be explained as the triumph of one side over another. That passage's title, 'Morality as self-division of human beings', resonates through his analysis of Christian saints. Nietzsche's key point is that these exceptional figures exhibited a divided personality; one part of them was continually at war with other parts. Such a figure looks 'upon his life as an ongoing battle and himself as a battlefield on which good and evil spirits struggle with varying success' (HAH 141; cf. 137). What really underpins the saint's excellence is the drive to dominate, which has been turned within and against different parts of the self (HAH 142). Any idea that saints are closer to the godly state of unegotistical action and motivation is refuted by Nietzsche's analysis. Indeed, this anatomy of the divided self of saints and ascetics brings them closer to ordinary human beings than to deities. Saints and ascetics turn out to be human, all too human.

Beyond Christianity

As the 'Destiny' aphorism, with its reference to unburdening the heart, illustrates, Nietzsche admits that not all of the Christian experience is gloom and doom. But he complains that when Christians do feel light, unburdened and happy, they attribute this to divine grace rather than seeing it as a respite from false and oppressive Christian teaching. The Christian 'can see in it only

---

[11] Salaquarda suggests, by contrast, that Nietzsche's criticism of Christianity becomes psychological in the 1880s (1996: 93). I don't think that his claim that 'Historical criticism remained Nietzsche's most important argument against religion up to the beginning of the 1880s' (1996: 99) can be sustained in light of this chapter's account of Nietzsche's views about Christianity.

the wholly unmerited radiance upon him of a luminous grace from above' (HAH 134).

Nietzsche is hopeful that the pall cast by Christianity will be lifted: with the advent of scientific knowledge, people will come to learn that religion is fallacious and so can be liberated from this Christian pessimism (HAH 135). He wants to embrace and enhance the human experience of self-love and joy, but without any reference to the divine. He hopes that when Christianity has been overcome, this swathe of positive feelings will be far more accessible because people will not have been weighed down in the first place by Christian teachings that demean them and render any goodness contingent upon divine love and mercy. The emancipation that he envisages following from Christianity's demise is described in the passage 'Sinlessness of human beings', where he writes that the doctrine of sin causes people 'collectively and even individually [to] take themselves to be much darker and more evil than is really the case' (HAH 124). Once the falseness of that teaching is uncovered, 'our whole sensibility is greatly relieved, and human beings and the world appear now and then in a halo of harmlessness that does us good from the bottom up' (HAH 124).

By ridding themselves of false beliefs, humans can attain a sort of self-acceptance that Christianity either discourages or, when it cannot be wholly suppressed, imputes to divine grace. This prospect of being freed from self-contempt is no doubt one of the inducements Nietzsche hopes will expedite Christianity's rejection, in addition to the epistemological realisation that it has no basis in reality. As this suggests, and in keeping with the epistemology-plus approach already imputed to Nietzsche in previous chapters of this book, chapter 3 sometimes implies that correcting the errors of reason will suffice to overcome Christianity, but at other times this transition appears more complicated. Section 135 illustrates the error-correction approach, asserting that once the 'confusion of reason and imagination' involved in Christianity is realised, 'one ceases to be a Christian'. Yet alongside confident pronouncements like this come other passages where Nietzsche is not wholly sanguine about the ease with which religion can be overcome. In the passage entitled 'Religious afterpains' he points to some of the difficulties of fully weaning oneself from religious beliefs and sensations. Mounting a rational critique and rejection of religious beliefs is one thing, but religious moods can be transmitted and experienced via music and art, for example, and this can be very seductive, even for one whose reason has rejected religion (HAH 131).

But even if it could be achieved, Nietzsche is not always wholly sanguine about the prospect of a future without religion, knowing that its false claims cannot be readily replaced with comforting truths. As the second passage in chapter 3 announces, 'humanity may bleed to death from recognizing truth' (HAH 109). This passage takes its bracing title from, and quotes halfway through, the poet Byron's line that 'Sorrow is Knowledge . . . the tree of knowledge is not that of life.'[12] This powerful 'Sorrow is Knowledge' passage ends by recognising that those who would become leaders and teachers of others cannot avoid suffering, which could imply that the painful truth need only be faced by some. This, of course, leaves what they teach others if not the painful truth a moot question. The section entitled 'Where being religious is advantageous' implies that some people might do well to remain religious; those who are 'sober and industrious', those who are servile, and those living 'empty and monotonous' lives (HAH 115). Nietzsche's major complaint here seems to be that groups such as these who benefit from religion should not impose it on or expect it of those who could flourish without it. It is, of course, possible that he is being mostly humorous and even sarcastic here, as he has a low opinion of the personality types listed as finding religion useful. A far more poignant statement on whether religion might persist into the future which does not mock Christianity or its followers comes in the aphorism 'Forbidden generosity'. It laments that 'There is not enough love and goodness in the world to allow us to give any of it away to imaginary beings' (HAH 129). This would suggest that he looks forward to the eradication of religion all together.

---

[12] Lampert points out that Nietzsche had admired the poem from which this comes, *Manfred*, since he was sixteen (2017: 181).

In *Nietzsche's Philosophy of Religion*, Julian Young observes that although HAH contains 'many scathingly anti-religious remarks . . . what remains to be decided is whether these remarks are preparations for a life with no religion or for a life with a *better* religion' (2006: 61, emphasis original). As we have seen here, most of Nietzsche's scathing remarks are levelled at Christianity in particular rather than religion in general. And it would, of course, be possible to look forward to a future without Christianity without thereby anticipating a future without religion at all. Yet as I read HAH, and in particular this chapter devoted to 'The Religious Life', the burden of its remarks suggests that Nietzsche has sufficiently imbibed the spirit of the Enlightenment to think that religion itself can be superseded (cf. Lampert 2017: 180). Young argues differently, contending that 'Nietzsche's future world is not based *purely* on science. It contains, too, a kind of religion' (2006: 71). Yet the one passage that Young finds from chapter 3 to buttress his argument is too ambiguous to do the work he needs it to: HAH 110 asserts that 'there is neither relationship, nor friendship, nor even enmity between religion and real science: they live on different stars' (HAH 110). That says, or even suggests, nothing about their future compatibility: they might coexist indefinitely, or over time the star of religion might fade.[13] The other passage Young draws from appears in chapter 5, 'Signs of Higher and Lower Culture', and recommends a double or bicameral brain (HAH 251). One side is devoted to science and the other to non-science. While non-science includes religion, it is not confined to religion – Nietzsche also locates art and metaphysics there. So that passage provides a fairly slender basis on which to support Young's thesis about religion's continuity. As we shall see, Nietzsche returns to this question of the future of religion in chapter 5 when he ruminates on what the signs of a higher culture are.

---

[13] Contrast Safranski, who also cites HAH 110 but finds there a Nietzsche who is 'a strict and uncompromising follower of the existing enlightened critique of religion' (2002: 192).

4
From the Souls of Artists and Writers

Having peered into the souls of Christian saints and ascetics in chapter 3, chapter 4 turns to those of artists and writers. Franco finds that most of the aphorisms in this chapter 'deal with art in general and not with specific historical styles or aesthetic attitudes' (2011: 41). But once again, the generic nature of the title misleads; as his examples illustrate, Nietzsche is not making claims about artists and writers from all times and places. His gaze rests securely on those from the Western tradition, from ancient times to the contemporaneous. This more limited purview befits HAH's insistence that scientific knowledge is historically aware, and eschews the large, essentialising and universalising gestures of metaphysics. In keeping with this spirit of attention to specifics, it will help to contextualise and clarify chapter 4's remarks to probe exactly who or what he has in mind when referring to art, artists and writers. Having catalogued that, this chapter then lays out his scientific approach to art which exposes the close affinity between art, religion and traditional metaphysics. Nietzsche tries to deflate myths about the artistic process. The chapter then segues into his account of the artistic genius. It concludes by reflecting on what Nietzsche thinks the role of art in a more enlightened future might be.

Who and what?

Nietzsche distinguishes the plastic arts [*die bildende Kunst*] from the verbal arts [*die redende Kunst*] (HAH 160; cf. 152). Although he offers no clear definition of either, his examples suggest that the plastic arts include both three-dimensional products such as architecture and sculpture and the visual arts such as painting. He refers to architecture in general (HAH 218), to that of the ancient and Renaissance periods (HAH 219), and to the Greek temple at Paestum (HAH 145) as well as Gothic cathedrals (HAH 220). He comments on the huge impact made by the seventeenth-century Italian architect and sculptor Gian Lorenzo Bernini (HAH 161). He also makes non-specific references to sculptors (HAH 160, 171). In addition to general references to painters (HAH 160, 173), examples in this chapter include the Italian Renaissance figures Raphael (HAH 162, 220) and Michelangelo (HAH 220)[1] and the seventeenth-century Spaniard Bartolomé Esteban Murillo (HAH 219).

When it comes to the verbal arts, Nietzsche seems to have in mind mostly novels (HAH 163) and poetry (HAH 152, 189), but he also makes a reference to oration (HAH 161) and several to theatre, which is, of course, both written and spoken. The poets he specifies include the Greeks Homer (HAH 154, 159, 211), Hesiod (HAH 170) and Simonides (HAH 154). More recent poets include Dante – although Nietzsche names only his work from the early fourteenth century, *The Divine Comedy*, and not the author himself (HAH 220). Lessing, the German poet from the eighteenth century, is mentioned (HAH 221), along with his compatriot and near-contemporary, Schiller (HAH 221). Schiller was, however, both poet and playwright and Nietzsche does seem to have theatre in mind in one of his invocations of Schiller (HAH 176). Being both poet and dramatist is a feature that Schiller shares with some of the other masters of the verbal arts whom Nietzsche identifies – Shakespeare (HAH 162, 176, 221) and Byron (HAH 221). In addition to these English writers, Nietzsche also refers collectively to French tragedy and to French dramatists (HAH 221), singling Voltaire out for notice among these as 'the last of the great dramatists who used Greek moderation to restrain a polymorphic soul' (HAH 221). The ancient figures he specifies who are relevant to

---

[1] Although Raphael was also an architect and Michelangelo an architect, sculptor and poet, Nietzsche refers only to their paintings.

drama in general and tragedy in particular are Aeschylus (HAH 159, 170) and Euripides (HAH 170).

Although neither a plastic nor a verbal art form, music is very important in Nietzsche's reflection on the arts. He refers to music in general (HAH 152, 171, 222), to modern music (HAH 221) and to opera (HAH 219). Specific composers mentioned are the sixteenth-century Italian Palestrina (HAH 219), the German Bach from the eighteenth century (HAH 219), and his German successor Beethoven (HAH 153, 173). But the category of the artist seems to embrace not just the composer but also the performer and even the conductor of music (HAH 171, 172). Music as an art form is bound to be important for Nietzsche's reflections because of his continuing intellectual and emotional engagement with two figures who go unnamed in this chapter on artists and writers – Richard Wagner and Arthur Schopenhauer.[2]

Handwerk observes that 'the "artist" described in general terms in HAH often turns out to refer in the notebooks specifically to Richard Wagner' (2013: 583; cf. Hayman 1980: 202). Franco likewise contends that, although unnamed, 'Wagner is his principal target' (2011: 39). Given the wide range of artists whom Nietzsche mentions in this chapter, I propose that it is the artistic genius and the cult surrounding him, more often than just 'the artist', who is the proxy for Wagner.

Art and science

Given HAH's enthusiasm for science, it should come as no surprise that this chapter ventures a scientific approach to art [*Die Wissenschaft der Kunst*] (HAH 145). What Nietzsche's scientific lens reveals is the close affinity between art, religion and traditional metaphysics. One passage asserts that 'artists of all ages . . . are the glorifiers of the religious and philosophical errors of humanity' (HAH 220). Another suggests that as enlightenment has slowly

---

[2] HAH 215 is, for example, a critique of Schopenhauer without naming him, for it rejects the idea that music has a special significance, that it represents our innermost being, or that it expresses the will.

chipped away at religious belief, some of the emotions and energies formerly directed towards religion have been channelled into art (HAH 150). Another illustration of art's connection with religion and metaphysics appears in the way that artists promulgate a myth of 'the sudden springing forth of perfection' of the artwork (HAH 145). A scientific approach must expose this illusion, with its 'erroneous reasoning and self-indulgence' (HAH 145). A closely related myth about the artistic process that Nietzsche believes science should dispel is that of inspiration. This serves as the artistic analogue of the religious belief in miracles. He underscores instead the perspiration dimension of artistic creation, with all the hard work, false starts and sheer effort that goes into aesthetic production. As he insists, 'All the great artists were great workers, tireless not only in inventing, but also in rejecting, sifting, reshaping, ordering' (HAH 155; cf. 156).

Indeed, throughout this chapter, many of Nietzsche's remarks seem to establish a dichotomy between art and science (HAH 160), just as he had previously posited such a clash between science on the one hand and religion and metaphysics on the other. The artist is interested in meaning, the scientist in truth. Artists drape themselves in myth, fantasy and symbol; scientists trade in 'sober, simple methods and results' (HAH 146). Art palliates suffering and hardship, whereas science seeks to reduce or remove it where possible (HAH 148). Art is backward looking, both in the sense that it reaches back to earlier times (HAH 147, 148) and that it represents an earlier stage of culture. Science, by contrast, both looks to and represents the future. Here Nietzsche seems to rely on a tacit and untheorised stadial view of history according to which societies progress sequentially through different periods of development. And just as art belongs to earlier phases of socio-historical development, so art and the artist are childish. Art also infantilises. As Nietzsche puts it, the artist 'does not stand in the foremost ranks of the enlightenment and the progressive masculinization of humanity: he has remained a lifelong child or adolescent . . . it becomes his task to juvenilize humanity' (HAH 147). Science is, by contrast, an adult-only activity. This connection between art and immaturity is also suggested in the final passage of chapter 4 where he writes that humanity will soon see art 'as a touching recollection of the joys of youth' (HAH 223).

Several of these pejorative views of art are collated when Nietzsche characterises the individual caught in art's powerful grip as one who

> comes to worship sudden stimulation, believes in gods and demons, sees spirits throughout nature, hates science . . . desires the overthrow of all circumstances that are not favourable to art with the vehemence and unfairness . . . of a child. Now, the artist is himself already a backward being because he lingers in games appropriate for adolescence and childhood: besides which, he gradually regresses into past eras. (HAH 159)

All in all then, Nietzsche's stadial view of history intersects with the depiction of art as childish as he suggests that art belongs to an earlier period of human development, and that at this earlier period humans were still as children. But these associations of art with infancy can only be polemical and directed at Wagner, for Nietzsche surely cannot maintain that the whole cast of artists he catalogues in chapter 4 are childish figures who represent forces of regression.

The genius

Just as ascetics and saints represent the most extreme form of Christianity in chapter 3, so the genius plays that role in this chapter's study of artists and writers. Nietzsche offers several observations on the figure of the genius. Most are not flattering, and there are grounds for suspecting that although this chapter's referent for the artist might shift, the account of the artistic genius is most likely to be code for Wagner. It is, for example, hard not to hear an allusion to Wagner in the claim that 'all great talents have the fateful tendency to crush many weaker forces and shoots and to lay waste . . . to all of nature around them' (HAH 158). For this reason Nietzsche believes that it is better to have a cluster of geniuses at the same time: they 'keep one another within limits;

their struggle usually leaves air and light for the weaker and more delicate natures, too' (HAH 158).

But some of Nietzsche's remarks about the genius seem less motivated by his hostile feelings towards Wagner, as, for example, when he writes of the seemingly genuine difficulty the genius faces in finding an audience. If such a creator 'stands at a very high level, there may not be anyone able to enjoy what he does; he offers food, but no one wants it' (HAH 157). If unable to find an audience, the solitary genius can take comfort in creative passion: 'he has more pleasure in creating than other people have in any other kind of activity' (HAH 157). No one wants the food, Nietzsche implies, because their taste has not been appropriately educated and elevated. Having a cluster of geniuses could also help with this problem, as a group of influencers would find it easier to raise the public's taste than any individual working alone. This benefit of having a cluster of geniuses within a culture is illustrated in HAH 170 as Nietzsche looks back to the Greeks. Their tragedians and poets were highly competitive and this had salutary effects for the quality of their work. He nominates Aeschylus and Euripides as striving to change the terms on which their art was evaluated. They defined new standards of excellence and persuaded others to agree to and apply them.

Entitled 'The sufferings of genius and their value', HAH 157 introduces the idea of geniuses of knowledge, such as Kepler and Spinoza, indicating that Nietzsche is thinking about this figure of the genius beyond the confines of art and not simply as a proxy for Wagner. Nietzsche compares the genius of knowledge favourably to the genius of art, for the former is less driven by ambition and envy and so less preoccupied with enjoying recognition, in the present at least. Having a greater eye for posterity than does his artistic counterpart, the genius of knowledge can hope that his current efforts will bear fruit in the future. This positive account of the genius of knowledge fits with HAH's overall remarks about the person of knowledge as modest and committed to the quiet labour of science. Yet he also deems the 'sufferings and privations' of the genius of knowledge to be 'genuinely greater' than that of the artistic genius, although he does not here explain why. My guess is that the genius of knowledge is more often and more fully confronted with stark and unpalatable truths about the world, whereas the artist, as indicated above, weaves fantasy and illusion and takes refuge from the truth in those fabrications. As Nietzsche says in HAH 151, 'Art makes the sight of life bearable by laying the gauze of indistinct thinking over it.' This could imply that the world that scientists see has something unbearable about it, and exposure to these painful truths could be the source of the genius of knowledge's greater sufferings and privations.

HAH 157 culminates in the evocation of a sort of super or triple-threat genius – a figure possessed of a genius for knowing and for doing and for morality. But having conjured such a paragon, Nietzsche retreats by suggesting that there is currently no way to even measure such a being. Yet from these dizzy heights, he moves precipitately within a few passages to what appears to be a deflation of what he calls the cult of the genius, or at least that part of it that perpetuates religious thinking about artistic works as the quasi-miraculous products of flashes of inspiration. As he did with the artist in HAH 155, here Nietzsche underscores the effortful, workaday aspects of the genius's creation in which the creator is always on the lookout for materials with which to realise his vision and is constantly sorting and sifting these. Nietzsche likens this labour to 'the activity of the inventor in mechanics, of the astronomer or the historical scholar, of the master tactician' (HAH 162). He concludes that when correctly understood, the work of the artistic genius is not so different from that of scientific geniuses.

This same insistence on the workaday or perspiration dimension of genius is on remarkable display in the very next passage, 'The seriousness of craft'. There Nietzsche outlines how much labour goes into artistic production, offering this time the example of the novelist. In its extraordinary detail, this passage reads like a handbook for aspiring writers, advising them to practise, practise, practise for at least a decade. Nietzsche's overarching point, however, is that geniuses are made not born, and they become geniuses through intense labour and effort and through working and reworking parts before forging them into a whole. The cult of genius, with its religious enthusiasms about creation, conceals this repeated and strenuous effort and striving. By offering his more deflationary, but also more accurate, picture of the genius as a labourer, Nietzsche is reminding such figures and their followers what 'purely human qualities have flowed together in them' (HAH 164). Just like saints, geniuses are revealed to be human, all too human. They also need to be reminded of the good fortune of their education and what they learned from 'the best teachers, models, and methods' (HAH 164).

HAH 162 is entitled 'The cult of genius, from vanity', but the vanity at the source of this cult turns out not to be that of the genius. Adopting the perspective of non-geniuses, this passage proposes that one of the reasons people are so willing to place artistic geniuses on pedestals is to soothe their own vanity. By locating these creators in a separate stratosphere, and distancing them from the rest of humanity, those who are not geniuses feel less diminished by comparison. As Nietzsche says, 'our vanity, our love of self, demands the cult of genius: for only if we think of genius as being quite far away from us, as a *miraculum*, does it not hurt us' (HAH 162). So the cult of genius attracts its followers because it flatters not only the artist but also the non-geniuses. But shortly after, in HAH 164, Nietzsche points out that this flattery can be dangerous and ultimately self-destructive for the genius. As the genius comes to believe his own press, his ego becomes massively inflated. He 'begins to reel and to take himself for something superhuman'. This makes the genius very hostile to criticism, irresponsible, superior to others and condescending. The example of the genius who becomes 'convinced of his own divinity' Nietzsche gives is Napoleon, but it is very hard to believe that he is not also thinking of Wagner here.

One effect of Nietzsche's efforts to deflate the religiously inspired cult of genius is to break down the distinction between science and art that he in other places seems so keen to erect. As we saw above, HAH 162 assimilates artistic production and creation to scientific modes of production and creation – the inventor in mechanics, the astronomer, the historical scholar. There are other moments when he allows art and science to meet rather than being cordoned off into separate domains. He characterises, for example, Renaissance and pre-Renaissance music as manifesting 'that basically scientific pleasure in artistic feats of harmonics and counterpoints' (HAH 219). It is also noteworthy that chapter 4's longest passage (HAH 221) includes abundant praise for Voltaire, but in this context it is for his skill as an artist. Nietzsche lauds his play *Mahomet*. Voltaire is definitely a paragon of scientific thinking and free-spiritedness throughout HAH, and his virtues as such also manifest themselves in his art. As mentioned briefly above, Nietzsche honours him as

> the last of the great dramatists who used Greek moderation to restrain a polymorphic soul that could encompass the greatest tragic thunderstorms . . . he was the last great writer who had a Greek ear, a Greek aesthetic conscientiousness, a Greek simplicity and charm in his handling of prose discourse; just as he was one of the last of those people who could combine in themselves the highest freedom of the spirit and an absolutely unrevolutionary disposition without being inconsistent and cowardly. (HAH 221)

But along with these examples of science and art fusing in productive ways, art can infiltrate science, and this causes Nietzsche some concern. For example, the intellectual character of the free spirit is tried at those times when art carries a metaphysical message. It may be 'that at one place in Beethoven's Ninth Symphony he [the free spirit] feels himself hovering above the earth in a starry vault, with the dream of immortality in his heart' (HAH 153). Hearing the siren call of what Nietzsche describes as the free spirit's 'lost love – whether we call it religion or metaphysics' causes great distress. In this same vein, 'deep pain' attends the realisation that in the past artists have been motivated to create by religious beliefs that can no longer be sustained. Nietzsche worries that 'the rainbow colors at the outermost ends of human knowing and imagining fade' (HAH 220), and it is not clear what can replace this once religion has declined.

Chapter 4's penultimate paragraph reflects explicitly on the place of art in an enlightened future. Asking 'What remains of art', HAH 222 begins by acknowledging that art's value or status depends in part on metaphysics. Anyone who believes in eternal truths and unchanging characters can believe that art manifests these things. However, adopting the historical outlook urged in HAH means that 'the artist can give his image validity only for a certain time, because humanity as a whole has come to be and is changeable, and even the individual human being is neither fixed nor enduring'. What art has always done, however, which does hold its value, is to affirm life's goodness. But Nietzsche allows that henceforth that affirmation could be conveyed by means other than art:

> We could give up art, but would not thereby forfeit the capacity we have learned from it: just as we have given up religion, but not the heightening of sensibility and exaltation acquired from it . . . the intense and manifold delight in life that has been implanted by art [would] still demand satisfaction after its [art's] disappearance. (HAH 222)

He does not here indicate what alternatives to art would convey these emotions, but he concludes this passage by claiming that 'The scientific human being is a further development of the artistic one.' This suggests that the scientist could in some way carry these functions and emotions forward. Although light on details, this passage does allow theoretically that art could disappear from human life or be so reconfigured as to be almost unrecognisable.

Chapter 4's final passage, 'Twilight of art', likewise suggests that art might be a thing of the past. Seemingly incapable of adulthood, art passes from childhood to death. Nietzsche predicts that 'We will soon view the artist as a magnificent relic . . . honouring a wonderful stranger upon whose strength and beauty the happiness of earlier times depended' (HAH 223). In this chapter at least, his under-developed stadial view of history seems to have the last word, with its idea that art could become an obsolete aspect of human culture. And it is noteworthy too that when Nietzsche champions Voltaire, it is all in the past tense. After him, the French 'suddenly lacked the great talents who would have led the way in developing tragedy from constraint into the appearance of freedom'; what he achieved with *Mahomet* has been 'lost once and for all to European culture by that break from tradition'; he represents 'the last great writer' capable of emulating the Greek aesthetic and 'he was one of the last of those people' with such admirable personal characteristics. So in these ways his panegyric for Voltaire functions more as eulogy than as an exemplar for free spirits of the future.

Once again, Young finds a different image of the future in HAH. On the one hand he acknowledges HAH's 'generally antipathetic stance toward art. Nietzsche calls it obscurantist, a lure back to the old metaphysics, a narcotic, emotional power without intellectual responsibility' (2006: 74). But Young infers that it is only art influenced by Christianity that will be superannuated (2006: 74) and that Nietzsche's critique is confined to '"romantic" art, metaphysical art, art that deals in world-transcendence . . . Wagner's art' (2010: 250). For Young, Nietzsche believes that there remains 'a vital role for art to perform' in the future (2006: 74; cf. 2010: 263). But his evidence for this comes not from HAH but from MOM (99, 172) and WS (170). This collapsing of what began as three separate works into one obscures the possibility that Nietzsche changed his mind about a future role for art, and that the later two writings offer correctives to his earlier views in HAH. Yet as we shall see in Chapters 10 and 11 below, that is precisely the arc of Nietzsche's thinking about art across these three works.

On those occasions when Young does not conflate the three works, he is able to recognise that HAH seems to dismiss art (1992: 72). In response to this, he criticises Nietzsche for failing to appreciate art's multiple functions and suggests that some of these could easily live on into the future (1992: 72). Franco's view of Nietzsche's attitude towards art in HAH is more accurate, for he finds that 'Art no longer belongs among the progressive forces in history, and . . . must be superseded as the fundamental activity of human beings' (2011: 40; cf. 44). The very next chapter provides more evidence to support this reading.

5
Signs of Higher and Lower Culture

As Cohen notes, chapter 5 lies at the centre of HAH and its 'discussion of the free spirit is at the centre of the book and thus highlights it' (Cohen 2010: 61; see also 194–5).[1] Franco also notes this chapter's central position,[2] but for him, what makes chapter 5 thematically central is that it provides '[t]he primary locus of Nietzsche's reflections on culture' (2011: 16).[3] Chapter 5's title harks back to one of HAH's very first passages, where Nietzsche announces that 'It is the characteristic mark[4] of a higher culture to esteem the small, unpretentious truths found by rigorous methods more highly than the blissful and blinding errors that stem from metaphysical and artistic ages and human beings' (HAH 3). This early passage suggests that the signs of a higher culture include respect for truth, science and reason whereas those of lower culture are a fascination with art, religion and metaphysics (cf. Franco 2011: 44). This chapter looks in more detail at what the signs of a higher culture are for Nietzsche, as well as what role the free

---

[1] Chapters 4 and 5 of Cohen (2010) provide a very helpful discussion of free spirits.
[2] And yet Franco treats the two volumes of HAH as a unity, which displaces this chapter from the centre of the work, physically at least. Franco (2011: 44–50) offers a treatment of some of the themes of this chapter.
[3] As this indicates, culture is, in Franco's estimation, the key organising concept for the whole of HAH (2011: 16, 54). See Abbey (2014) for my reply to his claim.
[4] Even though nothing substantive seems to be at stake here, I follow Hollingdale rather than Handwerk in translating *Merkmal* as 'mark' rather than 'sign', in order to flag that Nietzsche uses a different term (*Anzeichen*) in chapter 5's title.

spirit might play in bringing such a culture into being. Nietzsche is clear that the present is an interregnum and the future could go in more or less positive directions. Free spirits are vital forces for progressive change but they also face myriad obstacles in realising their potential.

Conservatism and change

Towards the halfway mark of chapter 5, Nietzsche observes that the era in which he lives feels like an interregnum, 'an interim state; the old worldviews, the old cultures, still exist in part, the new ones are not yet secure and habitual and hence lack decisiveness and consistency' (HAH 248). This image of a present caught between a past that must be overcome and a future as yet unclear recurs at the chapter's end as he urges his contemporaries not to regret their liminal condition: 'do not disdain it [the age] for still being religious; explore fully the extent to which you still have genuine access to art' (HAH 292). Although they have ultimately to be outgrown, having known religion and art confers benefits; if they were not loved 'like a mother and a nurse . . . we cannot become wise' (HAH 292). In both passages he consoles his readers about the current intermezzo while exhorting them to be brave [*tapfer*] (HAH 248) or to move forward with confidence [*guten Vertrauens*] (HAH 292). Although this chapter's final section ends on a buoyant note, the earlier passage concludes with the recognition that things could go either way from this interregnum – if the hope for progress is not realised, his contemporaries must attribute it to the damned (human) race to which they belong (HAH 248). Even though success cannot be guaranteed, Nietzsche is adamant that humans can no longer place their faith in the equivalent of miracles for salutary socio-cultural change. Humans 'must watch over the further destiny of culture with a sharp eye' (HAH 245). Precisely because people know that the important project of cultural renewal could fail, 'we are perhaps in a position to prevent the future from reaching such an end' (HAH 247). He devotes a lot of chapter 5 to reflecting on the forces that could contribute to this current condition of uncertainty turning out to be a prelude to a higher rather than to a lower culture.

Chapter 5 begins by outlining the characteristics of robust communities, for these are the things that make cultures 'secure and habitual', lending them 'decisiveness and consistency' (HAH 248). Common beliefs, enduring customs and individual conformity make communities strong and durable (HAH 224). But in generating stability, these forces promote, by their very nature, stasis and so do not prepare communities for change nor foster progress. Sources of innovation, by contrast, lie within those whom Nietzsche calls 'the more unconstrained, the much more uncertain and morally weaker individuals' (HAH 224). As he declares, 'the strongest natures hold the type fast; the weaker ones help to develop it further' (HAH 224).[5] Innovators earn these adjectives from the perspective of the more stolid community members (cf. Young 2006: 78 n. 20), for here unconstrained means not bowing to convention; uncertain means thinking twice (or more often) about social dictates; and morally weaker means not being entirely formed by community opinion and mores. A bit later in the passage he describes these weaker individuals as 'degenerate', but again, they only qualify as such from the standpoint of the fully integrated community members.[6] A little further on he applies some less, or perhaps just differently, loaded terms, calling those who deviate from social dictates 'more delicate and free'. As the term 'delicate' could signal, Nietzsche readily admits that many of these potential change agents sink without a trace, for the forces of conservatism they confront can prove too obdurate for them to make any impact. But occasionally their attempts to introduce novelty do have a productive effect, for some communities, or perhaps all communities at some time, prove strong enough to absorb and incorporate the challenge of novelty. Nietzsche

---

[5] Here I deviate from Handwerk's translation by rendering *halten den Typus fest* as 'hold the type fast' rather than 'maintain the type'.

[6] This passage buttresses one of the origin of morality accounts discussed in chapter 2. As we saw there, in HAH 96 Nietzsche claims that the designation 'good' originally applied to people who simply followed their society's customs and conventions. The greater the ease with which one conformed, the better the person, but the *sine qua non* of goodness is to act in accordance with custom whatever one's motivation or comfort level. Evil was, conversely, applied to those who flouted society's conventions. These customs and conventions arose in order to preserve the society, so the good person is one who contributes to that society's self-reproduction over time, while the evil one resists and disrupts it.

describes this dynamic thus: 'A people that has begun to crumble and weaken somewhere, but is on the whole still strong and healthy, can absorb the infection of what is new and incorporate it advantageously' (HAH 224).

Free spirits

This theory of social change sets the scene for the free spirit's re-entry into HAH. Although HAH is subtitled 'A Book for Free Spirits', until we get to chapter 5 this figure has only been explicitly mentioned twice. As we have seen, the first reference appears in chapter 1 when Nietzsche urges free spirits to practise radical scepticism about the foundations of philosophical thinking. He warns that free spirits can remain in thrall to the metaphysical tradition even as they think they are escaping it (HAH 30). The second reference also appears in the context of dangers and the risk of backsliding. Nietzsche cautions that the free spirit's intellectual character may be tried in those moments when art bears a metaphysical message and the free spirit hears the siren call of 'lost love – whether we call it religion or metaphysics' (HAH 153). Chapter 5's account of the free spirit likewise begins with terms that initially appear to be unpropitious, for the free spirit is one of the weak, degenerate characters who possesses the potential to disturb a stable community. But in the wrong conditions, a free spirit might have no impact whatsoever on the ambient society.

Nietzsche's definition of the free spirit reveals instantly how far such figures are from the strong, fully integrated community members who perpetuate culture, custom and convention. The free spirit 'thinks differently from what we expect of him on the basis of his origin, environment, his social rank and position, or on the basis of the prevailing views of the time. He is the exception, the fettered[7] spirits are the rule' (HAH 225). One of the things that makes such a spirit free is having 'freed himself from tradition' (HAH 225). Of course, thinking differently from others in one's society could be motivated by perversity or a spirit of rebellion or

---

[7] Again I deviate from Handwerk who translates *gebundenen* as constrained. Hollingdale's choice of 'fettered' strikes me as better in this case.

the desire to attract attention – as Nietzsche claims the fettered spirits are likely to think. But these alternative interpretations are refuted as he explains what it is that makes the free spirit exceptional compared to fellow community members. As further evidence of the enlightenment mood of Nietzsche's thinking at this time, we are told that free spirits demand reasons for things; others, by contrast, live by faith. The free spirits' demand for reasons means, moreover, that more often than not they are on the side of truth, or at least have 'the spirit of truthful inquiry' [*den Geist der Wahrheitsforschung*] on their side (HAH 225). As HAH 226 indicates, the faith by which the non-free spirits live might, but need not, be religious faith; it is fundamentally an unquestioning trust in one's society's conventions, customs, practices, beliefs and norms. This contrast between the free spirit and the typical community member reappears as the next passage emphasises that the strength and durability of a society and culture comes from 'the faith that the fettered spirits have in them' (HAH 227). Such faith consists in and is sustained by their unwillingness or uninterest when it comes to looking for reasons to justify social arrangements.

Those living such unreflective and fully integrated lives are also congratulated for the goodness and strength of their character (HAH 228). But Nietzsche points out that these qualities come about only because many options are occluded; successful socialisation produces individuals who follow their society's byways with little or no resistance. What society praises as good character is actually 'a narrowness of views that has, out of habit, become instinctive' (HAH 228). Free spirits are, by contrast, critical questioners of the things their societies take for granted. And by contrast with the fortitude born of compliance with convention, the closure of reflection and the foreclosure of other options, the free spirit always seems weak. Such an individual is 'acquainted with too many motives and points of view and therefore has an uncertain, inexperienced hand' (HAH 230). Yet if free spirits are to become vehicles of truth and progress in their societies, if they are to assert themselves 'and not perish without effect' (HAH 230), they must become stronger. Their strength will, of course, be different from that of the fettered spirits, for they have to push against, rather than assimilate themselves to, prevailing opinion and habitual practices.

So when Nietzsche's belief, mentioned above, that those hoping for a higher culture in the future should wittingly steer things in that direction meets his belief that free spirits can be forces for positive change, it comes as no surprise that the free spirit should assume a leadership role in shaping such salutary cultural change. Section 282, for example, asserts that the free spirit's task is 'commanding from a lonely position[8] all the scientific and scholarly people[9] who have been called to arms and of showing them the paths and goals of culture' (HAH 282). Their leadership task distinguishes free spirits from scholars for reasons Nietzsche outlines in section 250, which explains that even though some contemporary scholars want to be heralds of the new culture, they are still too caught in the old. 'The past is still too powerful in their muscles; they are still standing in an unfree[10] position and are half worldly priests, half the dependent educators of aristocratic people and classes, and furthermore are crippled and deadened by the pedantry of science and by outdated, uninspired methods' (HAH 250).[11] Contemporary scholars personify the interim condition outlined at the start of this chapter, for 'The ghosts of the past walk within them as well as the ghosts of the future' (HAH 250). Too implicated in the interregnum, they cannot lead the way out.

Ingenious

Given the leadership role that Nietzsche assigns to them, the question about how free spirits and their impact can be strengthened becomes important and timely. His reflections on this challenge rapidly bleed into a discussion of genius, for having asked

---

[8] I once again prefer Hollingdale's translation of *einem einsam gelegen Standorte* to Handwerk's 'isolated site'.

[9] Handwerk translates *wissenschaftlichen und gelehrten Menschen* as 'scientists and scholars'.

[10] Handwerk translates *unfreien* as 'constrained', Hollingdale as 'constricted'. But as the implicit contrast is with free spirits, 'unfree' strikes me as the best choice.

[11] My guess is that the scientists Nietzsche has in mind here are contemporary philologists who he typically characterises as pedantic and conservative. He is, after all, describing 'our men of learning' here.

'How does the strong spirit (*esprit fort*) come to be?' he immediately answers 'This is in an individual case the question of how to beget genius' (HAH 230). The very next passage classifies 'the emergence of the perfect free spirit' as a special case of 'the emergence of genius' (HAH 231). The term genius recalls his ruminations on this topic in chapter 4's account of artistic genius. In chapter 5, however, he seems to be using this term without reservation or critique, which reminds us that in chapter 4 he did also speak of the genius of knowledge without apparent discomfort or distance (HAH 157). Indeed, he calls this out quite directly in section 231, 'The origin of genius', inviting readers to understand the term 'without any mythological or religious flavour'.[12]

Because a strong free spirit needs 'energy', 'unbending strength' and 'persistence' (HAH 230), Nietzsche asks whence these qualities emanate. As was the case in chapter 4, he is clear that they should not be viewed as quasi-miracles, for that would lapse into a religious view of individual greatness. It would also imply that the way to cultivate genius is to wait and pray, which would be too passive an approach for him, given how much is at stake. Moreover, in 'Miraculous education', he indicates that the miracle method focuses only on the successes. What about all the cases of individuals who failed to achieve greatness or genius? Vast talent might have been squandered, yet this approach can neither acknowledge nor act to remedy that. As an alternative, 'An education that no longer believes in miracles' (HAH 242) will need to be designed around three issues: How much energy has been inherited? How much can be added to what is inherited? How can the individual occupy a place between public and private cultures?

Nietzsche offers an answer of sorts to the first and second issues posed by an education that no longer believes in miracles in this chapter's passage on 'Talent'. That brief reflection announces that in current conditions, many people have by nature access to many talents. The key to successfully discharging one's talents 'in works

---

[12] Franco, by contrast, does not distinguish between Nietzsche's critical and sincere uses of the idea of genius (2011: 49).

and actions' lies in the combination of 'tenacity, persistence, and energy' that one is both born with and trained for (HAH 263). He echoes this position in a later passage, claiming that when it comes to success, inherited talent matters less than does 'the degree of vigor that goes along with it' (HAH 272). Unbending strength, tenacity, persistence, energy and vigour turn out to be essential in part because Nietzsche is clear that whatever else it involves, becoming a genius incurs considerable suffering and torment. He likens it to being imprisoned and compelled to find one's freedom (HAH 231), while section 242 alludes to the genius enduring 'terrible circumstances'.[13] It is interesting to note that section 256 observes that having 'rigorously pursued a rigorous science' is a fertile training ground for some of these key qualities. What matters is less what one learns from the rigorous science than 'the increase in energy, in deductive capacity, in tenacity of perseverance; one has learned how to attain a purpose purposefully' (HAH 256).

The third question asked of an education that no longer believes in miracles is how an individual can develop a strong and individual identity while also being exposed to the myriad forces that make up modern culture. As we saw above, most cultures enable individuals to form strong characters by limiting their exposure to different influences. The cultivated person, by contrast, finds everything interesting (HAH 254), and many of the observations Nietzsche drops in about modern life – its pace (HAH 284–5), the number of languages people speak, its growing cosmopolitanism, the likelihood of air travel (HAH 257) – conspire to make it kaleidoscopic and potentially overwhelming. The challenge for the free spirit is to be exposed to, without dissolving into, modern culture's dazzling and dizzying diversity. It is interesting to note a later passage's suggestion that science helps to procure this sort of focus and concentration. 'Scientific natures . . . know that the talent for having

---

[13] HAH 233 might provide further evidence for this with its reference to mistreating and torturing people as a way of engendering genius. But having described this tortuous process that history 'seems' to recommend, he concludes by sowing doubt: 'But perhaps we have misunderstood.' Cohen offers a lengthy discussion of this (2010: 130–1) whereas Franco takes this passage at face value (2011: 49).

all sorts of ideas occur to them must be strictly curbed by the spirit of science' (HAH 264). Such natures encounter and take an interest in many things, but train their gaze on 'what is real, valid, genuine' (HAH 264).

A scientific education is one of the things that helps to strengthen free spirits and prepare them for a leadership role in improving their culture. Such an education would also appeal to their thirst for rational explanations rather than faith in social conventions. And both sets of observations belong to what I am calling the epistemology-plus perspective, where what matters is not just what scientific thinkers know but how they know, what sort of thinkers they are, how they live with their knowledge as well as how they come by it.

Contours of higher culture

In the event that enough strong free spirits arise to lead society out of its current impasse, what will the higher culture of the future look like? Answering this is by necessity speculative and indeterminate, as those who steer cultural progress will be the ones to determine its shape. But it is still meaningful to consider some of the general contours of a higher culture that Nietzsche identifies, and, conversely, what features will be marginal or absent. Several of the signs suggest that at this stage of his thinking, a higher culture will be devoid of religion, art or metaphysics, so again chapter 5 builds on remarks in chapters 2, 3 and 4 about the likely attrition of each of these forces over time. Nietzsche maintains, moreover, as we have also seen in the earlier chapters, that these three forces are closely intertwined and have been mutually reinforcing, so the atrophy of one is likely to affect the others. Section 265 begins with the declaration that 'Schooling has no task more important than teaching rigorous thinking, careful judging, and logical reasoning: therefore it must disregard everything that is not useful for these operations, such as religion' (HAH 265). This passage could support the reading mooted in Chapter 3 of this introduction and guide that religion will occupy no place in the future for Nietzsche, although of course, just to insist that religion be excluded from the curriculum is not tantamount to predicting or willing its demise in the culture at large. In section 234, however, he suggests pretty clearly that the future will be devoid of religion, writing that 'religious feeling . . . has had its time, and many fine things can never grow again because they were able to grow only from it' (HAH 234).

A little later in the same passage Nietzsche adds that 'Forces upon which art . . . depends could actually die out; the pleasure in lies, in imprecision, in the symbolic, in intoxication, in ecstasy, could come to be disdained' (HAH 234). He echoes this point about art, and adds religion to the mix, in HAH 239, warning that

> it is pure fantasy to believe that a new, higher stage of humanity will unite in itself all the merits of earlier stages and, for example, that it must also engender the highest form of art . . . What grew out of religion and in proximity to it cannot grow again if religion has been destroyed . . . (HA 239)

Chapter 5's final passage reiterates this idea that art and religion will be eventually superannuated: exhorting free spirits to move forward, Nietzsche urges that 'we must be able to look outward beyond them and be able to outgrow them' (HAH 292).

But this impression that a higher culture of the future will be dominated by a scientific approach to knowledge which has superseded metaphysics, religion and art is mitigated by the passage 'Future of science'. There Nietzsche imagines a time in which the scientific approach has become so dominant as to be ubiquitous, 'all the important truths of science . . . [have] become everyday, ordinary things' (HAH 251). Adopting once again the epistemology-plus perspective, he casts doubt not on the gains for truth that this would incur but on the quality of experience for the knowers. Learning from science affords less pleasure than actually doing it, so once scientific truths begin to accumulate, there will be more learning and less doing, even for the scientists themselves (cf. HAH 257). Contemplating this scenario, Nietzsche corrects for its disadvantages by stipulating that

> A higher culture must . . . give people a dual brain, two compartments of the brain . . . the one to experience science, the other to experience nonscience: lying next to

each other, without confusion, separable, each able to be closed off from the other; this is a requirement for health. (HAH 251)

Should this mandate not be met, Nietzsche warns that society will regress:

> [T]he interest in what is true will cease to the extent that it provides less pleasure; illusion, error, and fantasy will reconquer step by step the terrain they once controlled, because they are associated with pleasure: the ruination of the sciences and a sinking back into barbarism will result . . . (HAH 251)

The same image of science and non-science peacefully coexisting that Nietzsche evokes in HAH 251 via the dual brain is conjured later in chapter 5 where he describes the person

> who is as much in love with the plastic arts or music as he is enraptured by the spirit of science and who sees it as impossible to suspend this contradiction by annulling the one and completely liberating the other: the only possibility remaining for him is to shape himself into a cultural edifice big enough for both those powers to inhabit, albeit at opposite ends . . . (HAH 276)

Both passages suggest that despite those times when Nietzsche predicts that a scientific future will force art into retirement, he can also envisage a higher culture in which art continues to play a role. There is, however, at least at this point in his thought, no evidence that any such role remains for religion or traditional metaphysics.[14] And of course, the residual category of non-science which he

---

[14] It could look as if HAH 278 provides a third passage that argues in this vein, but that does include a continuing role for religion and metaphysics, as opposed to just art. The metaphor of the dance is intended to capture how a person can move back and forth between these different positions with strength and flexibility rather than 'staggering weakly back and forth between different impulses'. Yet as I read this passage, Nietzsche is referring to the present rather than the future: 'It should now be considered the decisive sign of a great culture.' The dance is the ideal image for how to negotiate art, religion and metaphysics on the one side, and science on the other in the current interregnum, with himself as principal dancer.

employs in HAH 251 could encompass things other than art. What occupies the non-science region of the brain has traditionally been the trio of religion, art and metaphysics, but the key features of this chamber are that it is a 'power source' [*die Kraftquelle*] (whereas the science compartment is 'the regulator'). This power source is home to 'illusions, one-sidedness, and passions' [*Illusionen, Einseitigkeiten, Leidenschaften*]. Later on the passage refers to 'illusion, error and fantasy' [*die Illuison, der Irrthum, die Phantastik*] which are associated with 'pleasure' [*Lust*]. Presumably these general forces of cerebral activity could be manifested in myriad different and potentially even currently unimaginable ways: they do not have to result in art, religion or metaphysics as traditionally understood and certainly not all three at once.

Safranski uses HAH 251 to illustrate his claim that Nietzsche's 'anxiety as to how far we can go along with the spirit of science without winding up in a desert comes through on several occasions' (2002: 200). More generally, he admires what this metaphor represents: 'The idea of a bicameral system flashes up again and again in Nietzsche's work and then vanishes, much to the detriment of his philosophy. If he had held to it, he might well have spared himself some of his mad visions of grand politics and the will to power' (2002: 200). It is easy to see why, citing HAH 251, Carol Nicholson infers that 'Nietzsche anticipated recent discoveries in neuroscience about the two-sided brain with astonishing prescience' (2012). But as Anne Harrington points out, localisation theory, or the idea that the brain has two hemispheres, began in the nineteenth century with the work of the phrenologist Franz Joseph Gall. Gall argued that the brain is divided into different regions, each with its own specialisations. This model of neuroscience thus included a division of labour within the brain. Nietzsche seems to have had some familiarity with the work of Gall – it is possible that he read about it in in Lange (Stack 1983: 289) or that it was in the ether. But however Nietzsche hit upon this idea, it amounts to his making use of recent scientific findings to allocate a role to science and to non-science in the future. Scientific thinking does not drive out its opposite; on the contrary, it is essential that non-scientific thinking or experiences remain part of the higher culture of the future. The role of science is to regulate these other forces, to cool them down somewhat.

Chapter 5 does offer two precedents for the achievement of a higher culture within the Western tradition – the Renaissance and, more distantly, Ancient Greece. Nietzsche hopes that the future will see a rebirth of the Renaissance (HAH 244), but his admiration for the Renaissance and aspiration for a new one could shed further light on this question of the future relationship between science and art. After all, as he acknowledges, the Renaissance boasted major achievements in both domains. HAH 237 describes this era as exhibiting 'an enthusiasm for science and the scientific past of humanity' and moves shortly after to praise for 'a whole array of artistic characters who, with the highest moral purity, demanded from themselves perfection . . . in their works'. In light of this historical precedent, it would be strange for him to insist that science and art in some form could not flourish together in the future.

The other model of a higher culture in this chapter is Ancient Greece, and that period likewise boasted achievements in the natural sciences and in the arts. In section 266, Nietzsche contends that there is inestimable value in the study of classics because in this way, and apparently only this way, do young people hear 'the abstract language of higher culture' (HAH 266). He admonishes that 'if the students only listen, their intellects will involuntarily be preformed along the lines of a scientific way of seeing things' (HAH 266). Another passage points out that this culture was very masculine, with women playing a minor role. Nietzsche describes the strong erotic bond between adult and adolescent males, and how this attachment relegated heterosexual romantic and sexual relations to the margins. Women's primary role was in reproduction. He concludes this passage on 'A culture of men' by observing that this restricted role for women 'kept Greek culture young for such a relatively long time; for in the Greek mothers, the Greek genius returned again and again to nature' (HAH 259). Nietzsche leaves it open as to whether this sign of a higher culture could or should be recreated in a higher culture of the future.

Shortly after this comes a long reflection on Greek culture in which Nietzsche contrasts its 'tyrants of the spirit' unfavourably with the 'oligarchs of the spirit' that he hopes will emerge in the future. Greek culture was marked by several figures with the powerful ambition to be the most important person of his time. He names Parmenides, Pythagoras, Empedocles, Anaximander and Plato in this context, while the only exception he acknowledges is Solon. These tyrants of the spirit are so named because each, 'believing himself to be the possessor of absolute truth, became a tyrant' (HAH 261). Each therefore saw other great figures as threats and rivals; they 'would have liked to eat one another raw; not a single spark of love . . . remained inside them' (HAH 261). Yet by contrast with the earlier passage about Greece's masculine culture, Nietzsche is clear that the tyrants of the spirit example should not be emulated: 'The period of the tyrants of the spirit is over.' The future needs oligarchs, rather than tyrants, of the spirit, which means a group of superior individuals who nonetheless see themselves as part of a group rather than as sovereign individuals in the way the Greek tyrants did. In a remarkable passage that warrants quoting at some length, Nietzsche describes these members of a spiritual oligarchy as forming

> a cohesive society, whose members recognize and acknowledge one another . . . The spiritual superiority that previously produced division and enmity now tends to unite: how could individuals assert themselves and swim on their own course through life, against the tide, if they did not here and there see others like them, living under the same conditions, and did not take their hands in a struggle . . . The oligarchs need one another, they have their greatest joy in one another, they understand their insignia – but nevertheless each of them is free; he struggles and triumphs in his own place and would rather perish than submit. (HAH 261)

Just as chapter 4 suggested that having a cohort of geniuses makes it easier for them to influence the wider culture, so this passage implies that one of the ways in which free spirits can strengthen themselves and increase their impact on society is through experiencing themselves not as isolated individuals but as part of a group with others who are waging similar battles. They seem to find strength in one another's very existence, but this is not any sort of group that requires individual subordination to the whole.[15]

This passage's long reflection on Greek culture mentions Socrates as one who initiated the rapid destruction of Ancient Greece's philosophical culture. Yet in an earlier cluster of passages about free-spiritedness (HAH 225–30), Nietzsche tacitly evokes the legacy of Socrates in a positive way, for free spirits are said to conduct the same sort of rational interrogation of their society's practices, norms and beliefs as he did.[16] As we shall see in Chapter 11, Nietzsche's attitude towards Socrates is also something that shifts across the course of these three works. His valorisation of rational scrutiny of what society takes for granted is also further testimony to the presence of the enlightenment spirit in HAH. And in this vein, Nietzsche cannot resist a further jab at Christianity because it did not promote or require the exercise of reason among its adherents, demanding instead 'faith and nothing but faith and passionately turning aside the demand for reasons' (HAH 227). HAH 265 associates this rationalist legacy with the Greeks and their 'scientific sense', but notes that it was in danger of being submerged in the Middle Ages. Nietzsche declaims that 'Reason in the schools has made Europe into Europe' and offers in this passage some orientalist remarks about how this rationalist tradition distinguishes Europe from Asia. 'Europe has been schooled in logical and critical thinking; Asia still does not know how to distinguish between truth and fiction' (HAH 265).[17]

---

[15] It is hard to square this passage with Amy Mullin's insistence that 'the free spirit is strongly associated with isolation' (2000: 384). Mullin helpfully suggests that becoming a free spirit happens in stages (2000: 385), yet shows no application of this developmental model to Nietzsche's own thinking about the free spirit. It is very possible that he changed his view about this figure over time and that HAH represents his very earliest ideas on these themes, which he might have revised as he went along. Mullin instead draws freely from across his whole oeuvre, as if all of his books were written at the same time or by someone who doesn't ever change his mind – i.e. not a free spirit. For a different view on the free spirit's isolation, see Daigle, who contends that 'the free spirit's search for truth can only be successful if he engages with others who can be his friends' (2015: 34).

[16] As Young observes, with HAH 'something close to "Socratism", the position of "theoretical man" deplored in *The Birth*, has now become Nietzsche's own position' (2006: 60).

[17] He appeals to the authority of 'the great naturalist von Baer' in making this sweeping statement.

If chapter 5 is clear that free spirits should play a key role in bringing a higher culture of the future into being, it is less clear about how this should be effected. We have seen a number of remarks above about how an education in scientific thinking can assist this evolution. But educational reform is a necessary, but not sufficient, condition of wider cultural change. When it comes to communicating with ordinary members of society, Nietzsche is frank about some of the challenges involved. He maintains that the identity of the free spirits is usually visible to all: 'proof of the greater excellence and keenness of his intellect is usually written so legibly upon the free spirit's face that the fettered spirits understand it well enough' (HAH 225). But he underscores the difficulty that they encounter in making themselves understood by ordinary community members. Fettered spirits are accustomed to thinking in terms of utility and so expect what the free spirit offers to be couched in this way. The former group will, understandably, interpret free spirits in their own terms, yet those terms are inapplicable to these exceptions. Nietzsche makes it especially clear that free spirits will be hard pressed to persuade the fettered ones that what they offer is advantageous. Indeed, he says, without directly explaining why, that free spirits will be unable to convince the fettered ones on this point (HAH 229). Section 227 even suggests that there is a direct conflict between what benefits the free spirit and what benefits the fettered ones, and they infer that what he stands for poses a danger to them.

This problem is compounded later in the chapter when Nietzsche admits that a higher culture does not 'increase happiness [*Glück*]. Whoever wants to harvest happiness and contentment from life need only keep away from higher culture' (HAH 277). This blunt admission that happiness is not one of the higher culture's promises helps to put this chapter's remarks on socialism into context, for otherwise they seem to sit uncomfortably in their surroundings and would be better situated in chapter 8's discussions of politics. But as chapter 5's passage on 'Genius and the ideal state in contradiction' explains, 'The socialists crave to produce a good life [*Wohlleben*][18] for as many people as possible . . . If this state were

---

[18] Hollingdale translates this as 'pleasure', but 'comfort' seems to me to be what Nietzsche is getting at.

ever attained, humanity would have become too feeble to be able to engender genius' (HAH 235). So from this we can infer that although a higher culture does not produce happiness or contentment for all, it does promote genius and supports the conditions necessary for the flourishing of excellence. Unlike socialism, the higher culture serves the exceptions and not the regular individuals. Widespread support for socialism would not, therefore, be the mark of a higher culture.

Nietzsche's blunt admission that happiness will not be one of the by-products of a higher culture should not be taken to suggest that the free spirit's life will be miserable – he nowhere signals that, at least not in HAH. Indeed, in keeping with the epistemology-plus perspective that I detect throughout this book, many rewards come with a life dedicated to the quest for knowledge. A whole passage is, for example, devoted to outlining the pleasure [*Lust*] in knowing (HAH 252). Nietzsche specifies three primary ones, while allowing that there could be more. One is the feeling of strength it provides. The second is the feeling of conquest over earlier ideas that one held. The third is the feeling of superiority it confers over others. It must be admitted that this third reward comes as a bit of a surprise, as Nietzsche normally portrays seekers after scientific knowledge as humble and modest, not rivalrous or vain. Two passages towards the end of the chapter reiterate Nietzsche's earlier ideas about how a life devoted to the pursuit of knowledge purifies and simplifies the emotions in a positive way (HAH 288, 291). So although the building of a higher culture might not disseminate happiness, it is not without other types of benefits.

The pluralist style of thinking in evidence here, by which I mean the insight promulgated by Isaiah Berlin that all good things might not be compossible and instead we might have to make hard and even tragic choices among good things, is something of a theme throughout HAH. In this same chapter Nietzsche attacks, for example, the assumption that the truth of an opinion guarantees that it will bring personal benefits or wider advantages (HAH 227). He had previously rejected the view, which he associates with all religions, that if a belief brings pleasure or happiness, it must be true (HAH 120; cf. 161). In chapter 4 he likewise jettisons the idea that if something is beautiful it must also bring happiness (HAH 149). The good, the true, the beautiful, the salutary and the useful should all be seen as not only different but potentially conflicting qualities. Nietzsche's mindset here is well captured in an aphorism from chapter 9: 'There is no pre-established harmony between the furthering of truth and the well being of humanity' (HAH 517). If asked, he would probably say that the Christian idea of God as combining all the virtues is a major source of this error that all good things can be realised simultaneously.

HAH 251's fearful image of barbaric backsliding into an earlier state when the achievements of the present are lost or at least buried is hard to reconcile with the stadial views of history Nietzsche sometimes espouses, even if only implicitly or incompletely. We saw such a stadial approach taken towards art in chapter 4, for example. Stadial views tend to be sequential and progressive, leaving little to no room for the sort of wholesale regression that so terrifies Nietzsche here. Yet this sort of regression is exactly what Nietzsche sees when he looks back at the eclipse of the Renaissance by the Reformation. In his estimation, the Renaissance was the instantiation of a higher culture. Listing its many qualities, including things such as 'liberation of thought' and 'disdain for authorities' that are indispensable to free spirithood, he concludes that 'It was the golden age of this millennium, despite all its flaws and vices' (HAH 237). But the Renaissance was overpowered and undone by the German Reformation, that 'energetic protest of the spiritually backward'. The Reformation 'threw humanity backward . . . and thus delayed for two or three centuries the complete awakening and supremacy of the sciences' (HAH 237). Such historical precedents remind readers just how much is at stake in the current interregnum and how urgent it is that signs of cultural progress be identified and strengthened.

6
The Human in Society

Nietzsche's title for chapter 6 – '*Der Mensch im Verkehr*' – does not translate readily into English. *Der Mensch* is, of course, easy, meaning the man, man, the human or humans. *Im Verkehr* is less straightforward, and can, as Handwerk indicates, mean 'In Relations with Others', although his translation deletes the first part of Nietzsche's original title. But *Im Verkehr* can also mean in social intercourse, in communication, in commerce, or in traffic. What these options suggest is that Nietzsche's topic for this chapter is the human in his or her wider social context, in association with people one knows but not intimately. Perhaps this explains why Hollingdale translates this as 'Man in Society'. I am closer to Hollingdale's translation than to Handwerk's but prefer the more inclusive 'The Human in Society'.

It warrants attention that Nietzsche's title for chapter 9 – '*Der Mensch mit sich allein*' – directly echoes that for chapter 6, '*Der Mensch im Verkehr*'. Chapter 9's 'Man/the human alone with himself' is then the alter ego of the man or human in society.[1] One question to arise immediately from the way these chapter titles so audibly echo one another is why Nietzsche separates them with two intervening chapters – one on Woman and Child (chapter 7) and one on the state (chapter 8). It could be that chapters 6, 7 and 8 all deal with humans in their interactions with others at different levels of intimacy or distance, whereas chapter 9 deals with the individual in isolation. But as we shall see, chapter 9 does not

---

[1] Hollingdale's translations capture this echo as he calls chapter 9 'Man Alone with Himself' whereas Handwerk chooses 'By Oneself Alone'.

deliver on the expectations created by its title, for many of its passages are not about the solitary individual.

This chapter begins by noting the relatively heavy use of the aphoristic form in chapter 6. It also observes the wide range of topics canvassed there, and connects the use of the aphorism, as traditionally conceived, with Nietzsche's more disjointed approach to his subject matter. But despite this, some common concerns do unite the material of chapter 6. One is the concern with how one appears to others and the competition for status to which this gives rise. Rousseau's concept of *amour-propre* is invoked as a way of making sense of this. I go on to propose that we use Nietzsche's own account of the complementary dynamic between benevolence and malice suggested in chapter 2 as a way of arranging some of this chapter's other insights into human motivation and interaction. This chapter concludes with an overview of Nietzsche's observations about friendship.

The French moralists

As we saw, chapter 2 is home to two modes for analysing morality: psychological observation that aims for perspicuous encounters with the depths and complexity of the human psyche on the one hand, and tracing the evolution of moral evaluations over time on the other. The latter typically requires longer passages to facilitate more detailed exposition. For the most part chapter 6 contains the former, taking snapshots of the psyche, and opens with HAH's first sustained run of aphorisms. Passages 293 to 335 are all genuine aphorisms – that is, short, pithy, standalone statements. From 336 onwards the passages grow longer and from 365 they are longer still, until by the end of the chapter Nietzsche is back to page-length passages.[2]

---

[2] But this is not to suggest that all long passages provide a historical perspective. Indeed, the only historical allusion I can detect in this chapter comes in HAH 354, which asserts, wrongly, that the Greeks were the first and the last for whom friendship was 'a problem worth resolving'. They might have been the first, but they were certainly not the last. But this historical purview is not used to illuminate anything about current friendship; instead Nietzsche veers away to express humorously his incomprehension that the Greeks used a superlative form of the term for friend to describe a relative.

In addition to the heavy use of the aphorism, the wit and playfulness of Nietzsche's insights display his affinity with and emulation of the French moralist tradition,[3] and in particular the work of the seventeenth-century writer La Rochefoucauld. As we have seen, Nietzsche pledges his allegiance to this tradition when proclaiming the necessity of in-depth and unblinking analyses of the psyche in chapter 2. He carries this out on priests and saints in chapter 3 and artists and geniuses in chapter 4. Chapter 6 seems to be about ordinary, generic, or perhaps unclassified human beings and the dynamics unleashed by social interaction. The wide range of topics covered in this context manifests affiliation with the moralist tradition too – flattery, sympathy, vanity, friendship, arrogance, dissimulation, giving and receiving, revenge, conversation, and speaking in public more generally. And although these are some of the themes threaded throughout the chapter, what chapter 6 also illustrates is that the more genuinely aphoristic HAH becomes, the more disjointed and discontinuous do its ideas seem to be. This discontinuity could be a further reflection of the work's affinities with the French moralist tradition, as the aphorisms of La Rochefoucauld appear to follow no particular order, while those of Chamfort most definitely do not as they were never prepared by him for publication.

This discontinuity and disconnection could also symbolise the fragmentation of the self that Nietzsche believes is likely to occur in society. Such dis-integration of the self in and by society is beautifully conveyed in a non-aphoristic passage just past the midway point of the chapter.[4] Entitled 'Pangs of conscience after social gatherings', section 351 asks

> Why do we have pangs of conscience after ordinary social gatherings? Because we have taken important things lightly, because in speaking of other people we have not spoken with complete truthfulness, or because we have kept silent where we ought to have said something, because we did

---

[3] And some of the aphorisms just strike me as funny and clever, devoid of significant social commentary. Examples include HAH 302, 303, 307, 315, 319, 334.
[4] Measured in page, not section, numbers.

not take an occasion to spring to our feet and run away, in short, because we have behaved in society as if we belonged to it.[5]

Amour-propre

One reason why the self dis-integrates in such social settings has to do with the pervasiveness of what Rousseau calls *amour-propre*. His 'Second Discourse' (*On the Origin and Foundations of Inequality Among Mankind*) describes this form of self-love as 'a relative and factitious sentiment, engendered in society, which inclines every individual to set a greater value upon himself than upon any other man, which inspires men with all the mischief they do to each other, and is the true source of what we call honor' (Rousseau 2002: 146). Although Nietzsche does not cite Rousseau here,[6] many of his aperçus reveal how concerned with and jealous of their standing in the eyes of others modern individuals are. For this reason social interaction becomes competitive, with people seeking to outdo one another and extract the regard of others, whether deserved or not.[7]

We see this competition most clearly enacted in Nietzsche's remarks about giving and receiving, whether the item dispensed be advice, courtesy, offence or gifts. Section 297 talks, for example, about having to 'refuse a gift because it was not offered in the right way'. This makes the person declining the gift feel embittered towards the would-be giver – without, of course, mentioning that said giver would also harbour hurt feelings about this failed exchange. Anyone who does succeed in bestowing a large gift should not expect gratitude, as the recipient 'has already been burdened too much by accepting it' (HAH 323). The idea here is

---

[5] This is not to suggest that all selves fragment through social interaction. In chapter 9 Nietzsche summons Goethe as 'someone who is able to live so very peacefully and cheerfully with himself, even amid the crowd' (HAH 626).
[6] Rousseau is mentioned in HAH 221, 463, 617. He was clearly on Nietzsche's mind at this point, so the connection I am drawing is not wholly adventitious.
[7] This competition that occurs within society can also help to explain the aphorism in chapter 9 that 'We are so glad to be out amid nature because it has no opinion about us' (HAH 508).

that an act of generosity is experienced as a display of superiority that creates a subsequent inferiority in the recipient, again betraying a preoccupation with one's standing vis-à-vis others. When unsolicited advice to a sick recipient is the 'gift', the giver feels superior, whether or not the advice is heeded. If a 'sensitive and proud' person, the recipient hates the advisor more than they hate their sickness (HAH 299). Note that these emotions have nothing to do with the value of the advice: it is all about people feeling superior or inferior to one another, with the former enjoying and the latter resenting that sensation. When people we don't like are courteous to us, we take offence even at their courtesy, according to section 309. The tug of war involved in giving and receiving is also laid out in section 348, 'Giving offense and being offended'. There Nietzsche suggests that it is better to give offence and then repent than to be the offended party. The offender exercises power in the act of giving offence but then displays goodness of character by apologising. The offended person is obliged to forgive no matter how they really feel, and that sense of compulsion outweighs any gratification that the apology might bring.

The concern with how one appears to others that is characteristic of *amour-propre* and the competition this gives rise to is also captured in the aphorism 'Presence of witnesses' (HAH 325), where Nietzsche asserts that a person is more likely to save someone who is drowning if there are others around who lack the courage to do this. It is reiterated in HAH 329, according to which 'People who do not feel sure of themselves in society use every opportunity of publicly displaying their superiority to anyone near at hand who is inferior . . .' HAH 341 writes of 'extremely conceited people' who feel they have not been shown due regard by others. They go to great lengths to convince themselves that the deficit is not real, but if they cannot persuade themselves of this, 'they give themselves over to an even greater rage'. These dynamics are especially acute in vain individuals, as conveyed amusingly in HAH 338's vignette 'Clashing vanities'. When two vain people meet, each is so concerned with the impression they are making on the other that they cancel one another out, each being left with no impression of the other at all. Each eventually realises that their efforts had no impact and then blames the other.

The rivalry that marks and mars social life is also evident in Nietzsche's several discussions of arrogance [*Anmaassung*]. He announces the paradox that 'Arrogance in those with merit gives even more offense than arrogance in those without merit . . .' This is paradoxical because one might assume that a more talented person had a better claim to be arrogant. But Nietzsche punctures this expectation by explaining that the merit of the meritorious person is already offensive to others and their arrogance piled on top of that makes them even more offensive in the aggregate (HAH 332). Although this passage is humorous, Nietzsche takes some time to provide a longer account of, and stern caution against, arrogance in HAH 373. Arrogant is 'anyone who wants to seem more important than he is or is considered to be . . .' Arrogance can infiltrate all corners of human interaction. Even otherwise positive things such as 'affection, signs of respect . . . benevolent familiarity . . . caresses, friendly advice . . . admission of errors . . . pity for others' can 'arouse repugnance' if tainted with arrogance. Nietzsche warns that people are very unforgiving of this trait, for in order to appear superior, the arrogant person has to humiliate others. Nietzsche concludes in the strongest of terms that 'there is no greater folly in our relations with other people than acquiring a reputation for being arrogant' (HAH 373).[8] Chapter 9's passage on arrogance suggests that talented people aged between twenty-six and thirty are most prone to this emotion, for they feel acutely the gap between what they are and how they are perceived. They may not be fully appreciated by others yet because their talents have not fully flowered (HAH 599).

There are some sections, however, when Nietzsche's analysis of humans in their social context steps outside this competitive arena. Two such moments invoke the refined [*feine*] or noble [*vornehme*][9] soul, recounting such a person's reaction to giving and receiving. In section 366 we discover that the noble soul does not feel burdened by receiving: such a one 'will gladly feel itself

---

[8] Sections 316 and 358 in this chapter also deal with arrogance.
[9] *Vornehme* can be translated as refined, so it is easy to see why Handwerk uses the same term in each passage. But I am following Nietzsche's lead by using different adjectives, as does Hollingdale, who also renders *vornehme* as noble.

obliged to be grateful and not anxiously avoid occasions in which it incurs obligations . . .' Such a person will also express appropriate gratitude. Lower or inferior[10] souls, by contrast, 'resist becoming obligated in any way'. Or if they cannot avoid it, they go overboard in their expressions of thanks. This idea that lower souls resist and resent feeling obliged to another, presumably because they fear that it compromises their standing, echoes a point made in section 330.[11] However, even though refined souls have no fear of obligation and the gratitude it entails, we learn from that earlier passage that they do not want to make anyone feel obliged to them. As this is an aphorism, Nietzsche does not explain it, but we might assume that refined souls know that not everyone wears obligation and gratitude as graciously as they do. Or it might be that while they suffer no discomfort from being 'in debt' to a benefactor, they do not want to place anyone beneath them.

Unsocial sociability

A useful way of arranging many of this chapter's insights into human motivation is by reference to the complementary dynamic between benevolence and malice suggested in HAH 49–50 and laid out in Chapter 2 of this introduction and guide. There I depicted benevolence and malice as micro expressions of sociability and unsociability respectively. Benevolence manifests 'good naturedness, friendliness, politeness of the heart' (HAH 49) among acquaintances, whereas malice betrays the opposite – a desire to hurt, harm or demean another. The aphorism's compact size makes it the perfect mechanism for putting small acts like this under the microscope. As this chapter's opening aphorism asserts, 'In our relations with other people [*im Verkehre mit Menschen*], a benevolent [*wohlwollende*] dissimulation is frequently required, as if we did not see through the motives for their actions' (HAH 293). Just as the term 'benevolent dissimulation' seems prima facie paradoxical if not oxymoronic (how can deception be good?), there is something ironic about the benevolence described here. One sees

---

[10] Handwerk renders *niedere* as 'coarser'; Hollingdale as 'baser'.
[11] Although the adjective Nietzsche contrasts with refined is *große* – i.e. coarse.

the apparently less than admirable motives of another person but pretends not to, presumably for their sake so that they are either not discomforted by having the motive or by being seen to have it, or both.

Yet thus far it looks as though chapter 6 is more concerned with malice than benevolence, because a preoccupation with one's social status can inspire behaviour that demeans others. But this chapter contains evidence of more benign social interaction too, in addition to that enacted by noble or refined souls. Section 301, for example, provides advice about the best way to assist an 'extremely embarrassed' person. This consists in 'praising them with conviction'. Section 316 prescribes knowing that 'we are always among deserving people' as the remedy for arrogance. Solitude can breed arrogance whereas association with worthy people dispels it.[12] Section 324 tells of a clever but polite person who finds himself in dull society. Being polite, he puts himself on their level and downplays his intelligence. He receives no thanks for this benevolence, however, except of course from Nietzsche. The passage 'Tactics in conversation' imagines two clever people seeking to please one another by creating opportunities for the other to shine. If both do this, but neither takes the opportunity, not wanting to outshine the other, 'the conversation as a whole proceeds without any wit or charm because each concedes to the other the opportunity for wit and charm' (HAH 369). This passage's self-cancelling dynamic provides the benevolent counterpoint to the two vain people who leave no impression on one another.

Section 359 also accentuates benignity, or at least its possibility in some people. Modifying the mantra that 'Every person has his price', Nietzsche observes that while everyone can be induced to do things they might not want to, the carrot need not be money. One must uncover what different souls find 'sweet and delectable' and appeal to that. Some people can thus be induced to act by 'philanthropy, nobility, charitableness, self-sacrifice' (HAH 359).[13]

---

[12] Contrast, however, section 625 on 'Solitary people' from chapter 9. There Nietzsche points out that people who spend so much time alone and who enjoy their own company tend to underestimate their value.

[13] Handwerk renders *Mildthätigen* as 'benevolence', but I follow Hollingdale and use 'charitableness' instead.

HAH 308 proffers advice in this same vein, this time about how to move a courageous person to do something. The strategy is to make whatever it is that you want them to do appear more dangerous than it actually is. This aphorism is somewhat ambiguous though, as at base it appears to recommend an appeal to the courageous person's desire to be seen as courageous and thus could take us back to the uneven and unstable territory of *amour-propre*.

And of course, what appears to be benevolent might not, upon closer inspection, be genuinely so. This is very clear in Nietzsche's account of 'Sympathetic people'. Those who are ever ready to sympathise with misfortune are less reliable when it comes to another's joy or good fortune. Dispossessed of 'their superior position' that comes from feeling sorry for another, they 'easily manifest discontent' (HAH 321). More bogus benevolence is logged in section 363 which attributes concern for the welfare of others, a sense of duty to and pity for the unfortunate and needy, to curiosity. Chapter 6 seems to provide more evidence of apparent benevolence that turns out to be closer to malice than apparent malice that turns out to be benevolent. One example of the latter comes, however, in section 355, 'Misunderstood honesty'. There Nietzsche explains that though the habit of prefacing one's remarks with '"as I said", "as I tend to say"' can be mistaken for arrogance, it is often just prompted by honesty.

The fact that social dynamics can be animated by benign or malign impulses is also apparent when section 300 distinguishes between two sorts of equality. Some pursue equality by bringing everyone down to their level, 'disparaging them, keeping secrets from them, or tripping them up'. Others want to raise everyone 'by giving them recognition, helping them, taking pleasure in their success'. Nietzsche's micro and personal examples here indicate to me that he is thinking about equality in social standing and dynamics rather than political movements.[14] As we shall see in chapter 8's discussion of politics, he has no time for political movements that promote equality of either sort – raising up or lowest common denominator – insisting instead upon the necessity of some form of elite that will perpetuate higher culture.

---

[14] See Corduwener (2013: 70) for a different, political interpretation of this passage.

Friendship

To further leaven this negative impression about what chapter 6 reveals about humans in their relations with others, it might be helpful to consider its reflections on friendship. Friendship is, of course, a different sort of interaction than most of those described above; it is more intimate, more particular and, we would hope, less infused with *amour-propre*. This chapter's first reference to friendship comes early and refers to friendship's failing. Section 296 observes that 'A lack of intimacy among friends is a mistake that cannot be censured without becoming irreparable.' A version of this point is made a few passages later, with section 304 saying that forcing another to be intimate betokens a lack of trust. When one feels trusted, intimacy is not so highly prized – presumably due to the assumption that it will flow naturally in a trusting relationship.[15] Friendship is the theme of the very next aphorism, where Nietzsche advises that the 'Equilibrium of friendship' can be recalibrated when a person is willing to blame themselves for difficulties. Section 327 also refers to friendship's frailty, asserting that 'There are few people who, when they are at a loss for subject matter in conversation, will not reveal the secret affairs of their friends.' This same note about friendship failing is struck in section 352 where Nietzsche observes that 'Even good friends sometimes give vent to their ill humor in an envious word; and would they be our friends if they knew us exactly as we are?' Thus far Nietzsche's discussions of friendship do not do much to equalise the chapter's tally of benevolent and malign human motivations, for its treatment of friendship alludes to its difficulties and challenges.

This jaundiced treatment of friendship as faulty and fragile changes somewhat with two long passages, one brief, almost passing remark and one more example of benevolent dissimulation. The briefest of these reflections appears in section 373, discussed above, which cautions against arrogance. Nietzsche slips into that passage the qualification that the only time it is permissible to

---

[15] The English translation conceals the wordplay in Nietzsche's expression, where trust is *Vertrauen* and intimacy is *Vertraulichkeit*.

appear proud is 'in front of friends or wives', for such familiars understand you and will not mistake pride for arrogance. Yet just as this remark conveys that we can feel well known and properly understood by our friends (and spouses), the section 'Demeanour when praised' makes room for benevolent dissimulation among friends. HAH 360 records that 'someone with a talented nature' will appear pleased by the praise of his friends when in reality he is indifferent to this. He feigns pleasure out of regard for his friends' feelings rather than any desire to deceive them: 'people want to cause pleasure with their praise, and he would distress them if he did not take joy in their praise'. So while there is pretence here among friends, it still falls into the register of benevolence.

A longer section, HAH 368, dissects 'The talent for friendship' by distinguishing within 'people who have a special gift for friendship' two types of friend, or two types of gift. One type is like a ladder, acquiring and discarding different friends for different stages of life. The sum total of that person's friends are likely to be very different from one another, reflecting how the person has changed across the course of his development. The other type of friend is like a circle. Once again, this type has diverse friends but simultaneously, not seriatim. The diversity of her friends reflects her own synchronic diversity. And those different friends can get along with one another because of their nodal shared friend. Nietzsche concludes this passage's positive treatment of friendship with the somewhat cryptic observation that 'the gift for having good friends is in many people much greater than the gift for being a good friend'. This remark is cryptic because we typically think of friendship as reciprocal, and that to have good friends you need to be a good friend in return. But once again here, right at the end of the passage, Nietzsche seems to be taking a somewhat deflationary attitude to friendship, suggesting that not many people succeed at being a good friend.

It is noteworthy that chapter 6's final and long passage, 'Of friends' (HAH 376), calls attention to friendship's fragility. Even close friends have different opinions or hold the same opinions with differing intensities. Friends can easily misunderstand one another. But rather than spiral into despondency about friendship, the passage offers a realistic account of this relationship. Yes, friendships do depend on some things going unsaid and perhaps even unnoticed. But the passage ends by proposing a reflexive turn; rather than be critical of your friends, become self-critical, and the more honest we are about our own weaknesses and shortcomings, the more tolerant should we be of those of our friends. 'And so let us put up with one another since we put up with ourselves' (HAH 376). This passage recommends a realistic appraisal of ourselves and thus a realistic acceptance of our friends, and in so doing represents the opposite of *amour-propre* where people strive to have others put a high value on them. Once again Nietzsche uses the term equilibrium or balance [*Gleichgewicht*] in this context of preserving friendships, just as he did in section 305. That section also enjoined awareness of our own failings as a salve to friendship. The goal of equilibrium or balance conjures a different spatial image of human relations than the hierarchical status consciousness that is so prevalent in wider social relations and that fuels *amour-propre*.

But perhaps Nietzsche's highest praise for friendship is reserved for HAH's last chapter. An aphorism in chapter 9 declares that 'Shared joy, not shared suffering, makes a friend' (HAH 499).[16] This aphorism shows that humans can be united by joy and thus provides an alternative to the modern, Christian-inspired emphasis on pity as the tie that unites. It also touches on the repeated theme of joy throughout these works, and shows clearly that this vital good can be shared, at least by some individuals.

---

[16] The English translation conceals the German wordplay, for shared joy is *Mitfreude* and friend is *Freund*. I have deleted 'is what' from Handwerk's translation so as to make the aphorism crisper. The 'rich capacity to share in the joys of others' is associated again with friendship in HAH 614.

7
Woman and Child

Just as chapter 6 situates the individual within a social context and analyses the impact of social relations on personal psychology, so chapter 7's title suggests that Nietzsche is going to consider women, or more worryingly, some essence of woman [*Weib*], in the maternal relationship. Such an essentialising view would suggest that there is something at the core of the female identity that does not change over time and that shapes and limits a woman's potential and possibilities. This would smack of the metaphysical tradition that Nietzsche is so eager to critique in HAH and would be significantly at odds with this work's insistence on history, development and change. Yet the title's use of the term 'Woman' belies the contents of this chapter, for on closer inspection we find diverse depictions of women in different conditions and at different stages of their lives. We encounter women as intellects, as unmarried individuals in quest of spouses, as wives, as well as as mothers. We also find reflections on men as intellects, spouses and fathers. Nietzsche sometimes even adopts the child's perspective on familial relations. So this chapter's title is not a reliable guide to its contents. It is interesting to note that Rée's chapter of aphorisms on similar topics is entitled 'On Women, Love, and Marriage', which is more expansive than Nietzsche's 'Woman and Child' but still not expansive enough to signal the many topics Nietzsche actually covers. My account of this chapter starts with Nietzsche's views on women and follows a developmental model, moving from girls as students to intellects to unmarried women to wives and finally to women as mothers. It then considers

Nietzsche's remarks on men in some of these roles, and moves thence to look at his remarks on familial relations from the child's standpoint. It considers why Nietzsche rules marriage and family life out for free spirits and concludes by briefly comparing his views on this range of topics with those of Rée.

The female intellect

Section 409's injunction not to extend to girls the sort of formal education that boys receive could smack of the anti-feminism that Nietzsche is often charged with. The traditional conservative recommendation, as expressed by Rousseau in *Emile* for example, is that girls be educated in a manner that prepares them for their supposedly natural domestic roles as wives and mothers. But the second line of Nietzsche's aphorism complicates any such impression as it provides his reason for not wanting girls to be educated in the same manner as boys. That education 'often turns spirited,[1] inquisitive, firey youths into – copies of their teachers' (HAH 409). This being an aphorism it is hard to glean with certainty what point Nietzsche is making, but one implication is that girls can manifest all of these attractive qualities and can, therefore, also have them distorted through the process of formal education. That would be a reason to keep them out of it. Another could be that were girls given formal educations, they too would become like their teachers, whoever those teachers were. And there is, of course, a sense in which the major purpose of the remark is not to reflect on girls but to be critical of education and the harm it does to youthful spirits and energies.

Some of Nietzsche's other claims about women's intellects also suggest greater possibilities than many traditional philosophers have allowed. If we consider Schopenhauer, for example, as a thinker whose work Nietzsche knew and whose views are not atypical for the time or the Western philosophical tradition more generally, we find claims such as 'One need only look at a

---

[1] Handwerk translates *geistreichen* as 'clever', whereas I follow Hollingdale in thinking that 'spirited' is more appropriate to the context.

woman's shape to discover that she is not intended for either too much mental or too much physical work.' '[C]hildish, foolish, and short-sighted . . . [women] are big children all their lives.'[2] Nietzsche by contrast, in section 411 on 'The female intellect', proclaims that women's intellect issues in 'perfect control,[3] presence of mind and utilisation of every advantage'. A bit further on we learn that while 'women have intelligence, men have feeling[4] and passion'. So although this is not the curiosity and spirit that section 409 might be imputing to girls, these are still somewhat atypical ways to characterise women's intellectual capacities, especially vis-à-vis men's. Section 411 goes on to claim that despite women's greater intelligence, men do more with their intellects because the intellect is basically passive. Men are spurred on by the 'deeper, stronger drives' that they possess but which women lack, so women cannot mobilise their intellectual abilities as effectively as men can. Men come out on top in the intelligence stakes because they are able to deploy their lesser intellects to greater effect. While Nietzsche can certainly be charged with essentialising women at many points in this chapter, here he also essentialises men. And such essentialising gestures are hard to reconcile with HAH's insistence up until now on a historical and scientific approach to knowledge, for essentialism is much more characteristic of the metaphysical tradition that Nietzsche is seeking to slough off.

This unusual passage on the female intellect turns into a reflection on seeking a heterosexual marriage partner, with Nietzsche asserting that when it comes to qualities of mind at least, both men and women can be prompted by homophilic urges. While ostensibly looking for a person of a different sex, what they really want is someone who shares their sex-specific qualities of mind.

---

[2] From his 1851 essay 'On Women'. He also says that 'women remain children all their lives', that they 'are instinctively crafty, and have an ineradicable tendency to lie' and that 'dissimulation is innate'. These are all essentialising and ontologising approaches to women. https://ebooks.adelaide.edu.au/s/schopenhauer/arthur/essays/chapter5.html (accessed 12 July 2019).

[3] Handwerk renders *Beherrschung* as 'self-control', but seeing no evidence of a reflexive in Nietzsche's language, I follow Hollingdale's translation.

[4] *Gemüth* is translated as 'spirit' by Handwerk but 'temperament' by Hollingdale.

Men are 'searching for someone who has great depth and feeling,[5] while women are searching for someone who has cleverness, presence of mind and brilliance' (HAH 411). Just a few passages later though, he depicts women's intellects in a way that is hard to reconcile with this passage. Adopting a much more traditional view of female judgement, Nietzsche says that women are led by their emotions: 'they are so accustomed to loving and to immediately feeling for or against everything' (HAH 416). This passionate and instant attachment to ideas or positions disables them from doing science, which requires, as we have seen from earlier chapters, a much cooler and more impartial mind. But how this view of women as too emotional can be compatible with his earlier position that they possess cleverness, presence of mind and brilliance while men have great depth and feeling is unclear.

Nietzsche does end this passage with the admission that this is the way things are and the concession that 'perhaps all this may change'. The passage's title is, after all, 'On the emancipation of women', so perhaps women will eventually be liberated from their traditional ways of thinking and enabled to do science. So once again we get a hint of historicism and the possibility that these features of women's intellects are the result of history rather than nature. Any hint of historicism is, by contrast, wholly absent from Schopenhauer's view, which repeatedly essentialises and ontologises women's characteristics, basing them all in women's unalterable nature.

Nietzsche's tendency to impute different intellectual essences to women and men is also somewhat undermined later in the chapter when section 425 depicts the 'Storm and Stress period of women'. There he predicts that in civilised European countries, women could over the course of the next few centuries be educated in ways that would equip them with the same mental and moral qualities and features, and weaknesses and shortcomings, as men. However, while this long process is underway, the period will be marked by dilettantism in the arts and sciences,

---

[5] As Nietzsche's term is a version of *Gemüth*, Handwerk again translates this as 'spirit'. Hollingdale in this instance uses 'feeling'.

bewildering chatter in philosophy, bipartisanship in politics, and general moral disintegration. Men will in their turn respond to this transitional turmoil with anger. This is not a pretty picture of the future and should perhaps be read in conjunction with chapter 5's portrayal of the interregnum that might precede the development of a higher culture. None of the consequences of women's entry into the public realm that Nietzsche sketches here sound compatible with or prophetic of a higher culture, but the idea that women could eventually come to have the same qualities as men is a distinctive feature of his argument and certainly contrasts with its more essentialising moments.

But whatever sort of future Nietzsche foretells here, this passage represents another of the places in chapter 7 where he explicitly applies a historical lens to women, allowing that their circumstances and characteristics could change over time. Given how central HAH makes history to scientific thinking, it is troubling how rarely Nietzsche's own depictions of women are historicising rather than essentialist. There is a further hint of historicising – but just a hint – in the aphorism 'Boredom', which reports that many people, especially women, have never really learned to work and so never experience boredom (HAH 391). I see this aphorism as hinting at a more historical approach to gender because learning to work is something that could change over time; learning to work is not some ontological capacity that women lack. It is, moreover, not just women who have failed to learn this, but 'many people', moving the analysis further away from gender essentialism. Section 412 indicates that women's failure to learn how to work has actually been a strategic choice, for they have used their cleverness to avoid work by rendering themselves dependent on men. This, of course, only makes sense if we follow Nietzsche by undervaluing or not even recognising as work the labour that many women have historically performed – that is, housework and child care. And to follow Nietzsche's logic we also have to accept that engaging in this work was a choice that women made based on their laziness. But however unpersuasive and unattractive this account of women's dependence on men might be, it is nonetheless not couched in essentialist or ontological terms; this dependence is portrayed as a choice and could, at least potentially, be unchosen at some later date.

Chapter 6 contained a similar observation about women's dependency and reluctance to work, but framed it in quite different, and more historicist, terms. Entitled 'The parasite', section 356 asserts that the preference to live in dependency on others so as to avoid work is symptomatic of 'a complete lack of refined sensibility'. Once again Nietzsche claims that this lack is more prevalent in, but not unique to, women, but adds that in their case it is 'also much more excusable (for historical reasons)'. While he does not enumerate those reasons, he explicitly acknowledges that historical forces played a powerful role in bringing about this outcome. And he has been adamant in earlier parts of HAH that pointing out that something is the product of history also signals that it could be changed.

Such historicisation of women's condition is also evidenced in section 342 of chapter 6 where Nietzsche describes them as speaking like 'creatures who have for millennia sat at the loom, or guided a needle, or been childish with children'. Once again, he treats men in the same way, showing how their contemporary voice carries echoes of traditional activities such as marksmen or swordsmen. And again, showing that a feature is the product of historical forces permits it to change. As women and men engage in different activities, so their voices will change. In passages like these, Nietzsche's remarks become compatible with proto-feminist readings of women's condition as socially conditioned and not at all reflective of their potentials, let alone any supposed essence.

Courtship and marriage

The way in which section 411 on the female intellect pivots to provide some thoughts on the quest for a marriage partner reminds us that at the time of writing, Nietzsche still considered himself, and was considered by others, as an eligible bachelor. During this stage of his life he was also witnessing some of his male peers getting married and could have been indirectly musing on their choices along with his own options and prospects. His reflections on courtship and marriage are not, therefore, wholly disinterested or abstract. Section 404 offers a powerful critique of women who look upon marriage as simply an exchange of female beauty for male wealth. His depiction of such women as 'courtesans' tacitly echoes Mary Wollstonecraft's attack on the way her society encouraged or required women to effectively prostitute themselves through the institution of marriage. Although both of chapter 7's passages invoke women's cleverness or cunning [*Klugheit*] to explain women's situation, section 404, by comparing women to courtesans, strikes a very different tone and carries much harsher social criticism compared to section 412, where women subordinate themselves to men in order to avoid work.

But chapter 7 also harbours an elevated view of the possibilities of heterosexual marriage. Indeed, in the last chapter of HAH, Nietzsche declares that 'Anyone who protests against marriage in the way that Catholic priests do will try to construe it in the lowest and meanest conceivable way' (HAH 598). He certainly cannot be accused of demeaning marriage, and at a number of points throughout this chapter he likens marriage to friendship. The chapter's second aphorism, for example, predicts that 'The best friend will probably obtain the best wife, because a good marriage rests upon the talent for friendship' (HAH 378). He is not, of course, suggesting that the two relationships are or could be identical; marriage obviously includes a sexual component that friendship traditionally does not. This could be what is behind section 390's claim that women and men can be friends but some degree of physical antipathy is needed for the friendship to last. This being an aphorism, Nietzsche does not spell out why this is necessary, but presumably without some physical antipathy, their relationship would evolve into a romantic and sexual one and thus surpass a friendship.

This question of what makes for a durable and effective marriage recurs in section 406, which defines 'marriage as a long conversation' and so counsels those considering matrimony to ask themselves 'do you believe that you will enjoy conversing with this woman all the way into old age?' Complementary advice about how to choose a spouse is offered in section 413, which counsels that the selection criterion not be physical appeal. Having 'the imaginative power to represent a face or a figure twenty years older than it is' could cure much infatuation. In this same vein, aphorism 389 describes love matches as having 'error as a father and penury (need) as a mother', suggesting that some other foundation for a successful marriage is needed.

That Nietzsche entertains an elevated view of marriage is most evident in one of this chapter's longer passages. Section 424, 'From the future of marriage', endorses an ideal of marriage 'in its higher form, as a friendship of the soul between two human beings of different sex . . .' He cautions that such a model of marriage will have limited room for sensuality, as its focus will be the partners' affective and intellectual bonds and shared activities. As such, it might be difficult to satisfy male sexual desire which, he is assuming, is more active and robust than that of females. The problem arises from the danger of overburdening the woman in the marriage. As he explains

> A good wife, who ought to be a friend, helpmate, bearer of children, mother, household head, and manager, who perhaps has to oversee her own business and official duties separately from her husband, cannot at the same time be a concubine: this would in general mean asking too much of her. (HAH 424)

Nietzsche's 'solution' is for the husband to seek sexual satisfaction outside the marriage, which, he seems to believe, is possible without disrupting the other more significant marital bonds. He observes that this reverses the practice in Periclean Athens where marriage was viewed as a vehicle for reproduction while stimulating female company was sought extra-maritally. His solution to the excessive demands that a higher model of marriage would place on the wife probably reflects Nietzsche's naivety and lack of experience more than anything else, but to his credit, he has given some thought to what role sexuality could play in a marriage modelled on friendship. Friendship has, after all, typically been seen as a non-sexual relationship, and so approximating the two poses a challenge when it comes to sexuality.[6] It is also noteworthy that this passage contains a lot of praise for heterosexual

---

[6] See Abbey and Den Uyl (2001) on the disanalogies between marriage and friendship.

relationships and thus does not depict women in a derogatory way. However it is to be achieved, Nietzsche recognises that men can desire and benefit from 'the charms of a sociability that liberated head and heart, a sociability that only the charm and intellectual flexibility[7] of women can create' (HAH 424).

Further reflections on how marriage could be reformed are offered in section 421, where Nietzsche proposes serial monogamy in contrast to the extra-marital sexual involvements envisaged in section 424. Entitled 'Occasion for female magnanimity', the passage explicitly considers marriage from the male point of view. Section 424 had, by contrast, looked at it from both angles – husbands' dual need for sex and for female companionship were weighed against the burdens that satisfying both would place on wives. Section 421 contends that in his early twenties, a man is best served by marriage to an older woman, 'who is spiritually and morally superior to him and who can guide him through the dangers of his twenties (ambition, hatred, self-contempt, passions of all kinds)'. One especially noteworthy point here is Nietzsche's admission that a woman can be ethically and intellectually superior to a man and could serve as his mentor in maturation. Her mentorship complete, the older woman's love would shade into the maternal, allowing her to feel no jealousy if, in his third decade, the man took a younger wife. He would in turn educate this younger woman, effectively passing on lessons from the older one. For the decades beyond the thirties, Nietzsche deems marriage as 'often harmful' and promoting 'regression in a man's spiritual cultivation' (HAH 421). He does not pause to comment on how the woman might feel about being discarded when her husband hits his forties, nor whether marriage is equally an impediment to women's spiritual and intellectual development. Both these lacunae illustrate again how this passage investigates marriage from the male point of view. Yet however limited or unrealistic Nietzsche's views might be, he clearly sees marriage as serving some sort of pedagogical function between the partners and is trying to think about how to maximise its benefits, for men at least.

---

[7] Handwerk translates *geistige Biegsamkeit* as 'spiritual resilience', but I follow Hollingdale's rendering of it as 'intellectual flexibility'.

Other noteworthy aspects of this imagined model of marriage are that it is not lifelong and no children are mentioned, which once again are departures from the dominant view of his time. This passage on female magnanimity also sheds light on an earlier aphorism from this chapter declaring that 'What is most certain to counteract the male sickness of self-contempt is . . . to be loved by a clever woman' (HAH 384). In isolation, this statement is ambiguous. The straightforward reading is that being loved by a clever woman will make a man feel better about himself. The explanation could be that the more clever a woman is, the more judicious will be her romantic choices, such that any man chosen by her should feel affirmed and this ego boost can mitigate his self-contempt. However, read in an ironic or even sardonic way, the passage could imply that familiarity with a clever woman will make a man feel better about himself because even a clever woman is still an inferior type of being. A man will hate himself less if he sees how much better he is than even a clever woman. But read in the light of section 421, the more straightforward reading becomes the more likely one. Both passages refer to men suffering from *Selbstverachtung* or self-contempt, and section 421 does not seem to be ironic in its claim that being mentored by an older woman can help a man in his twenties manage self-contempt among other dangers.

This is not to suggest that all of Nietzsche's remarks about marriage in chapter 7 dwell on its best forms and highest functions. The chapter also contains a number of critical and wry remarks about this institution. Nietzsche even includes a nineteenth-century version of the 'take my wife' joke when section 388 reports that 'Some men have sighed over the abduction of their wives, most men, however, because nobody wanted to abduct them.' Section 393 predicts that if married couples did not cohabit, 'good marriages would be more frequent'. The very next passage describes men as 'sinking a little' upon marriage whereas women 'are slightly elevated' (HAH 394). This passage ends, however, by recommending marriage to men 'who are too spiritual[8] in nature',

---

[8] Hollingdale translates *geistige* as 'intellectual' and this seems to be one of those cases where either is appropriate.

with the possible implication that carnal relations bring some balance to their personalities.

A number of other passages bring out the partners' selfish or self-serving motivations within marriage. Section 399, for example, declares that 'A marriage in which each person wants to attain an individual goal through the other person will last.' In this same vein, some women who love important men have to reconcile the conflicting desires to keep the man to themselves versus having their vanity stroked by public recognition of his importance (HAH 401; see also HAH 410). Section 430 offers an interesting twist on this exchange of self-interest model of marriage, arguing that some marriages work when the wife is willing to be treated as a 'sacrificial animal' for her husband by becoming 'the receptacle for the general disfavour and occasional ill humor' that others feel for him. What sounds to be self-serving on the husband's side and self-sacrificing on the wife's is, according to Nietzsche, actually an ambition on the wife's part to fulfil such a function. If so, this passage is just an elaboration on the theme of section 399, with two people realising their individual goals through marriage.[9] But not all marriages provide for complementary self-interest to be realised in this way. Other spouses see their relationship as a zero-sum game, such that one has to be the lover and the other the beloved. But each individual wants to feel him or herself as the beloved rather than the lover, resulting 'in scenes that are half amusing and half absurd' (HAH 418).

Parenthood

Nietzsche's remarks about marriage often point beyond the relationship between the spouses to the production of children. Indeed, the higher model of marriage he discusses in section 424 is 'entered into for the purpose of engendering and educating a new

---

[9] I imagine that the example Nietzsche has in mind here is Richard and Cosima Wagner. The husband is, after all, a man 'of renown and greatness' and this exchange will work only if the husband 'is enough of an egotist to put up with having this sort of willing conducting rod . . . near him' (HAH 430).

generation'. Such a segue from reflections on marriage to those on parenthood is overt in section 379, which announces that 'The unresolved dissonances of character and disposition in the parents' relationship resonate in their child's nature and constitute the history of his inner sufferings.' This brief passage clearly indicates the importance of choosing an appropriate spouse, as significant problems within the marital relationship get transmitted to the next generation. Its message is conveyed in more detail in section 422, entitled 'Tragedy of childhood'. There Nietzsche describes how 'noble-minded and ambitious people' can be thwarted by their parents. They might have 'a low minded father given over to pretense and deceit' or, like Lord Byron, 'a childish and wrathful mother'. The tragedy for the child comes in the knowledge that its worst and most dangerous enemy has been its parent.

Section 422's vignette of Byron's mother is, notwithstanding chapter 7's title, one of Nietzsche's few sex-specific remarks about women as parents. In this same vein, an early aphorism portrays most maternal love as a species of self-love: 'A mother generally loves herself in the son more than she does the son himself' (HAH 385). Note that he is not saying that mothers do not love their sons; rather he is saying that they love the reflection of themselves that they see in the son more than they love the son in himself, making this a question of rank-ordering the loves encompassed within maternal love. Nor is he claiming this about all mothers, as the modifier 'generally' communicates.[10] And there is some gender fluidity here if a mother can see and admire herself in her son, rather than her daughter. A passage towards the chapter's end says that mothers can only perceive 'the visible and palpable pains of their children' (HAH 434), suggesting that their offspring's more silent, inward suffering passes unnoticed. So the few observations that Nietzsche does offer about mother and child in this chapter are not at all romanticised and suggest that maternal love is not as altruistic nor as all-encompassing as it is sometimes portrayed to be.

---

[10] Aphorism 387 could also be read in this light, that mothers care about the way their children reflect them, but it could also just be read as saying that there are different ways of being a good mother.

As noted above, several of Nietzsche's remarks about the parent–child nexus are offered from the vantage point of the child, or rather of the adult who was once that child. Like sections 379 and 422, these passages reveal the ways in which having been a child continues to shape personality. Indeed, the passage immediately following section 379 makes the powerful assertion that 'Everyone carries inside himself an image of woman drawn from his mother' which determines the esteem in which women are henceforth held (HAH 380). This strong claim is expressed in language that could allow for the possibility that both males and females derive their attitudes towards women from their mothers. But if it is the case that one's mother provides the prism through which all women are henceforth seen, it would come as no surprise to discern traces of maternal love in all expressions of female love, as section 392 insists.

Nietzsche says even less about being a father than a mother, beyond the cryptic aphorism that 'Fathers have a great deal to do in order to make up for having had sons' (HAH 382). When writing about parents of either gender, he insists that they do not understand their children. This could be because they have too much experience of their children and are too close to them or because they take their children for granted and never stop to really think about them (HAH 423). Section 381 exhorts anyone lacking a good father to provide himself with one. Claiming that 'In the maturity of their life and of their understanding, the feeling comes over everyone that their father was wrong to have engendered them', section 386 could be the mirror image of section 382 in which fathers should make up for having had sons. It is interesting that this feeling is directed at the father rather than the mother, and Nietzsche's language is sufficiently gender neutral that this feeling that their father was wrong to have engendered them could be one that women experience too.[11] Although given its symmetry with section 382, it is more likely that those who experience this feeling are imagined by Nietzsche to be men and that this is a desire to annul the patrilineal line.

---

[11] Handwerk's translation is gender-neutral. Nietzsche refers to *den Menschen* as having this feeling, but Hollingdale imputes it to 'a man'.

So when we consider what chapter 7 has to say about men as parents, we can see why its title gives priority to women. Fathers should regret their paternity, their children may curse them for engendering them, and they have to be compensated for. It seems fair to conclude that while chapter 7 offers some glimpses into salutary relations between men and women, it has little good to say about parent–child relationships. This could reflect Nietzsche's own experience: his father died when he was five and he was raised by a mother with whom he had very little in common. And yet he was at this point hopeful that he might yet make a good marriage just as some of his friends had.

Free spirits

In what is HAH's most sustained suite of consecutive passages about the free spirit, the last eleven sections in chapter 7 turn explicitly to whether heterosexual love, marriage and family life can play any part in the free spirit's career. Despite having some positive things to say about romantic love and marriage in general, Nietzsche concludes that the free spirit cannot participate in these relationships.[12] Thus we are told in no uncertain terms that free spirits cannot live with women (HAH 426). Here Nietzsche's earlier remarks about that maternal dimension in one's experience of women is clarifying, because for him all women become associated with 'maternal care and vigilance' (HAH 429). Free spirits will find these things oppressive. Women are also said to want to serve, whereas free spirits do not want to be served (HAH 432), thus making them immediately incompatible. Essentialising women yet again, section 431 identifies their 'natural inclination . . . toward a peaceful, regular, happily harmonious existence and society'. This would impede the free spirit's progress towards truth and need for constant experimentation, for it would try to dispel the discomfort that both of these quests necessarily generate. In this same vein, women's desire not to see their husbands suffer as outlined

---

[12] Based on sections 427–32 only, Mullin concludes that free spirits 'find relations with others stifling, particularly relations with women' (2000: 396). On philosophers as being unsuited to marriage, see also GM, Essay 3, section 7.

in section 434 is also said to provide a check on what ambitious men can pursue, for as Nietzsche has already made clear in earlier chapters of HAH, some of that pursuit is bound to bring suffering and discomfort. This places women and their desire for 'a painless, comfortable present' at odds with their husbands' 'higher souls'. In these passages, women are portrayed as having a deeply conservative streak which also puts a damper on any 'free spirited, independent striving' (HAH 435). In all of these ways, the figure of the free spirit is gendered masculine, and consorting closely with women is incompatible with being or becoming such a spirit.

Yet there are other passages in chapter 7 that would dispute the natural inclinations imputed to women here. While the free spirit's desire for independence might be genuine, some of Nietzsche's own portrayals of women in this very chapter show that they do not all want to serve; some avoid work due to laziness; others achieve their own personal goals through marriage. Consider also section 425, which describes the chaotic effects women will create, in the medium term at least, as they start to pursue the same avenues as men. There is little evidence of any desire to serve there. Nietzsche's own example of (or perhaps speculation about) how Socrates' wife Xanthippe propelled him further into free spirithood by making his home inhospitable also gives the lie to his remarks about women always promoting harmony and rendering service (HAH 433).

Perhaps the most persuasive accounts of why free spirits cannot consort with women as potential spouses appear in sections 427 and 436. The free spirit must forego 'the happiness of marriage' because anything habitual is anathema. Because the free spirit must be able to change allegiance and love or hate where he formerly felt the opposite, an enduring relationship like marriage is unsuitable (HAH 427), although the staged model of marriage that Nietzsche outlines in section 421 could be more conducive. What is interesting about section 427 is that Nietzsche permits the free spirits' recurring need for change to also be a source of personal pain to them. Although he does not say this directly about marriage or other close relationships, this passage depicts the free spirit 'painfully rip[ping] apart the net around him again and again', and the numerous 'small and large wounds' this will open. Free spirits cannot cling to convictions and commitments, and this presumably includes commitments to enduring relationships.

The second of Nietzsche's more cogent explanations as to why the free spirit must forego marriage and family life comes in section 436, which outlines some of the demands that family life imposes. Here he is writing at a time when many female spouses and children were very dependent on a male breadwinner, yet free spirits would not want to be tied to any position in order to earn an income. So in Nietzsche's time, there probably was a real collision between being a husband and father on the one hand and being a free-spirited seeker after truth on the other, unless, of course, one was independently wealthy or married a person who was.

There is also a fear of excessive intimacy with anyone that pervades Nietzsche's depiction of personal relations. Just as parents can be too close to and too familiar with their children to really know them, so Nietzsche warns that too intimate association with anyone can ultimately prove corrosive. Whether by friends or romantic partners, 'the soul of a human being is eventually worn out by constant handling' (HAH 428). While these remarks are not confined to marital relations, they do apply to them and offer another explanation why a free spirit would avoid this.

One thing that emerges clearly from this suite of passages about the free spirit and family relations is that, as indicated above, Nietzsche does not consider women to be free spirits. Whether they have the potential to become so is a moot point and depends on whether one gives more weight to the historicist or the essentialising strands of his depictions of women. But for now it is clear that the category 'women' and the category 'free spirits' are mutually exclusive.[13]

Rée on women

Rée's aforementioned chapter 'On Women, Love, and Marriage' is the third chapter of his *Psychological Observations*. It comprises eighty-five numbered but not titled sections, with at least 90 per cent of

---

[13] As Mullin (2000: 384 n. 9) insists.

these being aphorisms.[14] The fact that so many of Rée's thoughts on these topics can be captured in the aphoristic form immediately suggests a certain superficiality to his treatment. And indeed there are times when Rée essentialises women and contrasts them with men as if they were quite different types of human beings. 'Dangers and women are like nettles – not [to] be grasped cautiously' (224). 'With women one does not converse, one only chats' (279). 'Women cry where men act' (290). Yet closer inspection reveals that there are a number of other places where Rée allows that men and women share some important drives and characteristics in common. Both are, for example, flirtatious, but men have many avenues for discharging ambition whereas coquetry is the only one available to women. 'The female sex is by nature no more flirtatious than the male; but whereas the ambition of men can motivate them in various directions, there exists for all the ambitious strivings of women only one direction: conquests' (239; cf. 240). This same idea that both sexes share a particular drive but women's avenues for expressing and exploring that drive are limited comes in the claim that both are interested in sexual variety, but because men are permitted to have pre-marital sex, they can explore this prior to marriage. Women, by contrast, are expected to have their first experiences of sex within marriage and this can pique their appetite for variety (241). Rée also says that men and women are equally envious by nature, but women are born competitors (301).

A long passage on coquetry opens with a gender-neutral definition: 'Whoever has the wish to be loved by as many people of the other sex as possible – without wanting to seduce, marry, or violate them or to achieve any positive advantage – is a coquette' (229). It likewise concludes with the gender-neutral claim that 'One takes pleasure in coquetry because it is pleasant to see people of the other sex at one's feet, but especially because one wants to be envied by persons of the same sex for one's conquests' (229). This suggests that coquetry is not simply about flirting with people of the other gender but also about gaining status in the eyes of others of either gender. Some of Rée's other aphorisms echo this

---

[14] The sections I deem too long to qualify as aphorisms are 229, 238, 241, 257, 265, 289, 306.

idea that our romantic attachments are powerfully influenced by the positive impact we think we are making on a wider audience or by some status advantage we feel ourselves to be gaining by this attachment (267, 284, 286, 291, 300).

Given these comments about men and women, it is no surprise to find that heterosexual romantic love becomes an arena animated by forces such as ambition, rivalry, status-seeking and vanity. Genuine love for or admiration of one's partner plays little role in Rée's analysis. As aphorism 223 declares, 'Few have loved. With most, a mixture of sensuality and vanity occupies the place of love' (cf. 262, 299). But it is noteworthy that some people do achieve what we can only infer is genuine love; Rée could have insisted that no one loves, but instead his choice of the term 'few' keeps the door open for some to experience this. This same tension appears in 250 which announces vanity to be 'the nurse of love'. But the second line of the passage concedes that 'there is a true love that needs no nurse since, like Minerva, it comes into the world already grown' (250). Yet despite these crevices of hope for genuine love, Rée shortly after announces that 'If, having come to know a noble, intelligent, and deeply sympathetic woman, we finally also achieve an intimate possession of her, we always lose more than we win' (228).

As this aphorism perhaps intimates, even for the few who might experience it, love is not a proper basis for marriage and has little chance of lasting in marriages based upon it. Rée's marriages are depicted as competitions between the partners, with no hint of the possibility of higher marriages that Nietzsche entertains. As he declares, 'In the marriages of our time, no feeling plays such a minor role as love' (235; cf. 243). Those who do marry for love 'are nearly always unhappy' (256). If one knew one's wife well before marriage, the marriage would never happen (281; cf. 270), just as for those who do marry, absence makes the heart grow fonder. As Rée puts it, 'the degree of married happiness stands in an inverse relation to the amount of shared daily life' (234). Consider also the aphorism that 'Every wife prizes most highly the qualities in men that are lacking in her husband' (226). It is followed immediately by the claim that 'Every wife is unhappy with her husband and knows another man with whom she would be happy' (227; cf. 295). Aphorisms 293 and 294 posit a contrarian antagonism between spouses. Rée's contribution to the 'take my wife' tradition appears in aphorism 252, which declares that 'Nobody would covet his neighbor's wife if he knew her as well as his neighbor does.' Note the emphatic use of 'every wife' and 'nobody' in these last three aphorisms – no exceptions allowed! But like Nietzsche, Rée also implies that marriage can be the vehicle for the complementary realisation of the spouses' goals when he writes that 'Every woman encourages the ambition of her husband, less because he stands out from other men through it as because she stands out from other women through it' (254).

And although Rée's chapter title does not include children, he makes three references to offspring. One resembles one of Nietzsche's claims by suggesting that one should have never procreated. His argument here is that when the children are grown, they will treat the parents either with or without forebearance, both of which are unpleasant (263). The other reference to children follows immediately to assert that grown children form an alliance with one parent against the other (264). This same competitive dynamic is audible in 278, according to which a mother not only ceases to criticise her children when the father starts to, but begins to defend them at that point.

Given that from the start HAH prides itself on its scientific and historical approach to moral and psychological matters, chapter 7 remains something of a mixed bag. Although it opens by invoking 'the natural science of animals' to establish the truth of its proposition that 'the perfect woman' is both a higher and a rarer type than the perfect man (HAH 377), it does not develop this, nor any other obviously scientific line of reasoning in any systematic way. The closest it comes to a scientific approach is when Nietzsche historicises women's condition. But however frequently Nietzsche fails to apply to women the scientific and historical mode of thinking that HAH champions, he is still more successful at this than his thought partner at this time, Rée. Briefly surveying Rée's treatment of these themes shows how much more complicated and variegated is Nietzsche's, notwithstanding the fact that Rée's own views are more subtle than Schopenhauer's.

8
A Glance at the State

Some unintended irony accompanies chapter 8's title, 'A Glance at the State' [*Ein Blick auf den Staat*], as this chapter provides the most sustained discussion of explicitly political subjects in all of Nietzsche's works. This so-called 'glance' is the closest Nietzsche comes to a treatise about traditional political topics in his whole corpus. Its forty-five passages treat democracy, political parties, political actors, the modern quest for equality, civil religion, socialism, revolution and war, as well as the state. Of course many, if not all, of his other works contain political remarks, asides and observations or contain material that has implications for political thought, but his views on conventional political topics are never before and never again assembled in one place like this.[1] And the fact of their concentration here provides us with a partial answer to one of the questions posed in the Introduction about whether HAH's chapter divisions carry any significance. In this case they clearly do, as the passages all revolve around some of the most significant conventional political topics.

The major unifying thread of chapter 8 comes from Nietzsche's reflections on the rise of democracy and egalitarianism in modern Western societies and the superannuation of older, more hierarchical, more elitist and exclusionary forms of politics. This issue, in turn, connects with some of the other questions already raised in HAH such as what a higher culture of the future might look

---

[1] For a briefer, but largely compatible overview of the themes in chapter 8, see Franco (2011: 50–4).

like, how it can be prepared for, and what role free spirits might play in paving its way. Nietzsche does not see free spirits as being political actors but as operating instead in the cultural sphere. Indeed, as we shall see, he posits a zero-sum relationship between political power and cultural attainment.

Democracy and equality

Nietzsche reflects throughout chapter 8 on what it means that the masses are now entering politics and expecting the state to cater to their interests as they perceive them. As he sees it, 'all politics is now a question of making life tolerable for the greatest number', based on that majority's understanding of what makes their lives bearable (HAH 438).[2] One of the first implications of this democratisation as he sees it is the dumbing down of political discourse; as the opening sentence of this chapter announces, all political parties are now 'compelled to transmute their principles into great frescoes of stupidity and to paint them thus upon the wall' (HAH 438). As this indicates, Nietzsche is not a great enthusiast for this aspect of democratisation and once again invokes Voltaire, applying to politics the French thinker's view that when the populace gets involved in reasoning, all is lost (HAH 438).

Although seeming to accept that the majority's definition of what makes their life bearable will steer politics, Nietzsche wants to confine this wave of democratisation if and where possible. He does not want their narrow-mindedness to become hegemonic, opposing the prospect that 'everything should become politics in this sense, or that everyone should live and work according to this standard' (HAH 438). Space must be created, or preserved, for those who do not want to participate in this movement nor share this mindset.[3] Although he does not mention his cadre of free spirits explicitly here, it seems reasonable to infer that they are the individuals who can remain aloof from this regnant democratic

---

[2] Drochon places Nietzsche's political thought very helpfully in its immediate political context and observes that German suffrage was among the most extensive of its time (2016: 76).
[3] Cf. Ansell-Pearson (1994: 90). This is an early example of Nietzsche rejecting the one-size-fits-all view that he later attacks vis-à-vis morality. Cf. for example BGE 202, 228.

view of politics and who do not need therefore to 'take the happiness of the many all that seriously' (HAH 438). The withdrawal of these types from mainstream politics is not permanent, however, for Nietzsche allows, in a very cryptic fashion, that every now and then they will emerge from their self-imposed isolation from the mainstream to connect with 'and to encourage' [*ermutigen*] one another. The majority will hear of these episodes, but what the free spirits communicate to one another will 'sound bad' [*übel klingt*] to mainstream ears, for they are not its intended audience. But after these periodic eruptions, those who do not belong to the majority retreat to their safe distance from the mainstream of political and social life. Jeremy Fortier offers a very helpful account of HAH's attitude towards politics when he writes that Nietzsche 'is not counselling the free spirits to be "apolitical" . . . [they] aim to be something closer to cultural critics (appraising the dominant culture at some distance from it)' (2016: 207).

What I am calling Nietzsche's concern with democratisation in modern Europe is my summary of what he says, not the actual term he uses, and is intended to cover more than just the majority's desire to express its will in politics. As I use the term, democratisation also refers to a more pervasive egalitarianism, whereby people think of themselves as one another's equals and expect the organisation of their social and political life to come more and more to acknowledge and reflect their status equality. In section 457 Nietzsche writes of the appeal to '"human dignity" . . . which feels that the hardest fate is not to be treated as an equal or to have less public esteem than someone else' (HAH 457). Critical of this ethos,[4] he redescribes it as a form of vanity [*Eitelkeit*] (HAH 457),[5] but for present purposes attention to his concern with human

---

[4] Corduwener (2013) also accentuates HAH's attack on equality.
[5] Elsewhere I have noted Nietzsche's interest in the idea of vanity in the middle period writings and suggested that it is a forerunner of his concept of *ressentiment*. Whether or not I am right about this, his repeated use of the term vanity certainly reflects the influence of Rée at this time. For Rée, vanity refers to the pleasure we take in the good opinion that others have of us and the displeasure in their bad opinion (Rée 2003: xviii–xix). In my estimation, Nietzsche uses the term vanity in a more consistently critical way than Rée does.

equality helps us to get a handle on some of his major foci in this chapter.

Very early in chapter 8 Nietzsche indicates that this egalitarianism or democratisation will not be conducive to the creation of a higher culture. On the contrary, such a culture 'can arise only where there are two different castes in society' (HAH 439). Society needs to be divided between the workers (presumably the majority) and a leisured elite. He acknowledges that this strong assertion of hierarchy's necessity will sound alien to contemporary ears, and given his repeated use of the term 'ears' in such quick succession, it is possible that HAH 439 sheds some light on HAH 438. Perhaps the truth of this necessity about two castes is one of the things that the free spirits utter to one another and which sounds discordant to the majority, precisely because of the latter's commitment to equality. But Nietzsche is also anxious to point out that membership in the leisured class is not all sunshine and lollipops. Although not forced to work, 'the caste of idlers', as he calls them, is the caste 'more capable of suffering and does suffer more, its pleasure in existence is less, its task greater' (HAH 439). He echoes this point towards the end of chapter 8, referring to 'the better, outwardly more favourably placed caste of society whose real task, the production of the highest cultural goods, makes their inner lives so much harder and more painful' (HAH 480).[6]

This declaration of the truth about the necessity of a caste-divided society ends with an appeal to the past: 'thus the fading voice of days gone by speaks to us' (HAH 439). But Nietzsche is also keen to point out that, unlike traditional aristocracies, membership in the sort of leisured class he endorses as necessary to a higher culture cannot be guaranteed by birth alone. The 'duller, less spirited individuals and families' (HAH 439)[7] are not equipped for these greater tasks of creating cultural goods nor for the inner suffering this work entails, and so should be demoted to the lower group. Conversely, any members of the lower group

---

[6] This point recurs in BGE, chapter 9, 276.
[7] Nietzsche's adjectives are *stumpferen, ungeistigeren*, which Handwerk renders as 'duller, less intelligent' and Hollingdale as 'obtuse, less spiritual'.

who show potential for this type of spiritual work can move up. His hierarchical model thus permits, indeed requires, upward and downward social mobility, although Nietzsche does not here specify any mechanisms by which this relocation would occur. HAH 439's implication that some people are ontologically better suited than others to manual labour becomes explicit in the passage Nietzsche labels 'My utopia' (HAH 462), where he dreams of a 'better ordered society' where hard labour and carrying out necessary tasks are assigned to those who are least adversely affected by this sort of work. Those who are more sensitive and correspondingly more vulnerable to suffering should have fewer or none of these chores. Once again, no allocation method is specified, so we do not know who decides where on the sensitivity and suffering food chain anyone stands, nor how the work that needs to be done is parcelled out. But Nietzsche is clear that this distribution of labour from each according to his ability to suffer from manual work does not mean that those with the fewest manual chores escape lightly. More liable to suffer than others, and having to bear their own particular forms of suffering, they will of necessity struggle. But their struggles will be ones for which they are dispositionally suited.

It's hard not to hear an echo of the Aristotelian idea of natural slaves here, according to which some people are just constitutionally more suited, physically and mentally, to engage in manual labour.[8] And indeed section 457 is entitled 'Slaves and workers', indicating that the phenomenon of slavery was on Nietzsche's mind in some form and to some degree at the time of writing. He notes the modern Western movement to abolish slavery, but in contrast to the abolitionist impetus, he compares the lives of slaves favourably to those of modern workers. He asserts that slaves enjoyed more security and happiness and worked less than do their modern counterparts in the paid workforce. Yet although he refers to the modern abolition movement, he is perhaps taking ancient slavery as his model rather than the more recent phenomenon of slavery and the slave trade in the United Kingdom and the United

---

[8] *The Politics*, Book I.

States, given his invocation of Diogenes at the end of the passage. The Cynic was 'for a time a slave and a tutor' (HAH 457).

But whether Nietzsche's template for thinking about slavery is ancient or modern, it is difficult for a contemporary reader not to be as shocked by what he says here as by what he doesn't say – that is, that slavery makes some humans the legal property of others. Whatever its problems, wage labour does not accord such *de jure* power over the worker to the employer. Nietzsche seems oblivious to the horrors and abuses of modern slavery and the slave trade. This is the passage in which he (twice) reduces the desire for equality and human dignity to vanity, yet it is hardly vanity alone, or perhaps at all, that inhibits one from wanting to be a chattel slave oneself or wanting others not to endure this. And one can, of course, be critical of the conditions of the modern working class without saying that its members are worse off than slaves. So from every angle, this unfortunate comparison seems wholly unnecessary.

As noted above, Nietzsche's reflections on the rise of democracy are accompanied by thoughts on the eclipse of older, more hierarchical, more elitist and exclusionary forms of politics. The fact that he is thinking about and modifying the traditional model of aristocracy is evident in chapter 8's third passage, 'Of blood lineage' (HAH 440).[9] He claims that what entitles male and female members of the nobility to be esteemed more highly than others is the fact that they are accustomed to the twofold art 'of being able to command and ... of proud obedience' (HAH 440).[10] Although this dual art is 'augmented more and more by hereditary transmission', he allows that the real driving force is the nobility's practical experience of commanding and obeying when he observes that 'Now wherever commanding is part of daily affairs (as in the world of business and industry), there arises something similar to these "noble bloodlines"' (HAH 440). However, even though there are avenues for practising the art of command in the

---

[9] Handwerk's translation of *Von Geblüt* is much more a propos than Hollingdale's 'Of the nobility'.
[10] This concern with the dual art of commanding and obeying reappears in BGE, chapter 9, 257.

modern world, what is being lost in this period of democratisation is the art of obedience, because humans expect to be treated as one another's equals and not as subordinates. One of the interesting implications of this passage is that aristocratic women practised this twofold art along with aristocratic men, unless, of course, we read Nietzsche as saying that men commanded while women obeyed. But that does not seem to be his point here; it is the ability to practise both that he prizes and which he believes 'will no longer grow in our cultural climate' (HAH 440), with its demand for status equality.[11]

This idea that it is not bloodline and inheritance as such that elevates the nobility, but instead their iterated experiences, is echoed in HAH 479, 'Wealth as the origin of a nobility of blood'. Nietzsche explains that what 'engenders an aristocracy of race' is the comfortable material and other conditions that wealth enables. Wealth can purchase leisure, quality education, freedom from manual labour, time for exercise and hygiene. A person with a noble disposition who is, conversely, forced to live in reduced circumstances will face an almost insurmountable battle to realise their nobility. (This passage thus sheds some doubt on the prospects of upward social mobility sketched in HAH 439.) But Nietzsche goes on to note that the amount of wealth needed to support a noble disposition is not something that increases exponentially; beyond a certain threshold, additional wealth becomes superfluous in supporting the conditions of a noble lifestyle.

In the section entitled 'Subordination', Nietzsche reflects more fully on the aforementioned attrition of subordination in modern Western society (HAH 441). He predicts that subordination will soon be unimaginable and that the loss of any experience of subordination will have detrimental effects. The only way in

---

[11] Such pessimism did not, however, prevent him from declaring in chapter 7 that 'Children from modest families must be educated in how to command, just as other children must be educated in how to obey' (HAH 395). This suggests some hope for the survival of this twofold art into the future, with each group of children being educated in the skill that their upbringing did not provide. The gender-neutral term *Kinder* is also noteworthy here, because Nietzsche could have said 'sons' or 'boys' had he wanted to confine this art to males.

which subordination becomes acceptable in modern culture is when it is contractually agreed to and based on self-interest. He opens his reflections on subordination by pointing out that it is highly esteemed in the military and bureaucratic state, and his very next passage reflects on the constitution of armies (HAH 442). One would think that he might support conscript armies precisely because they are not based on purely voluntary subordination or on anything like self-interest, and thus they run against the grain of what he takes to be a problematic strain in contemporary culture. Instead he bemoans conscript armies because they draft all manner of men indiscriminately and thus squander in war the finest along with the more ordinary. Indeed, the massacre of the more valuable individuals is intensified because not only are they as likely to be drafted as the mediocre ones, but once their military service starts, their valour and ambition make them more likely to put themselves in the front line and thus be killed.

Religion and politics

Entitled 'Prince and God', HAH 461 draws attention to one of the ways in which religion and politics have traditionally been imbricated, for princes were often seen as earthly representatives of God. Nietzsche points out that even though this tendency to divinise powerful individuals is declining, it can still sometimes break out and attach itself to powerful people in general, not just political actors. He detects the cult of genius, wherever it raises its head, as an expression of this tendency to invest the powerful with religious significance. His comments on that cult were first offered in chapter 4 in the context of artists, but one of the examples he gave there of a genius who becomes 'convinced of his own divinity' was Napoleon, indicating again the relevance of this idea to politics. Nietzsche's references to the cult of genius are typically critical, with HAH 461 offering a new reason to be suspicious of this phenomenon, for 'Wherever one strives to raise individual human beings into something superhuman, there will also be a tendency to conceive of entire classes of the people as coarser and lower than they really are.'

The longest passage of not just chapter 8 but the whole of HAH examines the relationship between politics and religion in more detail. Indeed, so uncharacteristically long is HAH 472[12] that at around its three-quarter mark, Nietzsche offers a précis of what he has said so far in the passage. 'Religion and government' opens by looking back to the time when government saw itself as the guardian, rather than the servant, of the people's interests. From that historical vantage point, Nietzsche surmises, the government will always think that religion should be maintained, for it can provide what government cannot; salve for the suffering private person. Religion serves a public function as well, as the community can interpret political power and political events through a sacred lens and impute higher meaning to these worldly matters. Detecting the hand of God in matters political, the populace is, moreover, more likely to comply with or submit to whatever is happening politically. So in addition to the consolations it can offer the suffering individual, religion has a unifying, legitimating and pacifying function within the political community. There are, of course, exceptions to this tendency, such as when the religious leadership finds itself at odds with the political rulers, but Nietzsche contends that political leaders, perceiving the value of having religion on their side, know how to win errant priests back.

Nietzsche then offers the fascinating observation that for political elites to adopt this attitude towards religion's value to the polity means that they simultaneously see themselves as above religion, understanding themselves as manipulating it for their own ends. He declares, intriguingly, that 'free-spiritedness has its origin here' (HAH 472). Looking back to what we learned about free spirits from chapter 5 can illuminate this somewhat surprising claim, for there we found that free spirits differ markedly from the fully integrated community members who unthinkingly perpetuate culture, custom and convention. Thinking differently from the majority of their fellow citizens, they liberate themselves from tradition. The mere fact that they reflect upon the dynamics of social and political life means that they do not live by faith as the majority does. Instead, free spirits are critical questioners of the

---

[12] I cannot join Franco (2011: 52) in calling this an aphorism. Ansell-Pearson calls this 'One of the major passages in HAH [and] absolutely central for understanding Nietzsche's political thought during this period' (1994: 86).

things their societies take for granted, and they demand rational accounts of social practices and beliefs. So while most members of the polity live within a religious outlook, the free-spirited rulers can take some distance from it and see religion as a phenomenon to be managed to their advantage.

But during the current period of democratisation, religion can no longer be used to manipulate the majority or to serve the ruling elite's interests. It must become instead an object of the popular will, allowing those in power only to mirror the attitude towards religion that the people have. No longer an instrument for use by the government, religion becomes a private affair and the subject of individual conscience. Nietzsche predicts that the first consequence of this turn away from civil religion will be an efflorescence of religions, because any previous suppression of some religious beliefs by the government in its quest for public unity has been relaxed. He further anticipates that the reaction to this proliferation of religions will be for 'every better and more gifted person to make irreligion his private affair' (HAH 472). At this point he imagines these better and more gifted people to also be political leaders, and as they turn away from religion, the still religious populace will turn away from them. This period of transition from a model of civic religion to its rejection by the rulers and the reaction of the people to that rejection could last quite a while, and Nietzsche predicts that its outcome will be uncertain. Religious political parties might be able to gain power and thus restore religion's public and political functions. But if they do not, the state will become ever more demystified and will come to be seen by different social groups as simply an instrument to achieve their goals. So once again we see the theme of the present being an interregnum, which was emphasised in chapter 5.

The next step envisaged by Nietzsche in this process is that, being reduced to the status of an instrument, the state itself loses any particular value in its population's eyes, and its previous supposedly core functions such as the protection of some of its citizens from the predation of others become contracted out to private companies.[13]

---

[13] Drochon identifies this as an important element in Nietzsche's political views from HAH through to his later writings (2016: 11).

In the service of self-interest, people might even seek to abolish the state and replace it with other institutions that can serve the same purposes. So the democratic state initiates a process of its own weakening and even potential dismemberment. Although many of Nietzsche's contemporaries react with 'fear and abhorrence' to this prospect of the state withering away, his historical perspective serves to remind us that there are different ways for humans to organise themselves politically. He imagines that such a development will bring in its wake 'all sorts of strange tales, some of them perhaps good ones' (HAH 472). His summary remarks on this point are even more optimistic as he assures readers that 'chaos is the least likely thing to emerge; instead, an invention even more to the purpose than was the state will triumph over the state' (HAH 472).[14] What Nietzsche foresees and endorses is a process of gradual evolution; he is not encouraging political groups to actively hasten the state's demise.

Socialism and nationalism

While Nietzsche appears here to be relatively sanguine about the possible gradual demise of the state, trusting to 'the cleverness and self interest of human beings' (HAH 472), one contemporaneous political movement that he was far from sanguine about was socialism.[15] As we shall see, socialism portends in a very different direction from the gradual superannuation of the state. Indeed,

---

[14] Here my reading departs from Corduwener's, for whom Nietzsche thought that the separation of Church and state 'would turn out differently, and worse, than was expected in his day' (2013: 71).

[15] Young argues that while writing HAH, Nietzsche was the least critical of socialism that he would ever be. He attributes this to the 'temporarily moderating' influence of Malwida von Meysenbug (2010: 233). But as we will see, Nietzsche is still staunchly critical of socialism from a number of angles during this time, and the passage that Young cites from Nietzsche's notebooks confirms rather than alters this in my interpretation. Young surmises that von Meysenbug would have been delighted by Nietzsche's remark that 'Socialism rests on the decision to recognize all men as equals and to be just to all of them: it is the highest form of morality' (2010: 233). But other remarks from this time clarify that he thinks this a bad decision based on a flawed and dangerous ontology, as humans are not equal. Socialism extends Kantian universalist morality into politics by treating everyone identically. In contrast to Young, I don't read any of this quotation as complimentary.

one of Nietzsche's criticisms of socialism, voiced in the very next passage, is that its agenda is to empower the state in the name of, and as a vehicle for, ensuring happiness for all. And based on what Nietzsche has just argued, the powerful socialist state could not appeal to religion to justify its existence (HAH 473). Yet as the power of the state grows, so he believes, the power of the individual diminishes, such that the socialist state would ultimately overpower the individuals it was putatively designed to serve (HAH 473).[16] By this logic, the state, which was originally formed as a means to protect individuals from one another, would so weaken those individuals as to make itself redundant, at least in terms of its original purpose. Its new purpose would be to produce 'a comfortable life for as many people as possible' (HAH 235).[17]

As part of its project of promoting human happiness, socialism also promises equal rights (HAH 451), but we have seen above the concerns Nietzsche harbours about such egalitarianism. Just as he has previously suggested that the push for equality was motivated by vanity, so here he adds that socialist equality is animated by the majority's 'hatred and envy' of those who are superior and whose task is to produce 'the highest cultural goods' (HAH 480). This insistence on a contradiction between socialism and the attainment of a higher culture connects with one of his criticisms of socialism aired in chapter 5. As we have seen, there Nietzsche claimed that because of its promise of equality and happiness secured through the state, socialism would kill the social and cultural soil in which genius grows: it would eradicate the great intellect and energy that genius needs (HAH 235).[18]

And just as Nietzsche repudiates socialism, so he condemns the other major political force of his time – nationalism. Nationalism

---

[16] This association of socialism with a powerful state is probably what explains Nietzsche's aside that Plato was 'a typical old socialist' (HAH 473). See also section 474 for a depiction of Plato as wanting a very powerful state. It could also be Plato's abolition of private property that makes him a socialist, as Ansell-Pearson points out (1994: 91), but that is, of course, just for the elite and not the mass of the population.

[17] Here I follow Hollingdale's translation of *ein Wohlleben* rather than Handwerk's 'a good life' to avoid any possible echoes of Aristotle's view on this.

[18] For other passages in this chapter critical of socialism, see HAH 446, 451, 452.

shares the socialist disdain for individuals who refuse to bow to collective political programmes. Just like socialism, nationalism is fuelled by hatred and envy of 'the prominent, self-made individuals who are not willing to let themselves be lined up in the ranks of those pursuing some mass action' (HAH 480). In lieu of nationalism, Nietzsche looks forward to the growth of pan-European sentiment, with chapter 8 containing his first invocation of the good European (HAH 475), an ideal carried into his later works. This passage, 'The European person and the destruction of nations' [*Der europäische Mensch und die Vernichtung der Nationen*],[19] observes how the material conditions of modern European life are themselves transcending national boundaries. These conditions include commerce and industry, the circulation of books and letters, a shared higher culture, and the movement of people who are not landowners. Assertions of nationalist sentiment might react against this practical exchange and intermingling, but they cannot undo it. And behind such expressions of nationalist sentiment Nietzsche detects not any genuine mass movement but rather 'the interests of certain princely dynasties and of certain commercial and social classes' (HAH 475). Both of these features – the material conditions that transcend national boundaries and the specific, limited groups that advocate nationalism – could explain why he dubs the nationalism of his time as 'artificial' (HAH 475).

Nietzsche also conveys his hope that the more transnational perspective and reality that currently exist will eventually dissolve the plague of anti-Semitism, for once the goal of preserving distinct nations is eclipsed by that of producing a robust pan-European race, the Jews with their many strengths and talents will be welcomed rather than abjured.[20] While the Jews' 'energy and higher intelligence' is confined within nation-states, it is bound to arouse envy and hatred, which are by now emerging as the twin

---

[19] I vary Handwerk's translation slightly by inserting 'person' after European.

[20] Nietzsche says that as soon as it is a matter 'of engendering the strongest possible European racial mixture, the Jew is just as usable and desirable an ingredient as the remains of any other nation' (HAH 475). Yet Menahem Brinker argues that this ideal does not appear until *Daybreak* 205 which 'spoke of the need to fuse the Jewish race with the other races of Europe for the advancement and betterment of European culture' (2002: 108).

forces behind so much political activity in Nietzsche's estimation. Although a major thrust of this passage is to attack anti-Semitism, it must be noted that some of Nietzsche's own remarks could, at the same time, be complicit in this. He says, for instance, that 'the youthful stock exchange Jew is perhaps the most repulsive invention of the whole human species' (HAH 475). These strong words are offered in the context of considering that every social group has unattractive qualities, but the stock caricature and hyperbole take that aim a bit too far in this instance. Nietzsche does go on to say that the history of the Jewish people 'has entailed more suffering than any other' and to confess that 'all of us share the guilt' for that, with 'us' presumably being the gentile population of Europe. He also thanks the Jewish legacy for having provided such individuals as 'the noblest human being (Christ))'[21] and Spinoza, 'the purest sage', along with 'the mightiest book, and the most effective moral code in the world' (HAH 475). And as I noted in the Introduction, he credits medieval Jewish scholars and free thinkers with preserving the banner of enlightenment by keeping Europe's intellectual link to ancient Greece and Rome alight.

Revolution

Whether taking the form of the gradual withering away of the state or the preparation of a positive, pan-European outlook, Nietzsche is at his most relaxed when imagining gradual political evolutions. This demeanour is evident in section 443 when he accepts that 'Our social order will slowly melt away, just as all earlier orders have done, as soon as the suns of new opinions shine with a new heat over humanity' (HAH 443). He is, conversely, very alarmed by revolutionary movements that foment rapid and radical change.[22] Nietzsche's fear of dramatic and radical efforts at reform or revolution is, moreover, in accordance with HAH's

---

[21] This is an early example of what becomes Nietzsche's characteristic tendency to emphasise that Christ was a Jew. Apart from historical accuracy, he no doubt accentuates this point to discomfort anti-Semitic Christians.
[22] Drochon suggests that Nietzsche's colleague at Basel, Jacob Burckhardt, was an influence here (2016: 76).

praise for science and its more incremental and modest approach to knowledge. In section 463, for example, he inveighs against the spirit of the French Revolution, seeing it as the betrayal, rather than the corollary, of the Enlightenment. A true student of Voltaire and admirer of his moderate nature would not endorse revolution.[23] Nietzsche thus redirects the Voltairean catch-cry *Ecrasez l'infâme*,[24] which was originally directed at the Catholic Church, its religious intolerance and its alliance with the French state, towards Rousseau's revolutionary followers with their belief in innate human goodness. What revolutionary moments actually unlock, instead of any stifled human goodness, are 'the most savage energies in the form of the long-buried horrors and excesses of the most distant ages' (HAH 463).[25]

An earlier passage from chapter 8 subdivides revolutionaries into two types: those motivated by immediate personal gain and those seeking to improve conditions for future generations. Nietzsche finds the latter to be more dangerous, because the former can be bought off and placated by savvy rulers. The latter, by contrast, think of themselves as more disinterested and principled, which enables them to feel superior to the supposedly self-interested defenders of the status quo (HAH 454). The very next passage, 'Political value of fatherhood', seems, prima facie at least, to be at odds with this, for there Nietzsche argues that some sort of stake in the future should be a prerequisite for political participation. Having children provides that stake because fathers (he makes no mention of mothers) have an interest in the happiness of their sons (he makes no mention of daughters), and so want to perpetuate the institutions most likely to secure this (HAH 455). But we have just seen that a future-oriented view of politics is more dangerous than one which treats it as a competition over resources. Maybe what Nietzsche is trying to say by juxtaposing

---

[23] As we saw in Chapter 4, he had previously praised Voltaire for being able to combine 'the highest freedom of the spirit and an absolutely unrevolutionary disposition without being inconsistent and cowardly' (HAH 221).

[24] Meaning 'crush/destroy the infamous'.

[25] Discussing this passage, Ansell-Pearson notes that Nietzsche 'never abandoned his fear and distrust of moral and political fanaticism' (1994: 84). He elaborates on Nietzsche's dislike of fanaticism and of revolution in Ansell-Pearson (2018: ch. 2).

these passages is that what matters is not so much whether one's view of politics is future-directed, but more how one sees the future growing out of and relating to the present. Those who support dramatic disruption between now and then differ markedly from those who hope for the conservation of current good things and who 'take the proper, natural interest in institutions and in their alteration' (HAH 455). He is not very explicit about this and it does require a granular reading of his prose, but this offers at least one way of reconciling two passages that otherwise seem mutually discordant.

Indeed, just as the passage vaunting Voltaire over Rousseau praises Voltaire's 'moderate nature, inclined to organizing, purifying, and reconstructing' (HAH 463), so the very next passage reminds us that the character traits that form free spirits render them 'moderate in action'.[26] These traits keep them cognisant of the only 'partial utility or the uselessness and danger of all sudden changes' (HAH 464). Here we witness once again the presence of what I am calling Nietzsche's epistemology-plus perspective in HAH, for he moves beyond thinking about knowledge in its own terms to speculating about how being a scientific knower should affect one's stance towards political matters.

Politics and culture

Yet while Nietzsche gestures towards the attitude that free spirits will adopt towards politics, it seems pretty clear from chapter 8 that he does not envisage this elite as themselves being political actors. Their salutary impact on society and preparation of a higher culture do not occur through conventional political channels. This introduces another way in which his new elite differs from traditional aristocracies, for the latter did typically have a hand in governance. Chapter 8's penultimate passage is clear about the fact that this new elite will not engage directly in politics, for Nietzsche writes that just as war wastes the lives of talented young men, so participation in politics squanders the skills of those who should be following other, higher paths. He refers, for example,

---

[26] I depart here from Handwerk's 'makes us moderate in our actions' and am closer to Hollingdale's 'action tends to moderation'.

to 'all the more noble, more delicate, more spiritual plants and growths in which this nation's soil had previously been so rich [being] sacrificed to this coarse and gaudy flower of the nation' (HAH 481). This is, to be sure, the conclusion of a passage about 'Great politics and its costs',[27] and by great politics Nietzsche has in mind the military might of the state coupled with its strength in trade and commerce. So what he says here about involvement in grand politics being a waste of the time, talent and energy of more spiritual individuals might not apply to all forms of politics.

However, at a number of points throughout chapter 8 Nietzsche seems to assert a zero-sum relationship between any sort of politics on the one hand and high cultural attainment on the other. In section 465, for example, he declares that 'Culture owes its highest achievement to times of political weakness.' Looking back to his much-admired Greeks he finds this same clash between political and cultural greatness. He opens the section 'The development of the spirit [*Geist*], feared by the state' by pronouncing that, 'Like every organizing political power, the Greek polis resisted and mistrusted the growth of culture [*Bildung*] . . . Culture therefore developed despite the polis' (HAH 474).[28] With these statements in mind, it becomes easier to see the passage outlining the costs of great politics as also positing a necessary conflict between politics and culture, and not just great politics and culture. As Nietzsche says there, 'the political blossoming of a people almost inevitably brings with it a spiritual impoverishment and exhaustion, a lessened capacity for undertaking works that require great concentration and single mindedness' (HAH 481). His injunction to free spirits is therefore to 'Live as higher human beings and always do the deeds of higher culture – then everything that lives will acknowledge your rights and the social order, whose summit you represent, will be proof against every evil eye and hand' (HAH 480). This exhortation to higher human beings to stay out of politics also means that,

---

[27] Hollingdale's rendering of this as 'grand politics' is just as plausible. This term is in turn associated with the political project of the Prussian statesman Otto von Bismarck (Drochon 2016). Drochon argues that Nietzsche's rejection of this grand politics 'is remarkably consistent over the course of his writings from *Human, All Too Human* to his last notebook' (2016: 9).

[28] Franco sees in this an important thread of continuity between HAH and Nietzsche's later views (2011: 50). See also Ansell-Pearson (1994: 95).

in effect, chapter 8, like chapters 1 and 2, closes with a personality profile of the free spirit, for such a person should not get directly involved in politics.[29]

Chapter 8's reflections on war also shed some light on this issue of the relationship between politics and culture. Section 444 posits an inverse relationship between war and culture: 'war is a time of sleep or winter for culture'. As both of these metaphors indicate, Nietzsche also holds that culture can come back better and stronger after a period of war. And war is a political phenomenon closely, albeit not exclusively, associated with 'great politics'. Just over thirty passages later, he elaborates on these thoughts to offer a strong statement that war is 'indispensable' to cultural achievement when it alternates with it (HAH 477). Although war and culture cannot flourish simultaneously, Nietzsche suggests that periods of war are necessary preludes and postludes to periods of cultural excellence. Although he does not repeat his sleep and winter imagery here, the logic is the same – that after a period of war in which culture recedes, culture can come back stronger. So while this passage reports that war 'destroy[s] the fields of delicate cultures, [it] will afterward under favourable circumstances turn the wheels in the workshops of the spirit with new energy' (HAH 477).

This longer passage on the complementary alternation between war and culture offers a reason for this that was absent from the briefer section 444. Nietzsche's logic is that war channels and discharges the violent passions, and cultural creation 'simply cannot do without passions, vices, and acts of malice' (HAH 477). Although this passage dubs war as indispensable in its title, Nietzsche does offer some surrogates for war such as gladiatorial contests and persecution of the Christians in the case of the Romans and adventures to foreign parts in the case of contemporary England. And while one could imagine that HAH's enthusiasm for science would lead him to endorse the 'dangerous voyages of discovery, circumnavigations, [and] ascents of mountains undertaken for scientific purposes' that the English pursue as productive alternatives to war, he concludes

---

[29] Yet unlike those earlier chapters, it does not literally end with this; its final section is an aphorism (HAH 482). But the parallel comes from the fact that the last two lengthy sections of this chapter counsel higher human beings against political participation. Franco wrongly calls HAH 481 'the concluding aphorism of the chapter on the state' (2011: 54). Cf. Fortier (2016: 206–7) on the role that HAH assigns to free spirits vis-à-vis politics.

that what these possible surrogates actually demonstrate is that there is no substitute for the 'temporary relapses into barbarism' that war brings.

This strong statement on the necessity of periods of war for periods of cultural excellence sheds, in turn, new light on one of Nietzsche's passages about socialism. Section 452 points out that while the socialists are correct to complain that the current distribution of property is unjust and based on unjust precedents, they fail to see that all of the past is unjust, based as it is on 'force, slavery, deceit, error'. Everything we inherit is therefore the legacy of unjust acts and relationships. He concludes that what socialism needs is not 'the forcible redistribution of property, but instead the gradual transformation of sensibility; the sense of justice must become greater in everyone, the instinct for violence weaker' (HAH 452). On the one hand, such a gradual transformation would recommend itself to Nietzsche more than a sudden redistribution of property because of his mistrust of rapid and radical change mentioned above. But on the other hand, the weakening of the violent instincts anticipated here would diminish the conditions for cultural greatness. And so this passage provides a variation on his aforementioned reason for rejecting socialism, for here we find that even in its best form, the change in sensibility it requires would provide no outlet for the passions that Nietzsche thinks make cultural greatness possible.

Whatever we can glean from chapter 8 about Nietzsche's attitude towards conventionally political questions at this time, one thing is crystal clear. For him, the ethos and institutions of politics are important not just in themselves but also because they provide the template for other relationships. As he declares in 'New and old conception of government' [*Neuer und alter Begriff der Regierung*],

> the relationship between people and government is the strongest model for other relationships, the pattern from which interactions between teacher and pupil, head of household and servants, father and family, commander and soldier, master and apprentice have instinctively taken their shape. (HAH 450)

It is hard to imagine a stronger statement about the impact and importance of politics, and the power Nietzsche attributes to politics here, whatever form it takes, poses a challenge to those who insist that he was uninterested in the political.[30] He goes on to observe that 'All these relationships are now being slightly reformulated under the influence of the prevailing constitutional form of government: they are becoming compromises' (HAH 450). The reason they are becoming compromises is democratisation: as people come to perceive themselves as one another's equals and as traditional hierarchical justifications for authority relations fade, so the bases of interaction become choice and self-interest. Individuals engage with one another along the contract model of social and political exchange: give something up to get something back.

It has become something of a commonplace in the secondary literature that during his middle period writings, Nietzsche was more accepting of democracy than he later became.[31] Based on the evidence of this chapter alone, it seems that he is only willing to tolerate democracy if its effects can be cordoned off such that higher human beings can continue to do their thing without democratic encroachment. As Ansell-Pearson puts it, 'He now seems to think that democracy does not inevitably mean the death of high culture and noble values provided the two – culture and politics – can come to an agreement about the ends of each and that space is provided for the practice of both' (1994: 90). It is easy to see why Hill argues that the middle period writings suggest that 'In many respects, Nietzsche would leave society and state as they are, focusing his interest on a minority who will achieve liberation independent of politics' (2007: 39). But in so far as democracy is accompanied by a commitment to some degree of egalitarianism, we can see that even in HAH, Nietzsche insists upon the need for a firm division between two castes. And if one of the conditions of the creation of a higher culture is the separation of society into two castes, as he insists in this chapter, then democracy's egalitarianism and his commitment to a higher culture cannot easily coexist.

---

[30] For just one expression of this view, see Brobjer (2008b).
[31] Bruce Detwiler (1990) was one of the first commentators to advance this view. See also Ansell-Pearson (1994: 85). Drochon describes without endorsing this view (2016: 71).

9
Conclusion to HAH: Alone with Oneself

A more literal translation of the title Nietzsche gives chapter 9 – '*Der Mensch mit sich allein*' – would be 'Man (or the Human) Alone with Himself'. Hollingdale opts for 'Man' but using the more neutral term 'the human' captures the echo in the common English translation of the book's title – *Human, All Too Human*. Handwerk translates the title as 'By Oneself Alone' which has the advantage of gender neutrality. My choice of 'Alone with Oneself' retains gender neutrality while also conveying the image of the plural self that Nietzsche develops in these works. 'With Oneself Alone' would also do this work.

As I noted in the Introduction, chapter 9 contains the largest number of genuine aphorisms in HAH, MOM or WS. As was the case with chapter 6, the wit and playfulness of Nietzsche's insights display his affinity with and emulation of the French moralist tradition. Chapter 9 is, moreover, the most miscellaneous collection of ideas in any chapter of HAH, at least in the eyes of this reader. Many of the aphorisms do not, moreover, obviously relate to the chapter's title and could just as easily belong in chapter 6, which situates the individual within society.[1] Chapter 9 is thus a noteworthy exception

---

[1] See, for example, passages 492, 493, 495, 496, 497, 502, 507, 509, 524, 525, 533, 536, 540, 548, 549, 550, 557, 561, 562, 567, 571, 583, 589, 595, 605, 614. One passage that does belong in a chapter with this title is the charming 625 on 'Solitary people'. It points out that some people are fine with their own company, but because they spend so much time alone, they tend to underestimate their own value.

to what we have found in HAH's other chapters, which is a considerable degree of thematic integrity. But only by running the experiment that this introduction and guide has, and by taking a careful and sedulous chapter-by-chapter approach to HAH's contents, can we identify both the dominant tendency and this departure from it. Because chapter 9 does not, in my estimation, exhibit sufficient thematic integrity to warrant consideration as a unified chapter, I focus here on the way in which Nietzsche chose to conclude HAH by emphasising convictions as impediments to truth and to the free spirit's quest for knowledge.[2]

Thus despite chapter 9's general miscellany, a powerful thread unites the last suite of passages, stretching from 629 to 637. These passages delve into the theme struck at chapter 9's outset when Nietzsche declares convictions [*Ueberzeugungen*] to be 'more dangerous enemies of truth than are lies' (HAH 483). The sections comprising this suite are also passages or paragraphs rather than aphorisms, as the term is traditionally used, which illustrates once again that when Nietzsche wants to mount a sustained argument, he reaches beyond the aphoristic form. It is also noteworthy that while passage 629 is entitled 'Of conviction and justice', the following eight passages (630–7) remain untitled, from which we can infer some continuity of topic. Indeed, Nietzsche ends section 629 with an invitation to 'examine how convictions arise and . . . whether they are not greatly overestimated', thereby implying that what is to follow is part of that examination. And in accordance with the epistemology-plus perspective that I uncover in HAH, his broadside against convictions proceeds on three fronts simultaneously. These are 1) the epistemic, 2) the social, and 3) the ethical or attention to personal character.[3]

Nietzsche opens these reflections on the importance of being willing to change one's opinions by observing that what often

---

[2] Other passages that I deem to be noteworthy from this chapter have been located in the chapter where their theme was first or most discussed.

[3] Adhering to convictions is also discussed briefly in section 511, where those who are busy remain true to their convictions, no doubt due to a lack of time to scrutinise them. Those 'who work in the service of an idea' also lack the time for such scrutiny, but Nietzsche also indicates that they lack the incentive to reconsider the idea they have committed to. In both cases, being convinced is associated with lack rather than being a positive state.

creates conviction in the first place is a strong passion. And here he is talking about commitments not just to ideas but also to religious beliefs, other people, political forces or artists. The expectation that a person retain their loyalty to the person, thing or idea that might have been forged in a rash of emotion is wholly inappropriate according to Nietzsche: instead, 'we must become traitors [*Verräther*], act unfaithfully, forsake our ideas again and again' (HAH 629).[4] And as the paradox of Nietzsche urging people to become traitors and infidels indicates,[5] there is great social disapprobation attached to changing one's views and allegiances. But he points out that the social admiration for people who remain steadfast in their convictions assumes that people only change their opinions for base reasons such as self-interest or fear. He sets out to overturn this presumption and to make the act of changing one's commitments appear not just acceptable but admirable, whereas remaining steadfast becomes suspect. The sort of anti-dogmatic practitioners of science that he both lauds and advocates will be ever willing to reconsider the things they hold to be true. And as this indicates, his suspicion of convictions applies no matter how the initial attachment was formed: even beliefs formed in calm and rational ways must be subject to continuous review.

Section 630 begins by treating convictions from an epistemological point of view. In order for any commitment to a belief to be valid, three things are necessary: that

1. absolute truths exist;
2. there is a perfect method for uncovering those truths;
3. in each case, that reliable method was the route to that truth.

As an advocate of science, Nietzsche cannot accept any of these premises. As we saw in HAH's earlier chapters, he believes that historical knowledge must dislodge and ultimately replace the faith

---

[4] I follow Hollingdale rather than Handwerk by translating this as 'become' rather than 'be' traitors, as that seems closer to Nietzsche's point that this will be an ongoing process.

[5] His later concern with using words 'on which for ages a disparaging purpose has been stamped' (BGE, chapter 9, 259) applies here too.

in metaphysical and religious certainties. He also insists that the methods for getting to knowledge are in great need of refinement, precisely because the new era of enlightenment is still in its infancy and thus far religion and metaphysics have dominated approaches to knowledge. He is also conscious of how long a training in scientific styles of thinking can take (HAH 635). So purely as a matter of correct epistemology, convictions cannot be defended.

But this is not to deny that they have hitherto served some useful purposes, and once again we see how easily Nietzsche moves from epistemological matters to broader issues – in this case the social effects of convictions. In the past, firm attachments to beliefs have generated 'humanity's mightiest sources of strength' (HAH 630), with individuals sacrificing their lives for their political and religious commitments. But conversely, action on the basis of convictions has also ignited much violence and harm. Indulging in some counterfactual speculation, he muses upon how much more peaceful history might have been had people felt less convinced of their beliefs. There would, for example, have been much less religious persecution because both, or all, sides to any religious dispute would have to admit that their beliefs were more frail than they thought and not worth punishing or being punished over (HAH 630).

Continuing this theme of convictions and religious persecution, section 633 observes that one major difference between the present and the Reformation is the current unwillingness to use political means to effect religious persecution. Nietzsche applauds this as evidence of 'a higher culture', thus recalling chapter 5's terminology about what a better future might look like and how it can be ushered in. Today those who respond in an angry or domineering way to a difference of opinion evoke that earlier time and arouse the suspicion that they would resort to violent means to suppress that difference were this option available. Nietzsche deems the current more moderate and tolerant outlook to be a decisive improvement, and again links that progress to the growth of scientific styles of knowledge:

> we no longer concede so easily to anyone that he might possess the truth: rigorous methods of inquiry have disseminated enough mistrust and caution that everyone who

advocates opinions violently in his words and actions is felt to be an enemy of our present-day culture, or at least to be a backward person. In fact: the pathos that we possess the truth counts for very little today in relation to that admittedly milder and less resonant pathos of searching for the truth, which does not grow weary of relearning and examining anew. (HAH 633)

This remarkable passage weaves together the three sorts of critique of convictions noted above: the epistemic ('rigorous methods of inquiry'; the 'pathos of searching for the truth'), the socio-cultural ('an enemy of our present-day culture') and the ethical ('a backward person').

Indeed, Nietzsche has already depicted those who cling to convictions as backward [*zurückgeblieben*]: anyone who remains 'attached to the belief in whose net he became entangled . . . [is] a representative of backward cultures' (HAH 632). Far from manifesting greater reliability, integrity and attachment to principles, then, the convinced person is here redrawn as lacking 'cultivation . . . [and as] hard, injudicious, obstinate, without gentleness, always suspicious' (HAH 632).[6] Unable to comprehend the existence, let alone the content, of other points of view, the convinced person's only contribution to the project of cultural improvement is that by being such a stolid and immovable force, he provides staunch resistance to those who would think differently. And in having to resist such a force, those others become stronger themselves. Section 634 shows again how Nietzsche, in keeping with the historical perspective adopted throughout HAH, is willing to concede that cleaving to convictions has been beneficial in the past. Then each inquirer believed in his truths and believed them to be absolute, but those truths were incompatible with those of other inquirers. This collision fostered their closer interrogation. As he puts it, 'the methodical search for truth is itself the result of those ages in which convictions were feuding with one another'

---

[6] *Bildung . . . hart, unverständig, unbelehrbar, ohne Milde, ein ewiger Verdächtiger.* I substitute 'obstinate' for Handwerk's (and Hollingdale)'s 'unteachable'.

(HAH 634). But for society to move forward in the progressive way Nietzsche hopes for in this enlightenment phase of his thought, convictions must henceforth be eschewed.

As another illustration of the ethical or character-focused attempt to critique and transvalue convictions, Nietzsche attributes 'the desire to be seen as consistent through and through' (HAH 608) to vanity. As he explains, the vain person is centrally concerned with what he thinks other people think of him (HAH 545), and vanity is not an admirable motive in Nietzsche's book.[7] What he does admire, by contrast, is that 'virtue of cautious reserve' and 'wise moderation' (HAH 631) that accompanies a more scientific and tentative approach to knowledge. This is amplified as section 614 describes the many virtues of the person who 'claims no privilege in being alone in recognizing truth, but is instead filled with a modest mistrust . . .' Once again recalling the terminology of chapter 5, this is 'an anticipatory person who is striving toward a higher human culture' (HAH 614). Section 635 likewise applauds 'the cautious and modest scientific sensibility', contrasting it with the more bombastic outlook of thinkers who present themselves as geniuses.

This echoes chapter 4's critique of the figure of the genius, although that figure is primarily an artistic one. But as we saw, Nietzsche does not repudiate all ideas of genius, referring favourably to geniuses of knowledge such as Kepler and Spinoza (HAH 157). And just as chapter 5 also revealed that the term genius can be used in a positive way by Nietzsche, so in HAH 636 he conjures and praises the figure of the genius of justice. The genius of justice opposes convictions and strives instead to 'perceive things clearly' [*rein erkennen*]. But as part of this process, the genius will give convictions their place, as we have seen that Nietzsche tries to do, by observing some of the benefits they have yielded in the past. As this indicates, his concern here is epistemic, rather than political, justice. Indeed, in the very next passage Nietzsche invokes a 'we' who should 'kneel down

---

[7] Vanity goes on to become an aspect of slave morality, for having no autonomous sense of self, the vain person must rely on the opinion of others for his sense of self-worth (BGE, chapter 9, 261).

before justice as the only goddess that we acknowledge above ourselves' (HAH 637). Such knowers 'stride from opinion to opinion', and by the end of this passage we see him addressing directly the paradox noted above, for such knowers are now 'noble traitors [*edle Verräther*] of all the things that can ever be betrayed'.[8] Their infidelity has been redeemed and ennobled.

Chapter 9's final passage, and that of HAH as Nietzsche originally conceived and published the book, offers a vignette of the person pursuing the sort of scientific knowledge HAH advocates. In this way it follows the pattern of chapters 1, 2 and 8. And interestingly this final section, 638, is one of the passages that suits chapter 9's title, for the seeker after knowledge portrayed here is, initially at least, very much a solo figure. He is also a wanderer, as the passage's title indicates. Indeed, 'the wanderer', 'the free spirit' and 'the philosopher' seem to be synonymous labels in this passage. The wandering seeker after truth not only does not know his final destination, but he does not see himself as having one. No final goal exists for him. He journeys on, taking in all he sees around him, without becoming attached to any place. This allegory of the wanderer thus enacts chapter 9's critique of convictions.

This journey will know its share of difficulties, and there will be times when the wanderer longs to cease moving and feels oppressed by his journey and all it reveals to him. But to compensate for this suffering and to alleviate this solitude, there will also be 'rapturous mornings' which disclose 'swarms' of dancing Muses. The wanderer will also enjoy 'equanimity' in his 'morning soul' when 'good and bright things are thrown out to him . . . the gifts of all those free spirits who are at home amid the mountains, woods and solitude' (HAH 638). In these ways, the knower's solitude is ultimately tempered by the sight of the Muses and the gifts of fellow free spirits. And the very image of the dancing Muses who appear before the knower's eyes and who thereby provide him perhaps comfort, perhaps inspiration, suggests once again that art has not been wholly banished from Nietzsche's vision

---

[8] I have modified Handwerk's translation from 'betrayers' to preserve in English the way this passage echoes HAH 629.

of a more enlightened future, despite what he often implies in chapter 4. To modify one of my comments on chapter 2, if this is Nietzsche advocating a new science, he is the artist of that science. Indeed, this closing image of HAH can be seen as presaging the more hospitable attitude to art that we find in MOM and WS.

This remarkably fecund conclusion to HAH contains themes and images that the book has already touched on, such as the joy and equanimity that come from the free spirit's knowledge. It also harbours ideas and images that Nietzsche will develop in later works, such as the figure of the wanderer and the matutinal metaphors: 'rapturous mornings' [*wonnevollen Morgen*], 'his morning soul' [*Vormittagsseele*], 'the mysteries of the dawning day' [*der Geheimnissen der Frühe*], 'the philosophy of the morning' [*die Philosophie des Vormittages*]. It is also possible that the idea of the solitary knower, 'at home amid the mountains, woods and solitude', provides a precursor to Zarathustra. In these ways, HAH's closing passage is at the same time an opening to his future works.

10
Mixed Opinions and Maxims

> Changed opinions do not change the character of a human (or only very little); but they do in fact illuminate individual sides of the constellation of his personality . . . (MOM 58)

About half the length of HAH, *Mixed Opinions and Maxims* was published in 1879 as an addendum to HAH. As Jeremy Fortier (2016: 208 n. 18) reports, this is clear from the work's title page, which places *Human, All Too Human* at the top in larger typeface than the words 'Appendix: Mixed Opinions and Maxims', which appear halfway down the page.[1] Its title could echo 'Mixed Thoughts' [*Vermischte Gedanken*], one of the chapter titles from Rée's 1875 publication *Psychological Observations*. Like Rée's chapter, MOM is a collection of opinions and aphorisms, although it is much longer than Rée's work. MOM's passages are offered without any chapter structure or guidance about how they might be related to or separated from one another. This can give the appearance of the ideas being 'a fairly random collection of bits and pieces' (Young 2010: 275; cf. Handwerk 2013: 568), and in some cases this is correct. Yet in several instances we find a run of passages on the same or related topics, lending this work more cohesion than initially meets the eye. What is more, most of MOM's contents can be assimilated to the chapter titles of HAH: this work

---

[1] See the following link to the title page, https://www.maggs.com/menschliches-allzumenschliches-ein-buch-fanduumlr-freie-geister_227324.htm (accessed 11 July 2019).

introduces nothing new in terms of topic.[2] This is not to deny, however, that some of the topics familiar to us from HAH are treated differently in MOM: I agree, for example, with Young that Nietzsche changes his views about art from one work to the next. As Young reports, 'whereas art, in *Human*, is consigned to the realm of glorious memory, in *Opinions*, Nietzsche recovers his sense of its indispensability' (1992: 73; cf. 82, 84; see also Franco 2011: 44).[3] Nietzsche's change of mind on such an important topic within such a short period of time provides but one illustration of the Introduction's claim about this being a period of immense intellectual transition, fermentation and experimentation for him.

Franco's claim that MOM's aphorisms 'are arranged in exactly the same order as the original [HAH]' (2011: 15) strikes me as mostly but not entirely correct.[4] For the most part in this chapter I track MOM's major ideas and concerns as they appear in the text chronologically and organise them using the relevant chapter titles from HAH to illustrate their thematic and chronological mirroring of that work. However, if there is a strong thematic connection between earlier and later passages within MOM, I break sequential continuity to acknowledge that. The major topics explored are epistemology, morality, religion, art, gender and politics.

Of first and last things

The first thirty-three passages of MOM take up the themes of HAH's first chapter, with its rejection of traditional forms of knowledge such as metaphysics and religion, and its advocacy of an alternative historical approach to knowledge which Nietzsche

---

[2] Hayman reports that some of the material for MOM came from notes that Nietzsche had made the previous year, while some of it was newly prepared (1980: 207). My point is that whatever Nietzsche says about things, no new topics are introduced. Cf. Handwerk (2013: 561, 567) on the continuity between HAH and MOM (and WS) and (2013: 569) on the clusters of thematically related passages that could serve as chapters and the parallels with HAH's chapter structure.

[3] I don't agree with Young's explanation for the change, however. He argues that HAH, with its focus on the scientific person, neglected the question of value (1992: 74). As my discussion of Nietzsche's epistemology-plus perspective indicates, I cannot agree that HAH neglected the problem of value.

[4] Cohen (2010: 196–8) also notes the echoes from HAH but does not make as strong a claim about this as Franco does.

depicts as a type of science.[5] MOM's opening section is directed at 'those disillusioned with philosophy'. The best way to make sense of this is that Nietzsche is anticipating possible reactions from readers who have followed his journey in HAH, with its rejection of traditional metaphysics. He is trying to encourage them not to abandon philosophy altogether but to put it on the newer, more scientific, more historical footing that he adduces. Such a philosophy of the human, all too human need not mean selling philosophy 'off right away at the lowest price' (MOM 1). The very next passage speaks to those who are following his journey to this new mode of philosophising, as he laments how hard it is, when one is aiming for conceptual clarity, 'to deal with things that are only partially clear, hazy, striving, intimated' (MOM 2). MOM's third passage offers some resolution to the previous two, for those who, like Nietzsche, realise how much they have been deceived by the false promises of traditional metaphysical philosophy 'will defiantly embrace even the most hideous reality' (MOM 3), presumably because it is reality, unlike the philosophical fictions of the past. They will not devalue a philosophy that treats of the real, even though it might not be as beautiful or alluring as traditional philosophy.

And just as chapter 1 included HAH's first reference to free spirits, so these figures make their appearance early in MOM. Distinguishing between free spirits of the past and those of the present, section 4 measures the progress of free-spiritedness by quoting Voltaire who, as we have seen, is much admired throughout HAH on multiple axes – his art, his style of thinking, his political moderation. However, on this occasion Nietzsche invokes Voltaire only to supersede him, claiming that the Frenchman's belief that error also has merit is now recognised as a piece of 'involuntary naïveté' (MOM 4). This implies that for today's free spirits, error is without merit, making this sound like one of the more positivistic statements of this phase in Nietzsche's writing. Its very title – 'Progress of free-spiritedness' – indicates his faith in the possibility of a growth in free-spiritedness over time and once again bears witness to the enlightenment flavour of his thought at this time.

---

[5] The one passage that does not fit this schema is MOM 24.

Continuing this theme about the shape that philosophy should now take, section 20 advises that 'The belief in truth begins with doubting all the "truths" that have previously been believed' (MOM 20). Thus even the truths of former free spirits like Voltaire should come to be doubted. Section 7 also reflects on the possibility of attaining the truth by outlining the provisional nature of knowledge in the first instance. With Nietzsche's more scientific approach to knowledge, and its disavowal of convictions, one 'could, in the strictest sense, never speak of the truth, but instead only of probability in its various degrees' (MOM 7). But Nietzsche takes this point in a somewhat surprising direction to ruminate on the knowers' reactions to the necessarily provisional character of truth. The fact that those who delight in this news prefer uncertainty to certainty leads Nietzsche to speculate whether they are afraid that the bright light of the truth might one day shine on them and show them for what they really are. Or, invoking the Platonic metaphor of the cave, he muses whether their being accustomed to the twilight causes their 'Hostility to light'. It is hard to know what is going on with this passage other than Nietzsche casting doubt upon the motives of those who pursue his preferred scientific path to knowledge. It definitely contrasts with HAH's typical praise of such knowers as modest, moderate and unpretentious.

Section 11 might shed some light on the surprising turn that the 'Hostility to light' passage takes, for there Nietzsche insists that a truly free spirit will think freely 'about spirit itself' (MOM 11). This can mean uncovering 'dreadful facts about its source and direction'. Although he does not even gesture towards what those dreadful facts are in this passage, it does illustrate that he does not shy away from darker underbellies of even developments that he admires and welcomes. This is, of course, entirely in keeping with the genealogical sensibility he sketches in HAH, which frequently exposes the less than desirable sources of many things highly esteemed today. Instead, MOM 11 goes on to grapple with the label 'pessimist of the intellect' which has been attached to free spirits who look unblinkingly and see things that are not so wholesome. This same theme is taken up later in MOM where Nietzsche points out the murky origins of science. It has not always been held in the high repute it is today (at least by some). As he points out, 'everything good has at one time been new, hence unfamiliar, contrary to custom, immoral' (MOM 90). We hear Nietzsche's more usual type of praise in the much later section 206, 'Why scholars are nobler than artists'. Nietzsche's explanation is that scholars 'must be simpler, less ambitious, more sober, quieter, not so concerned for posthumous fame, and able to forget themselves in things that rarely seem to the eye of the many worth such a sacrifice of personality'. He goes on to declare that being this way weakens the scientists' will; they stay cool by comparison with the internal combustion of poets. Living at these lower temperatures means that scientists bloom earlier than poets do, and Nietzsche says that they know this about themselves. Because they sparkle less than artists, they seem to be less gifted and are taken for less than they are. This explains why vanity would be alien to scientists, for as we have seen in HAH and will see again in MOM, vain people care pre-eminently about their status in the eyes of others.

Other echoes of this more usual type of praise for scientists resonate in MOM 25, which declares that 'Anyone who does not have the courage to allow himself and his work to be found boring is certainly no spirit of the first rank, whether in the arts or the sciences.' It warrants attention that the need for this courage to be found boring holds across the arts and the sciences and thus provides some evidence of a point to be encountered more fully below – that is, that art and science are not as strictly differentiated from one another in MOM as they typically were in HAH.

The later passage MOM 211 echoes some of these depictions of the free spirit. Nietzsche reminds readers that in earlier times, 'this name was hung upon [people] as an insult' and was accompanied by 'public distrust and abuse'. Anyone aspiring to be a free spirit today should 'pay homage' to their predecessors and their struggles. So once again, at a time when Nietzsche emphasises historical knowledge as a key to understanding, he urges that contemporary free spirits or would-be free spirits become aware of their own history. And such historical awareness brings to light the free spirit's membership in a wider community that expands across time and also brings certain duties, such as paying homage to the ancestors. Nietzsche also reiterates here the idea that because of their commitment to the pursuit of truth and suspicion of all convictions, free spirits must remain untethered and at liberty to pursue 'freedom as the strongest drive of our spirit'. In opposition to those other 'fettered[6] and firmly rooted intellectuals', free spirits must embrace the ideal of 'spiritual nomadism' (MOM 211). This image obviously looks back to the conclusion of HAH where, as discussed in Chapter 9 of this introduction and guide, Nietzsche casts the new philosopher, the free spirit, as a wanderer. And this image is, of course, carried over into his next work, *The Wanderer and his Shadow*.

Section 12 makes it clear that at least at this point in the development of scientific knowledge, the terms science and metaphysics cannot be combined (MOM 12). Section 10 casts doubt on the motives of traditional philosophers who Nietzsche describes here as philosophers of the veil and 'world obscurers',[7] and who are thus also very far from being dazzled by the bright light of truth. These metaphysicians resist and resent the philosophical development that he champions as it becomes more and more historical. They react by 'throwing stones and filth' at anyone who agrees with Nietzsche that 'all of philosophy has henceforth fallen to history' (MOM 10). Such traditional philosophers are also the subject of section 5 which identifies one (but only one) of their original sins. This consists in making absolute and eternal claims out of observations that began as limited and partial. And before long he has resurrected some of the criticisms of Schopenhauer familiar to us from HAH – his metaphysics of the world as will, his belief in individual free will, and his commitment to unchanging character. His faulty philosophy is once again aligned with

---

[6] Again I follow Hollingdale in preferring 'fettered' as a translation of *gebunden* over Handwerk's 'constrained'.

[7] Nietzsche's phrase is *Schleier-Philosophen und Welt-Verdunkler*. Handwerk renders this first term as 'veil-making philosophers', while Hollingdale calls them 'veil-philosophers'. I prefer 'philosophers of the veil'. Both translators render the second term as 'world-obscurers' but *Verdunkler* could also translate as 'darkeners' or 'blackeners'. (Indeed, both translate the term in MOM 303 as growing dark.) This would also work given Nietzsche's criticism of traditional philosophy for holding reality in such low esteem. Some evidence of this view appears in MOM 1, for example.

art when Nietzsche charges Schopenhauer with using a 'poetic metaphor' in asserting the world to be will (MOM 5). As a practitioner of this new style of philosophy, Nietzsche feels himself to be not poor in spirit as traditional philosophers would see him, but as the denizen of 'the heavenly kingdom of change, with spring and fall, winter and summer' (MOM 17). The phrase 'heavenly kingdom' is obviously used here ironically, for Nietzsche's realm is, as he acknowledges, one of continuous change and not at all eternal. He celebrates himself as one 'who is forever being newly transformed by history' and who harbours within him 'not "one immortal soul," but many mortal souls' (MOM 17).[8] This echoes the point made in HAH about the self as plural (HAH 57, 521).

On the history of the moral sensations

With section 33, Nietzsche returns to Schopenhauer and expands the discussion to include the scrutiny of moral motives. Thus section 34 takes up the theme of egoism, asking whether the mark of moral action really is to be self-sacrificing. Nietzsche suggests that this alone cannot be what renders an action moral, as self-sacrifice is 'present in every action that is done with deliberation, the worst as well as the best' (MOM 34). Conversely, MOM 37 points to the prevalence of egoism even in those emotions that are supposed to be most self-denying such as love, for we love the perfected image of ourself that we project on to the other person. This exposure of the role of egoism in love does not doom Nietzsche to a wholly jaundiced view, however, for MOM 75 defines love as 'understanding and rejoicing in the fact that someone else lives, acts, and feels in a different and opposite way than we do'. Based on a recognition and appreciation of another and his or her difference from the self, this definition of love celebrating difference is far from the image of self-projection on to the other outlined in MOM 37. Nor does love defined this way

---

[8] Handwerk finds here an allusion to Jacob Burckhardt (Nietzsche 2013: 449 n. 22), but it could just as easily be Nietzsche speaking of himself.

presuppose any ego-free affection for the other. Nietzsche insists that even self-love fits this definition of love loving difference, for if the self really is multiple – as the claim above about multiple mortal souls indicated – then self-love requires embracing one's own diversity (MOM 75).

In this same vein of reflecting on what role, if any, egoism has in moral life, MOM 91 points out that actions undertaken with egoistic motives can still produce good outcomes. So the presence or absence of egoism cannot be the key ingredient in determining an action or emotion's moral character. Egoism is returned to in a later brief passage where Nietzsche accuses the idea that the ego is always hateful of containing 'the most senile thing that has ever been thought about human beings' (MOM 385). The other side of this normative coin – that one should love one's neighbour as oneself – is 'the most childish'.

This same part of the text where Nietzsche returns to Schopenhauer and starts to ruminate on morality includes two passages about the difficulty of really knowing a person's moral character. On the one hand we must be able to grasp the best and worst that they are capable of, but this is hard to discern (MOM 35). And on the other is the fact that our moral character is shaped by things that don't happen, tests to which we are never put (MOM 36). Both of these passages suggest that we can never be confident in knowing anyone's moral character – that of others or our own.

But from then on we get a long series of mainly traditional aphorisms, and in becoming more staccato in style, the text also becomes less focused. It ranges across a number of themes that fit under the umbrella of moral psychology such as our old friend vanity. In MOM 38, for example, Nietzsche points out that vanity causes people to deny their vanity. Simultaneously vulnerable and invincible, vanity just gets stronger when wounded (MOM 46). Humans cleave to the belief in free will because of vanity (MOM 50). The theme of vanity recurs later in MOM too, for example when Nietzsche says that giving a vain person a public platform can be received with ambivalence: on the one hand, their vanity appreciates the opportunity to occupy the limelight, but on the other, being given that by another person, unless that person is manifestly above them in social standing, offends their vanity (MOM 234). This aphorism illustrates well the earlier claim about vanity's simultaneous vulnerability and invincibility. As in HAH, the defining feature of vanity turns out to be a preoccupation with the impression one makes on others, rather than with what one really is (MOM 64, 74; see also 240, 263 for references to vanity).

Another familiar theme that appears in this section is the human capacity for joy. The aphorism 'To have great joy' declares that 'Anyone who has great joy must be a good human being.' This does not mean that the joyful person is the most clever, although he does possess what the clever person seeks (MOM 48). And just as we saw that an aphorism in chapter 9 of HAH declares that 'Shared joy ... makes a friend' (HAH 499), so here Nietzsche echoes that sentiment to insist that 'to imagine the joy of others and to rejoice in that is the highest privilege of the highest animals and accessible even among them only to the choicest exemplars – and thus a rare *humanum*' (MOM 62).

Nietzsche's interest in friendship also carries over into MOM, with a cluster of passages in fairly close proximity to one another exploring this topic. MOM's first depiction of friendship encourages the appreciation of diversity within this relationship. This short passage opens with an unnamed speaker urging '"You go toward the morning: and so I will head toward the evening"' (MOM 231). Nietzsche comments that this feeling represents 'the high mark of humanity in closer relationship with others', and underlines its value not just in relations between equals but also between leaders and their followers or teachers and students. This short passage effectively affirms the definition of love offered in MOM 75 which, as we have just seen, defines love as celebrating difference. Ten passages later, 'Good friendship' (MOM 241) reaffirms the importance of difference and distance within friendship. The ingredients for this relationship include respecting the friend even more than we do ourself, but loving him slightly less, which fits with Nietzsche's insistence that the ego cannot and need not always be suppressed. But he recommends that while we should appear to be intimate with the friend, in reality we should hold 'ourselves back from real, genuine intimacy and any confusion of I and you' (MOM 241). Such confusion of the self and the friend that Nietzsche cautions against represents the Montaignean model of friendship, by comparison with which Nietzsche is much closer to the Emersonian model which also recommends distance and diversity between friends.[9] This same sentiment receives beautiful expression in the passage 'In parting': 'Not in how one soul draws near to another, but in how it distances itself from the other, do I recognize its relation to and togetherness with the other' (MOM 251).[10]

But along with these powerful testimonies to friendship's beauty, Nietzsche also records instances of its frailty and failure. Thus MOM 242 describes what happens when one friend changes a lot but the other does not: such friends become 'ghosts of our own pasts' (MOM 242), reminders of who and how we used to be. Given the changes in Nietzsche's life at this time, it is hard not to read this passage autobiographically. Friendship's attrition is also traced in MOM 247, which warns that as soon as we find someone forcing themselves to be attentive to us, we should realise that they do not, or no longer, love us. This warning sign can, of course, also be applied reflexively: when we notice ourselves expending effort to be attentive to a friend, then the relationship is atrophying. MOM 259 is a companion passage to both of these, for it describes what happens when long-time friends see one another after an extended separation. No longer sharing the same interests, they feign concern for things that are by now matters of indifference to one or the other. Sometimes both see this occurring but, probably to honour their past friendship, play along nonetheless. Just as a friend one has grown away from becomes ghost-like, so their conversation resembles 'those in the realm of the dead' (MOM 259). Three more passages point out, and warn against, friendship's flaws. MOM 252 counsels readers not to discuss their friends lest one talk away the feeling of friendship. The harm that too much talk can do friendship reappears in MOM 260, which advises against being friends with idle people, for having nothing

---

[9] For a fuller discussion of these themes, see Abbey (forthcoming).
[10] Handwerk translates *Verwandtschaft und Zusammengehörigkeit* as 'relation to and affinity with'. Were it not so ungainly, I would coin the term 'belonging together-ness' for the latter, as it fuses unity and diversity in a powerful way.

better to do, they are likely to talk about you to others and also try to interfere in your affairs. MOM 263 effectively advises against becoming friends with vain people, for in order to prop themselves up, they will not hesitate to mistreat you.

Interestingly, all of MOM's comments about friendship are communicated in aphoristic form. Indeed, the same pattern identified in chapter 2 of HAH recurs in this part of MOM. On the one hand, Nietzsche serves up psychological observation of the sort inspired by the French moralists that aims for perspicuous encounters with the depths and complexity of the psyche and that can often be delivered in aphoristic form. But on the other, he traces the evolution of moral evaluations over time, and for that he typically needs longer passages that host more detailed exposition. Thus in a longer passage, MOM 89, he returns to the theme of custom's role in morality, and the function of morality being to preserve the collective. The next passage, which is paragraph-length rather than an aphorism, folds science into this, for as a force that questions collective, taken-for-granted morality, science was initially eyed with suspicion (MOM 90).

The religious life

Christianity becomes the focus with section 92 and remains so for the next six passages.[11] MOM 95 claims that its great attraction over other religions is that Christianity places the idea of love at its centre. This makes it appeal to those who have some experience of love, no matter how fleeting, as well as to those who feel deprived of love. The very next passage claims that the Christian injunction to love one's enemies also makes people happy – whether possible or not, the belief that one could and should love one's enemies is attractive. Christians get a boost out of the feeling that they are experiencing some of God's divinity in loving all their neighbours in this way. MOM 96 thus offers a very different take on Christianity than most of what we find in

---

[11] There was an earlier reference to Christianity, however, in MOM 8, but that is in connection with Pilate's riposte 'What is truth?'

HAH, for there the accent was on Christianity making its adherents feel chronically inferior to their all-powerful, all-knowing, all-loving God. That outlook is typified in HAH 119 which claims that Christianity burdened the heart in order to claim the credit for unburdening it though God's grace. This more typical stance towards Christianity does, however, return towards the end of MOM 98 where Nietzsche draws attention to the contradiction between the glad tidings of the gospel and the miserable demeanour of most Christians. As he urges them: 'if your belief makes you blessed, then behave as if you were blessed too! Your faces have always done more damage to your belief than our reasons!' The Christians' general demeanour allows Nietzsche to ask: 'If Christ really did intend to redeem the world doesn't it seem that he has failed?' (MOM 98).

MOM 97 takes up the question from chapter 4 about the future of Christianity directly and offers an unusual take on this. Nietzsche suggests that Christianity's continuing hold on people will vary from region to region. Those where adherence is mostly intellectual will yield first. He identifies this with the north and he probably has Germany in mind here as the passage begins by talking about the spread of Protestantism. Its demise in those regions where the attachment to Christianity is primarily sensuous – regions in the south – will take longer. This series of reflections on Christianity concludes with MOM 98 wondering how the works of science could ever compete with what Christianity offers, including in terms of certainty. As Nietzsche asks, 'Aren't all honest scientists "poor in spirit" in relation to what religious people proclaim of their "knowledge" and of their "holy" spirit?' (MOM 98). To address this challenge of science's pallid appeal compared to Christianity's, he develops a new articulation of what doing science involves. In the first place, its knowledge brings both pleasure and utility, so the idea of science being purely impersonal or disinterested is diminished. He goes on to insist that scientists are motivated in part by 'belief, love and hope', which are comparable to the emotions that draw followers to Christianity. A further reward is that within 'the republic of scientific human beings' each individual scientist who is 'inventive, happy . . . honest and hardworking' enjoys great significance.

So scientific activity creates a sense of belonging to a community where one is reciprocally respected and valued. (With this remark we see that free spirits are located in communities that are both synchronic and diachronic, for as discussed above, MOM 211 explicitly situates the free spirit within an intergenerational community of free-spirithood.) So notwithstanding its image, science can appeal to the unscientific parts of the human psyche – it can draw in the whole person and not just the detached, impersonal knower. Here again we witness what I have called Nietzsche's epistemology-plus perspective on knowledge, for he attends to the ethical and experiential dimensions of knowing. In addition to the truth value that science yields, here Nietzsche is outlining what sort of character traits the pursuit of this form of knowledge requires and fosters. He discusses what it will feel like to seek and acquire such knowledge and what sort of rewards it will return in addition to the growth in knowledge. And, as noted above, this passage ends with some epistemology-plus considerations about Christians too, with Nietzsche suggesting that they are not very good ambassadors for their cause. This is captured in his remark, cited above, that 'Your faces have always done more damage to your belief than our reasons!' (MOM 98).

Some of these themes are revisited and developed in a trio of later passages about Christianity. After a passage about the necessity of knowing history, MOM 224 returns to the genesis of Christianity and asserts that it can only have taken hold within a degenerate culture. At that time its appeal was primarily emotional rather than rational, with Nietzsche contending that 'the voice of reason and philosophy' was no longer audible. It spoke to the majority 'born with servility of soul and the sensuality of the aged' (MOM 224). It is, by contrast, anathema to 'young, vigorous, barbarian peoples', as Nietzsche sees the ancient Germans as being. The impact of his point here is to say that there is something alien about Christianity to the German tradition and thus to bring discomfort to proud German nationalists who are also Christians. But in weakening the barbarian soul with its impact, Christianity also inadvertently kept the ancient world alive, for barbarian cultures typically destroy previous cultures. Nietzsche also engages in some counterfactual speculation here, wondering whether the pre-Christian Germans could have found their way eventually to a higher culture without Christianity's intervention. By the end of the passage he concedes that what such a culture might have looked like and whether it could ever been attained must remain unknowable.

MOM 225 touches upon Christianity's truth value and concludes that whether Christian beliefs in God and Jesus are true is of secondary importance, for their effects are the same whatever their veracity. Nietzsche likens this to the belief in witches, which has the rhetorical effect of reducing Christian belief to the level of superstition. He closes the passage by gesturing towards the occasions in which Christians wait, in vain, for divine intervention but then mine their religion for 'excuses and reassurances' to explain divine inactivity. The combined effect of these two passages is to convey that Christianity cannot appeal to reason, while the emotions it appeals to are those most likely to be felt by weak, depleted individuals who are easily duped. Although he has not yet come out and declared Christianity to be a form of slave morality, as he does in BGE and GM, we can see how Nietzsche is paving his way to that position.

The final passage in this trilogy reaches back to the Reformation, and even to a time before religious war broke out. A more benign and peaceful form of Christianity is seen by Nietzsche as emanating from Italy but, driven by his ego and his 'suspicions and sinister fears', Luther insisted on the doctrine of justification by faith as being his creation, for which he demands full credit. As this passage unfolds it echoes the point of MOM 225 which is that this is a battle over beliefs which do not hold any truth value, such as original sin or justification by faith alone. Nonetheless 'the world was set ablaze . . . over opinions that do not correspond to any things and any realities at all' (MOM 226). I detect a sense of sadness and futility as Nietzsche recognises all the violence done in the service of these false beliefs, and find this passage to resonate with his reflections in chapter 9 of HAH on the violence and harm that convictions have caused. In HAH 630, he observes that 'It is not the conflict of opinions that has made history so violent, but the conflict of belief in opinions, that is, of convictions.' And as we have seen, he speculates about how much more peaceful history could have been had people felt less convinced of their beliefs. There would have been much less religious persecution of the type that followed the Reformation because all sides to any religious dispute would have to admit that their beliefs were more fragile than they thought and not worth harming or being harmed over (HAH 630).

And yet, just as in HAH Nietzsche conceded that convictions have, in the past, fuelled 'humanity's mightiest sources of strength' [*die mächtigsten Kraftquellen der Menschheit*] (HAH 630), so in MOM 226 he finds consolation too, using similar language to express it. At the time of the Reformation, there arose 'sources of energy so powerful [*Kraftquellen so mächtig*] that without them all the mills of the modern world would not have been driven with the same force'. He does not, however, specify what components of the modern world were driven by this powerful energy nor offer any counterfactual speculation about whether they could have come about through other, less destructive channels.

From the souls of artists and writers

MOM 99 pivots the discussion towards aesthetics, where it remains until the end of MOM 126.[12] This suite of connected passages starts with one entitled 'The poet as a signpost to the future' and ends with one entitled 'Earlier art and the soul of the present'. The title of MOM 99 alone suggests a positive answer to the question of whether art could persist into a more enlightened future. Nietzsche recommends that the poet's new role be to focus on human, rather than divine, splendour: such a creator 'will compose and recompose images of beautiful human beings'. Such images will, he hopes, stimulate 'imitation and envy' in their audience and thereby 'help to create the future'. Nietzsche unfolds this idea of an art that reflects, inspires, and perpetuates the best in humans as he envisages:

> Strength, goodness, mildness, purity, and an unintended innate sense of moderation in the personages and their actions . . . knowledge and art flowing together into a new

---

[12] MOM 122 does not fit this schema.

unity . . . all of this would be the inclusive, general, golden background upon which now, for the first time, the delicate differences among embodied ideals would make up the actual painting – that of an ever-increasing human majesty. (MOM 99)[13]

He points to Goethe as a source for this poetry of the future. This idea of an art of the future that depicts the best in humanity is reiterated in section 114, which predicts that 'the good poet of the future will represent only the real and completely disregard all the fantastic, superstitious, halfway sincere, faded subjects upon which earlier poets displayed their powers'. This conveys Nietzsche's new view that art can be disentangled from the religion and metaphysics it has hitherto been wrapped up with. But he is clear that such poets of the future will portray 'a select reality', which is, presumably, that which is most laudable about human beings or at least that which ultimately affirms the human, even if it takes a detour through their less noble parts.

The need for art to engage with the real recurs in MOM 135 where Nietzsche writes of the poet who is not enamoured of reality. Any artist not inspired by reality will sire 'hollow-eyed and all-too-frail-limbed' creations. These remarks about an art of the future that will depict and celebrate the human are part of what informs my more optimistic reading of the phrase 'human, all too human' in the Introduction to this work. These remarks were, of course, published after the predecessor book was given its title, but as noted in the opening remarks of this chapter, Nietzsche conceived of MOM as an addendum to HAH. This makes it not unreasonable to look to this companion work for clues about the meaning of the earlier title, to say nothing of the fact that he ultimately gave the two-volume amalgamation that title.

Nietzsche's model for a culture that handles reality productively is Ancient Greece (cf. Handwerk 2013: 537), which could imply that art's entanglement with religion and metaphysics is a

---

[13] In Handwerk's translation, this passage also contains a celebratory reference to 'a shining heaven' that is 'mirrored in faces and events'. But Nietzsche's term is *Himmel* which Hollingdale translates, correctly in my view, as 'sky'.

legacy of Christianity. As he describes in MOM 220, the Greeks did not deny the less attractive elements of human life but found a way of weaving them into their cultural creations. 'They allowed for a moderate discharge of what was evil and questionable . . . and did not strive for their complete annihilation' (MOM 220). Nietzsche even links this 'most comprehensive regard for the reality of everything human' to their ability to excel as 'natural scientists, historians, geographers, and philosophers' (MOM 220). This indicates clearly that this outlook on reality is not confined to Greek art but ramifies throughout the culture as a whole. He even speculates that Homer and his predecessors might have been the source of the Greek embrace of reality which, in turn, suggests that at least in this case, a particular approach to art fosters science and other areas of inquiry. In the contemporary case, conversely, the implication is that the arts should be inspired by science in its turn towards the human, all too human.

The possibility of art and science sharing things in common is revisited in MOM's celebration of Laurence Sterne. Goethe honoured Sterne 'as the freest spirit of his century' (MOM 113) and with such a resounding recommendation, a book dedicated to free spirits must pay some attention to this English author. Nietzsche offers abundant praise for Sterne as a writer and a person. But what is noteworthy here is that thus far the free spirit accolade has been confined to philosophers, or philosophers such as Voltaire who are also artists. The fact that a writer like Sterne could so thoroughly embody free-spiritedness is further evidence that Nietzsche's appreciation of art has changed somewhat from HAH.

Nietzsche closes this cluster of passages on aesthetics by suggesting an ongoing place for art in a more enlightened future because each new generation infuses old artworks with its own meanings. Each generation that brings past artists back to life in this way by animating 'the older works as their own souls see fit' at the same time honours those previous artists. As if to mimic this process of reanimation, he ends the passage by resurrecting Beethoven to imagine how the composer would react to such appropriation and reinterpretation of his creations. Nietzsche has Beethoven approving or at least accepting of it: 'That is neither I or not-I, but some third thing – yet it seems right enough, even if not exactly right' (MOM 126). The fact that artworks are not tied to the circumstances or meanings of their creation allows a religiously or metaphysically inspired artwork to occupy a place, albeit a different place, in a less or non-religious or metaphysical culture of the future.

MOM's reflections on art are interrupted by three passages which consider the reading and writing of aphorisms, with the text enacting itself as these reflections are conveyed in aphoristic form. As we saw in the discussion of chapter 2 of HAH, Nietzsche lamented how inexperienced his contemporaries were in reading and appreciating aphorisms (HAH 35). MOM contains more reflections on this genre and its reception than did HAH, so perhaps Nietzsche is responding here to some of the reactions that HAH received. MOM 127 upbraids inexperienced readers for assuming that aphorisms contain ideas only in embryonic form. Nietzsche contends, to the contrary, that they can be 'the fruit and harvest of much long thought' (MOM 127). Readers who think in the way he describes both misunderstand the aphorism's meaning and effectively criticise its author for putting his thoughts out in an 'immature and unripe' condition. MOM 128 cautions readers against inferring that because thoughts are communicated in aphoristic form, the work itself is fragmentary. MOM 129 chastises a different group of readers: the author's friends. Scouring the aphorism to find something personal about the author, and reducing its meaning to that, they leave with nothing more than they came with.[14] The final passage in this clutch of confessional or reflexive aphorisms complains about readers who praise one of an author's books over another. These readers do not seem to realise that praise couched in this way does double duty as criticism, making it hard for the author to receive it with gratitude (MOM 130). I describe these aphorisms as interrupting Nietzsche's reflections on art, but maybe they are really part and parcel of them, for as a writer, he might also see himself as an artist. If so, this points to yet another way in which MOM allows science and art to dovetail in a manner largely alien to HAH.

---

[14] MOM 153 and 156 also counsel against conflating an author with his or her work.

MOM 165 and 168 are also reflexive passages, with Nietzsche commenting again on the aphorism's interpretation. Section 165 makes another observation about how inexperienced readers think that if they understand an aphorism immediately then it must contain nothing new. Section 168 suggests that a good aphorism can convey an eternal truth, which seems somewhat paradoxical given Nietzsche's professed suspicion of such truths at this time. It also represents the mirror image of his criticism of one of the philosopher's original sins which, as relayed above, was to transform observations that began as limited and partial into absolute and eternal claims (MOM 20). In this case we are supposed to accept that observations that are eternal can wrongly appear to be limited and partial. Once again these reflexive passages appear as part of a run of comments about aesthetics, so perhaps we can reasonably infer that Nietzsche counts himself among the artists at this time.

Nietzsche returns explicitly to the theme of art in section 131 and stays with it until section 179. One of the first things we notice in this extended part of the text is the direct reference to Wagner, who went unnamed in HAH even if some of its reflections on art, or on the cult of genius, were inspired by or directed at him. In MOM 134 Nietzsche portrays Wagner's music as creating the sensation that one is swimming rather than dancing. This is 'perhaps the most essential of all his innovations'. Nietzsche is critical, albeit in a fairly restrained or indirect way, of this by pointing out that 'complacent imitators' of his art can cause the music to degenerate. Although Wagner is not named in MOM 159, he is probably the composer Nietzsche has in mind when generalising about modern music, for section 134 was also about modern music. And once again Nietzsche refers to the dangers of modern music enticing those who are otherwise 'moderate and noble' to overindulge. Even if minimal, such intemperance, when repeated, can undermine spiritual health. For this there is no cure other than to shun the source, which is, of course, exactly what Nietzsche had done relatively recently by ending his relationship with Wagner.

This threat seems to have been averted, however, in a later passage which reports that 'The level headed person, secure in his own understanding[15] can profitably spend a decade among fantasists and abandon himself to a modest madness in this torrid zone' (MOM 204). The benefit to such a person from such immersion is the way it enhances cosmopolitanism of the spirit [*Kosmopolitanismus des Geistes*], allowing one to say with greater confidence that 'nothing of the spirit is alien to me' (MOM 204).[16] Once again, although Nietzsche does not name Wagner, it is hard not to read this as thinly veiled autobiography. It cannot be a coincidence that the passage describes 'a decade' spent among fantasists, when Nietzsche met Wagner in November 1868 and their final meeting took place in November 1876. While not a full decade, this is close enough. Nietzsche's terminology in this passage is, moreover, telling. His verb for being among these people in both the title and the text of the passage is *untergehen*, which can translate as drowning. This in turn reminds us of the imagery of swimming (rather than dancing) that he associates with Wagner's music. More precisely, he says there that hearing modern music is like 'going down into the sea, gradually losing our secure grip upon the bottom, and finally surrendering ourselves to the billowing elements' (MOM 134). But even if *untergehen* here is not meant to evoke something as specific as drowning, it does capture some form of descent into this zone.[17] His terms for those who inhabit the torrid zone are also telling; the title of the passage calls them *die Schwärmer*. Handwerk translates this as 'dreamers', but that is probably too benign to capture Nietzsche's intention. Hollingdale calls them 'fanatics', but the term could also be rendered as 'enthuasiasts' or 'visionaries'.

---

[15] Nietzsche writes of *Der besonnene und seines Verstandes sichere Mensch*. Handwerk renders this as 'A person who is prudent and confident of his own understanding'; Hollingdale as 'The thoughtful man who is sure of his reason'.

[16] I translate *nichts Geistiges ist mir mehr fremd* in this way to retain the resonance with Terence's 'nothing human is alien to me'. Handwerk and Hollingdale preserve the *mehr* in the original by giving us respectively 'nothing of the spirit is foreign to me any longer' and 'nothing of the spirit is any longer alien to me'. Handwerk also notes this allusion to Terence (Nietzsche 2013: 469 n. 264).

[17] Although Nietzsche uses this term twice, its potential significance is obscured by both Handwerk and Hollingdale, who render it more neutrally as 'spending time with' and 'going among' respectively.

These latter three terms are also often used in conjunction with religious excess, which could once again serve to illustrate art's implication in religion and speak to Nietzsche's ambition for a non-religious art of the future.

Wagner is named again in MOM 171, which is a passage critical of both him and Schopenhauer, at least by implication in the philosopher's case. About a third of the way through this lengthy passage, Nietzsche protests that music is

> not a universal, timeless language . . . but instead corresponds exactly to the amount of feeling, of warmth, and of time that a quite specifically individual, temporally and geographically delimited culture carries within itself as its inner law . . . (MOM 171)

Indeed, at the start of this passage he portrays music as a cultural latecomer, and at its end he insists that, if anything, music has a shorter shelf-life than many other artistic forms. In between these three general claims about music – it arrives late in a culture, it finishes early, and it is not universal and timeless – he devotes quite a bit of time to unpacking the specifics that have gone into Wagnerian music. Wagner's music is portrayed as an unruly pastiche that presses images and characters from traditional sagas into the service of the composer's own inclinations, with the addition of 'the medieval Christian thirst for ecstatic sensuality and asceticism' (MOM 171). It is the fruit of a culture that is fading, along with its strong nationalist sentiment. Wagner's music is alien and hostile to the spirit of the Enlightenment, to pan-European sentiment, and to what Nietzsche characterises as 'Anglo-American sobriety in the reconstruction of state and society' (MOM 171). As we saw in chapter 8, Nietzsche was at this time a critic of programmes of radical and sudden political change, making sober reconstruction laudable. In addition to emphasising that Wagner's music is neither universal nor timeless, Nietzsche underscores that this is not, or need not be, the music of the future. If anything, it is a reactionary art form that should find little foothold in an enlightened future. In wrapping up this attempt to contain Wagner's impact and importance, Nietzsche once again breaks down any strong barrier between art and science by announcing that 'among all the creations of human artistic sense . . . ideas . . . are the most lasting and durable' (MOM 171). This locates philosophy within the human artistic sense, and means, of course, that the artistic work that Nietzsche is currently engaged in – writing philosophy – will be more lasting than Wagnerian music.

MOM 169 provides a lengthy reflection on what sort of art is valued today. Nietzsche finds that most people have simple aesthetic tastes which are simply satisfied. His elitism comes to the fore in his assertion that 'Only among exceptional human beings does there exist a need for art in the high style at present' (MOM 169). There is, however, another group of potential connoisseurs whose needs fall somewhere above simple, *volkisch* art but are not as elevated as those of exceptional human beings. These are all people who are in some ways dissatisfied with themselves, with Nietzsche supplying an intriguing cast of examples. They include the cultivated person who cannot abandon the comforts of religion, the half-noble person who cannot realise full nobility of character, the rich person who thinks himself above work but is too limited for any other achievement, the girl who cannot create a satisfactory 'circle of duties' for herself, the woman who married too quickly, anyone who entered a profession too early and has been unable to develop other sides of themselves, and 'all the unfinished artists' (MOM 169). I find it hard not to believe that this is a sort of mini *roman-à-clef*, and that we would see a number of figures from Wagner's circle characterised in a general way here.[18] This motley population has a need for art that is, as aforementioned, different from that of Nietzsche's higher human beings: this population needs art as a form of escapism from their unsatisfactory lives and selves. But art can also amplify and dignify their situations, allowing them 'to reinterpret on a grand scale the mistake of their lives and characters as a mistake in world destiny' (MOM 169). Nietzsche's important takeaway from this passage is the contrast he posits between the Ancient Greeks' attitude towards art and that of his contemporaries. The latter are drawn

---

[18] Note that two passages later he refers to Wagner's 'adherents' (MOM 171).

to art by 'their annoyance with themselves', whereas the Greeks expressed 'their own well being and health . . . their pleasure in themselves led them to art' (MOM 169). We are left to infer that this would also be the case with higher human beings today who need art; their need would not derive from personal shortcomings or disgruntlement, but they would be drawn to forms of art that reflected and celebrated their strengths. Once again we see another way in which MOM makes room for art, or some art at least, to have a creative and constructive role in a more enlightened future.

A similar but more general contrast with the ancient outlook is drawn in section 187, where Nietzsche claims that the ancients 'knew better how to rejoice', whereas moderns know 'how to sadden ourselves less'.[19] The ancients 'found new reasons for feeling well and for celebrating festivals', whereas moderns focus on 'eliminating pain and removing sources of displeasure'. Although critical of the modern negative attitude towards pain and suffering as compared with the Greeks' more affirmative embrace of joy, Nietzsche does not despair of it. He allows instead that this might serve as the foundation upon which future humans 'will once again erect the temple of joy' (MOM 187).

This impression that MOM sees art as having a creative and constructive role in a more enlightened future is compounded in sections 172 and 173, where Nietzsche continues to envisage what an art form of the future might look like. It would emulate the classicism of Greek art, for one thing, rather than the heady Romanticism of contemporary art.[20] The latter unchains the will whereas the former tamed and disciplined it (MOM 172). The sort of art suited to the future is exemplified not by the Greeks alone but also more recently by Calderón, Racine and Goethe. Such art is 'the surplus of a wise and harmonious mode of life' (MOM 173). This passage does, however, not entirely repudiate Romantic art, which expresses the 'bubbling over of heated and brightly

---

[19] Handwerk translates *betrüben* as 'depress'.
[20] As Young points out, this amounts to a return of the idea of Apollonian art from BT, although without that terminology. Young provides some useful background on the Weimar classicism that Nietzsche was effectively echoing (1992: 76–8).

colored things from an untamed chaotic soul' (MOM 173). This sort of art can satisfy the needs of youth and 'women who lack a good employment for filling their souls' (MOM 173). And just as MOM 169 referred to the needs of higher human beings, so these passages clearly elevate a more classical form of art. It warrants attention that, whereas in HAH art as such tended to be associated with childhood, immaturity and backwardness, in MOM Nietzsche distinguishes among types of art and even portrays the classical or neo-classical artist as a teacher of adults [*Lehrer der Erwachsenen*] (MOM 172). Nietzsche thus echoes here the idea from MOM 169 that different groups within society harbour needs for different types of art. He is also, of course, relegating Wagner's music to a particular and inferior audience.

When MOM defines art's function as embellishing life, as making us 'tolerable and, wherever possible, pleasing to others' (MOM 174), we can see that the need for art will never disappear. Art 'restrains and reins us in' and makes social intercourse more harmonious. Another of its functions is to 'conceal or reinterpret everything ugly', and this too addresses a need that will never go away. Nietzsche makes it clear in this passage that the aesthetic impulse to beautify is in the first instance directed at humans themselves. What we think of as artworks are but a narrow product of this broader impulse. This same idea echoes in section 102, which also depicts the aesthetic impulse as something that can be directed at humans and not limited to the work of art. But in this case Nietzsche records the failure of that to happen, citing the artist who pours so much into his work that he has no energy left over for 'becoming more beautiful and better as a person . . . [for] creating himself'. What could prevent this restriction of the artistic impulse to the work of art and not the artist is great ambition on the part of the artist, a desire to show 'that he has himself grown in proportion to the growing beauty and greatness of his works' (MOM 102). But the passage's closing lines entertain the possibility that working on the self and working on one's art is a zero-sum game, with effort directed at one being unavailable to the other. If this is so, we could expect great artists not to be great individuals also. It must be noted that Nietzsche poses this as a question, just as the title of this passage, 'An excuse for much guilt', could suggest that this separation between working on the art and working on the self is a false one. However, the term *Entschuldigung* can also be translated as 'apology', which makes it sound less artificial, although his use of the term guilt [*Schuld*] could, on the other hand, signal that Nietzsche is holding artists responsible for choosing to focus on the quality of their work to the neglect of their character. Maybe the relationship between working on oneself and working on one's art is an open question for artists of the future to explore. If the subject of art henceforth becomes the human, all too human, that could help to wear down the barrier between the artist and the work of art.

One thing that MOM does make clear is that art should henceforth be construed in a de-divinised way: the poet should not be seen, by himself or others, as 'The mouthpiece of the gods' (MOM 176). This resonates with HAH's discussion in chapter 4 about how aesthetics has been infiltrated by religious myths and misconceptions, allowing the genius to become 'convinced of his own divinity' (HAH 164).[21] And as in HAH, so Nietzsche offers in MOM a more deflationary, but also more accurate, picture of the artist, reminding the poet in this instance that spiritual wisdom comes from ordinary life and social relationships, from the human, all too human. What appears in poetry is nothing 'wholly new and miraculous', but instead the reweaving of elements of ordinary life (MOM 176). It is interesting to consider in this context MOM's claim that the original mind does not need to see something new but can look with fresh eyes on that which 'is old, long familiar, seen and yet overlooked by everyone'. The original mind sees this material 'as if new' (MOM 200).[22] Nietzsche notes further that what usually permits this widely familiar material to be seen anew is chance (or accident), thereby further deflating any grandiose understanding of the creative process. But it should be noted that in explaining originality in this way, Nietzsche once again does not distinguish between artistic and other forms of creativity, talking instead about 'genuinely original heads' [*die eigentlich originalen Köpfe*].

---

[21] Although the example Nietzsche gives of such a genius is Napoleon, it is, as I noted in Chapter 4, very hard not to believe that he also has Wagner in his sights.
[22] Based on Nietzsche's *wie neu sieht* I shorten Handwerk's translation from 'as if it were new'.

Finally, if we compare the inventory of artists and writers named in chapter 4 of HAH with MOM's discussion of aesthetics, we find several of the same figures referred to in both. Listed in order of frequency of reference, they are Goethe (MOM 99, 113, 170, 173, 227, 298, 302), Schiller (MOM 126, 170, 227, 336), Beethoven (MOM 126, 170, 171, 298), Sophocles (MOM 162, 170, 173), Homer (MOM 173, 189), Hesiod (MOM 188), Bach (MOM 298), Michelangelo (MOM 144), Shakespeare (MOM 162) and Palestrina (MOM 171). Nietzsche introduces a number of writers in MOM: the English authors Sterne (MOM 113) and Milton (MOM 150), Frenchmen Diderot (MOM 113) and Racine (MOM 171, 173), the Spanish Golden Age writer Calderón (MOM 170, 172), the Germans Kotzebue (MOM 170) and Klopstock (MOM 150) and the Greek poet Theocritus (MOM 173). Composers mentioned for the first time are the German Handel (MOM 171, 298), the Austrian Mozart (MOM 171, 298) and the Italian Rossini (MOM 171). The French painter Claude Lorraine (MOM 171, 177) is also invoked. Yet notwithstanding these new names, the general point about chapter 4 applies here too: even if he generalises about art, Nietzsche is not making claims about artists and writers from all times and places. His focus rests securely upon a selection from the Western tradition, from ancient times to the contemporaneous.

Nietzsche's discussion of aesthetics reaches a turning point at section 179 where he talks about art but also moves beyond this. This passage shares something of the flavour of HAH chapter 5's insistence that the current period is an interregnum. Here Nietzsche sees the present as productively poised between a past it can enjoy and a future it can mould. Looking back, cultural products from earlier ages can still be appreciated. Looking forward confronts us with the fact that 'for the first time in history' there is the prospect of 'ecumenical human goals that span the entire inhabited earth' (MOM 179). As this massive vista opens, it is accompanied by the sense that humans have the strength to undertake these challenges without 'supernatural assistance . . . humanity can henceforth do with itself whatever it wants' (MOM 179). This grand horizon combined with the strength to match ushers in some reflections on education, and on how humans can be prepared for these magnitudinous tasks (MOM 180, 181).

Woman and child

The passages from sections 272 to 292 include about a dozen aphorisms about women where the duelling historicist and essentialising strands of HAH's depictions of women as identified in Chapter 7 of this introduction and guide reappear. The first of these sections, 'On the spirit of women', sounds as if it smacks of essentialism but ends up pointing in the opposite direction. This passage tracks the movement of a woman who, out of love for a man, sacrifices her own spirit. Through this sacrifice she comes to inhabit a new space, originally alien to her, which brings her closer to the man's character. In this shift, 'a second spirit immediately grows up within her' (MOM 272). Nietzsche begins the passage by claiming that this sort of change displays a woman's 'spiritual strength', so he might think that not all women are capable of this transformation. But the fact that some, or even many, are is a sign that the expression of gender is affected by opportunity. It is not a fixed and ontological property.

MOM's very next passage also traces the metaphorical movement that heterosexual love can stimulate, contrasting the experience of some men with that of some women when it comes to sexual desire. Such desire can sometimes elevate a man, bringing him 'to the height where all desire grows still: a place where he truly loves and dwells in a better state of being' (MOM 273). For what Nietzsche calls the good woman, by contrast, sexual desire is experienced as a descent out of true love and as a form of degradation. He comments sympathetically and admiringly on the willingness of a woman in a good marriage to make this journey. His depiction assumes, of course, that sexual desire comes more readily to men than to women, which betrays a fairly common form of gender essentialism, and one that was also manifest in chapter 7 of HAH. But he does allow that, through love, some men can overcome this sort of sexual desire, which takes his observations beyond crude essentialism. His remark that the good woman 'degrades herself in her own view' could likewise gesture towards her initial distaste for sex as being a matter of her socialisation rather than any innate biological difference. But either way, in both of these passages we find echoes of the elevated view of the possibilities of heterosexual marriage from chapter 7 of HAH. Another interesting aphorism about heterosexual love comes in MOM 287 which explains that a man's deep passion for a woman is ignited less by sensuality and more by her combination of 'weakness, neediness and . . . insolence'.[23] The man reacts by feeling 'touched and offended at the same moment' (MOM 287), which is surely a very creative angle on romantic chemistry.

Nietzsche's other passages, however, are largely devoid of the innovative perspectives on women that can be retrieved from these three. MOM 274 writes of nature having fully 'finished its work' in women. 'The perfect woman of every age is the idleness of the creator on every seventh day of culture' (MOM 274). It is hard to know how seriously to take these references to nature or the creator completing their work – neither fits with the scientific view promulgated in MOM and HAH. Nietzsche is perhaps being ironic; as there is no creator to finish its work, women are destined to be forever works in progress, which would suggest a very positive appraisal by Nietzsche's own standards. MOM 276 takes how and when a woman laughs as a register of her cultivation, but the sound of her laughter is an expression of her nature. MOM 278 imagines how much better the world would be if 'the dissatisfied, the bilious and the grumblers' were precluded from having children, adding that this advice 'belongs in a practical philosophy for the female sex'. Nietzsche's odd assumption here seems to be that women are the gatekeepers of reproduction. MOM 282 continues to essentialise women, suggesting that by talking so much about the people they feel sorry for, they effectively carry 'the bed of the invalid into the public marketplace'. This is, of course, a critique of a certain brand of pity as much as it is of women who practise it. MOM 292 advises women on their appearance. Those wanting to be deemed beautiful should take care not to be seen as pretty. The idea seems to be that pretty is pleasing and popular, whereas the woman who wants to attract the sort of man 'whose soul is large enough to take in something great' should aspire to be more uniquely appealing.

---

[23] Handwerk translates *Uebermuth* as 'presumptuousness'; Hollingdale as 'high spirits'. But it is hard to know what would be offensive about high spirits; 'presumptuousness' makes it easier to see, but 'insolence' makes it even easier.

Nietzsche does not, interestingly, offer specific guidance about how women can avoid being pretty so as to be appreciated as beautiful by Mr Right.

MOM 284 is the first in a number of short reflections on women and knowledge that occur in this part of the text. It accuses women and artists of having 'wholesale souls' because they believe that anyone who could refute them would, and so mistake silence for consent. Nietzsche's alignment of women and artists here is more characteristic of the dismissal of artists seen in HAH than of his more nuanced treatment in MOM. A passage shortly after portrays women as disgusted by the truth and seeking to punish anyone who opens their eyes to it (MOM 286). MOM 290 contends that women make new knowledge or new experiences into an ornament for themselves.[24] Men, by contrast, treat such novelty as a ploughshare or a weapon. Duncan Large identifies this as Nietzsche's first use of the ploughshare image in his published writings. By being associated exclusively with men, the ploughshare becomes 'a phallic instrument, a man's tool, and by associating it with a "weapon", Nietzsche is already figuring it as dangerous'.[25] But Nietzsche's exact words here state that men use new knowledge or experience 'as a ploughshare, perhaps also as a weapon', so the association of the ploughshare with weaponry is contingent rather than automatic. A tool used to break up and turn over ground in agricultural work, a ploughshare is not necessarily dangerous, just as something's value as a weapon would depend for Nietzsche on the nature of the conflict. But however we interpret this imagery, men are said to do something active and potentially productive with new knowledge, whereas women use theirs for self-decoration. This makes it hard to read this passage as anything other than an essentialist criticism of women. While it does also essentialise men, it appears to do so in a more positive way. Yet it is not hard to imagine vain men reducing their new knowledge or experiences to self-adornment, given their preoccupation with how they appear in the eyes of others, so this generalisation rings untrue to things Nietzsche says or implies elsewhere in MOM and HAH.

---

[24] Hollingdale's translation of *machen einen Putz für sich zurecht* is clearer than Handwerk's 'attire'.
[25] For a fuller discussion of this image in Nietzsche's writing, see Large (2014).

Women are again essentialised in the very next passage, which asserts that a woman 'cannot refrain' from savouring the triumph when she is told she is correct. Men, by contrast, 'are generally ashamed of being right' (MOM 291) – but note that Nietzsche's qualification indicates that this need not apply to all men. He does not explain this odd claim about men feeling shame at being correct. He does, however, try to explain women's revelling in their triumph by reference to their not being used to 'being victorious' in this way; for them it is an unusual experience to be told that they are right. This could, of course, signal that women rarely are correct, or that they are rarely told that they are, which are not identical phenomena. And if Nietzsche is making the first point – that women are usually just wrong about things – it is unclear whether he would attribute this to their being less intrinsically intelligent than men or being less educated. The latter could, of course, be a product of history and custom and thus could be rectified. And at least this passage makes room for men who might flout their victory in being told they are right. Once again, it is not hard to imagine vain men touting such success, given their preoccupation with their standing in the eyes of others.

Few of MOM's aphorisms about women are especially innovative or insightful; with the notable exceptions mentioned above, most of the material just seems to recycle hackneyed stereotypes. MOM is, if anything, less of a mixed bag than chapter 7 of HAH was deemed to be, for the stereotyped depictions of women occupy more space here than they did in that earlier work. MOM's remarks on women are not especially free-spirited if we recall that by Nietzsche's own definition, the free spirit 'thinks differently from what we expect of him on the basis of his origin, environment, his social rank and position, or on the basis of the prevailing views of the time' (HAH 225).

A glance at the state

MOM's reflections on politics appear to start at section 303 when Nietzsche writes of the masses beginning to rage and of reason growing dark. In this way it echoes that part of the opening passage of HAH's chapter 8, which applies to politics Voltaire's view that when the populace gets involved in reasoning, all is lost (HAH 438). The suspicion that MOM 303 is alluding to democratisation is compounded by the fact that the very next passage is obviously about politics, referring to revolution, property and socialism. Nietzsche advises the rich members of the bourgeoisie to live moderately and unpretentiously, to avoid excessive displays of wealth, and to support luxury taxes. Those who would resist his advice show themselves to be the mirror image of the socialists, with one side possessing property and the other wanting to. He accuses the rich of trying to fuel envy of their wealth and the lifestyle it affords, with the spread of socialism showing that they have succeeded. The middle of this passage gestures towards what the appropriate use of and attitude to wealth is. It should not be mistaken for well-being. Used in the right way and for the right purposes, rather than externally and to arouse envy, wealth 'would be more shared, benevolent, equitable, helpful'.[26]

Nietzsche's rich contemporaries who are so worried about the threat of a socialist redistribution of wealth could reduce that threat if they adopted this stance towards their possessions. As we have seen, chapter 8 of HAH enumerated several criticisms of socialism, but it is interesting to note that while MOM is still concerned about socialism, here Nietzsche is more critical of the rich than of socialists. He does, in the last passage in this cluster, describe the German socialist as dangerous, but this is because the socialist does not know what he wants (MOM 324). This presumably only reinforces the responsibility of the rich not to fan the flames of socialism by ostentatious displays of wealth and the arousal of envy.

Nietzsche returns to this theme of how to possess wealth rightly in MOM 310, contending that wealth should not be viewed as an end in itself. Only those with the spirit to enjoy wealth properly should possess it, but a person with spirit would be satisfied with a moderate endowment, seeing it as only a means to other, more important ends. This issue is taken up again in section 317 where Nietzsche points not just to the futility of amassing too much wealth but also the way in which this enchains its possessor.

---

[26] This is my rendering of *mittheilender, wollwollender, ausgleichender, nachhelfender*.

With a great deal of wealth or property to attend to, 'the property becomes the master, the owner the slave' (MOM 317).

In addition to socialism, MOM is also critical of nationalism, just as HAH was. Nietzsche describes the national differences that nationalists set so much store by as 'only to the smallest extent something enduring (and even this, not in a strict sense)' (MOM 323). Anyone interested, as he is, in changing culture need pay little attention to national character. It is, after all, something that changes over time, and a people that is moving forward will soon break out of what appears to be its national character. The most capable Germans, at least in Nietzsche's estimation, have taken 'the turn toward un-Germanness' (MOM 323). The very next passage undercuts the idea of nationalism by recounting the many regional variations within Germany (MOM 324).

Other passages in this portion of MOM take up conventionally political topics such as political parties (MOM 305, 306, 308, 314), tyranny (MOM 307), the press (MOM 321), bureaucracy and education (MOM 320), voting systems (MOM 318), and commanding and obeying (MOM 11), although here those arts seem to have been relegated to different strata of society, unlike in HAH 440. One interesting thing about MOM's comments on politics is that the passage entitled 'On the rule of those with knowledge' nods towards the possibility of a more enlightened politics. Designing a voting system for the legislature, Nietzsche refers to what could happen if 'the belief in the supreme utility of science and of those with knowledge were finally to enlighten even the most malevolent and to be preferred to the now-reigning belief in numbers' (MOM 318).[27] He does not stipulate how the growth of reason could improve politics, noting only that it could. But this allows for free spirits to influence politics in some fashion, just as this gesture towards a more enlightened politics poses a stark contrast with MOM 303's talk about mass involvement and the darkening of reason. It also hints towards a possible shift of position from HAH where it was pretty clear that free spirits would play no political role. But these are just gestures: there is no fully worked-out political philosophy in MOM.

---

[27] Handwerk translates *Herrschaft* as 'mastery'; Hollingdale as 'hegemony'.

Conclusion

We saw above that MOM 259 recounts what happens when long-time friends see one another after an extended separation. No longer sharing the same interests, they feign concern for things that are by now matters of indifference and their conversation resembles 'those in the realm of the dead' (MOM 259). As the closing passage of MOM confesses, Nietzsche himself has conversations with those in the realm of the dead, but these are friends with whom he still shares important interests. He identifies his interlocutors as 'Epicurus and Montaigne, Goethe and Spinoza, Plato and Rousseau, Pascal and Schopenhauer' (MOM 408). These are, obviously, not all thinkers from the past with whom he agrees on everything: on the contrary, he imagines them debating with one another on things they disagree about. But these are the eight thinkers that he imagines himself to be in dialogue with as he works out his own ideas. As is clear from the presence of Plato, Rousseau and Schopenhauer, his choice of internal interlocutors includes antagonists, which is eminently compatible with the idea that the free spirit should never rest on their beliefs and be every ready to reconsider them. So present are these eight to his imagination that the living can seem spectral by comparison. This passage reprises the conclusion of HAH where Nietzsche depicts the knower as a lone wanderer whose solitude is nonetheless tempered – in this case not by dancing Muses but by the internalised voices of great thinkers from the past. 'They are the ones with whom I must come to terms when I have wandered for a long time alone' (MOM 408).

11
The Wanderer and his Shadow

If someone ever wants to be somebody, he must give honor to his shadow, too. (MOM 81)

Jeremy Fortier argues that when first published, WS was presented as more of a standalone work than was MOM. For evidence of their different statuses in this regard he turns to their title pages: when published in 1880, the title page of WS made no reference to HAH, displaying just its own title and author (2016: 208 n. 18; cf. Young 2010: 277).[1] MOM's title page, by contrast, was dominated by the title of HAH, and, as noted in the previous chapter, specified that this new work was an addendum to HAH. Further evidence that Nietzsche conceived of WS as a more independent work than MOM lies in the fact that one very distinctive, and indeed unprecedented, aspect of WS is the way it is bookended by dialogues between the eponymous Wanderer and his Shadow. We find nothing like this in HAH or MOM.

Yet like those of MOM, and unlike those of HAH, WS's passages are assembled without any chapter structure or guidance as to how they might be related to or separated from one another. As was also the case with MOM, there is considerable thematic cohesion across several sections, with many portions of the text exhibiting a run of sequential passages grappling with the same or similar topics. However, on the whole, there seems to me to be

---

[1] A copy of the title page can be found here: https://www.maggs.com/menschliches-allzumenschliches-ein-buch-fanduumlr-freie-geister_227324.htm (accessed 11 July 2019).

more miscellany in WS than in MOM and, unlike Franco, I do not find its passages to be arranged in exactly the same thematic order as that of HAH's chapters (Franco 2011: 15). The presentation of material in this chapter is, therefore, different from that of the chapter on MOM, whose structure does to a large degree mirror that of HAH.

I begin by examining who or what the eponymous Wanderer and his Shadow represent. I go on to identify and describe what I call an ethic of care of the self in this work. I reflect on whether Nietzsche forwards a new understanding of philosophy in WS. His continuing critique of free will is outlined and his views on equality, punishment, aesthetics, politics, gender, religion and pity are laid out.

The protagonists

It is easier to answer the question of who the titular Wanderer is than to know who or what the Shadow represents. As we have already seen in HAH and MOM, Nietzsche casts the free spirit as an intellectual itinerant, untethered to convictions and commitments. As discussed in Chapter 9 of this introduction and guide, HAH's very last passage is 'The wanderer' (HAH 638), with 'the wanderer', 'the free spirit' and 'the philosopher' appearing to be synonymous labels in that section. The wandering seeker after truth not only does not know his final destination, but he does not even see himself as having one. In this same vein, MOM 211 writes of 'Free moving spirits' who embrace the ideal of 'spiritual nomadism'. Fortier argues that the Wanderer's identity does not become clear until the closing dialogue 'which indicates that the wanderer is the author of the book, Nietzsche himself, in conversation with his shadow' (2016: 211). But that the Wanderer is a free spirit, and that Nietzsche himself identifies with free spirits, should be clear to anyone who has read the previous two works.

Who or what this Wanderer's shadow is is less immediately obvious. According to Young, the Shadow signifies death (2006: 79). I have argued that the Shadow represents embodiment (Abbey 2012). In a note from spring–summer 1878, Nietzsche muses that 'If someone wants to have his own corporeal personhood, he must not resist having a shadow as well' (Nietzsche

2013: 320, 28 [53]). Accepting one's humanness means accepting embodiment and that means accepting one's shadow. Yet the denial or downgrading of embodiment has been part of the religious and metaphysical traditions that Nietzsche so roundly criticises at this time. His dismissal of those traditions includes a full-bodied acknowledgement of embodiment. And, of course, these two proposals are not incompatible, as embodiment entails death. My attention to embodiment is more encompassing than Young's, as embodiment brings much more than finitude in its train. As a third possibility, Fortier argues that 'the shadow represents what the wanderer, (i.e. Nietzsche) typically neglects about himself, and even what he simply fails to understand about himself' (2016: 211).

If we look at what the Wanderer and the Shadow actually say to one another in their opening exchange, we can distil some different or perhaps additional connotations for what the eponymous Shadow might stand for. The first words in their dialogue go to the Shadow and contain the initially surprising claim that he has not heard the Wanderer speak for a long time. The Wanderer's reported silence conjures him as a solitary figure, which is consistent with the closing passage of HAH, although there we also see that solitude being occasionally punctuated, just as there are moments throughout his work when Nietzsche depicts the free spirit as part of a longer and wider tradition. The Wanderer reacts with surprise and initial confusion to the Shadow's overture, wondering whether a weaker version of himself is speaking. The Wanderer then equates the human shadow with vanity, suggesting here a fourth possible meaning of the Shadow as this darker, less admirable part of the psyche that we would prefer not to recognise.

But as the exchange unfolds, it becomes apparent that the Shadow is not co-extensive with vanity but rather stands for all the supposedly darker things about human existence that Western philosophical knowledge since the Christian era has tended to shun. These include but go beyond vanity, and are things that Nietzsche's more honest and more searching approach to knowledge does not eschew or deny. This fifth approach to what the Shadow signifies is suggested by the Wanderer's attestation of how he loves to hear the Shadow speak: 'I love the shadow as I love the light . . . They are not opponents: but rather, hold each other lovingly by the hand . . .' This declaration of love inspires the Shadow to affirm its identity as 'The shadow that all things display when the sunshine of knowledge falls upon them.' The remarks from both parties evoke the mistrust of supposed antitheses that we have seen in HAH: as mentioned in Chapter 2 of this introduction and guide, in contrast to traditional philosophy, Nietzsche allows that things appearing to be diametrically opposed to one another could actually be intimately related to one another or differ in degree rather than kind. His historical approach also permits that, over time, a force can arise from its opposite (HAH 1).

Matters become even more interesting when the Wanderer admits to having many questions for the Shadow, implying that the free spirit still has much to learn about what has typically been seen, or ignored, as the darker side of human existence. This despite the fact that, as the Wanderer's penultimate contribution to this opening conversation indicates, 'Up to now, people have perceived in my views more shadow than me.' It is also instructive to note that by the end of the conversation the Wanderer's attitude towards the Shadow has shifted from surprise to friendship. All this suggests that the Shadow stands for those forces, motivations, events and so on that have typically been occluded by mainstream philosophy, but which Nietzsche's inquiries will continue to befriend.

Indeed, not much further into the text we find a statement that reflects what I am calling Nietzsche's genealogical sensibility, which has already been on display in the previous two texts. Section 3 of WS writes critically of exalting the origin by believing that 'what stands at the beginning of all things is most valuable and essential'. As we saw in Chapter 2 of this introduction and guide, Nietzsche's forays into the origins of moral valuations often reveal the outcome to be far removed from the provenance. One of the deflationary effects of his historical approach is to show that what appears now to be lofty can have much more banal origins, and even origins that would appear distasteful by the current standards of that moral value or practice. Anyone who believes contrary to this, insisting that 'good could only come from good and grow out of what is good', is characterised as a 'moral fanatic' in WS 70. We find the suspicion of supposed antitheses expressed in WS 67, which attributes opposites to 'ordinary, imprecise observation', whereas Nietzsche maintains that 'no opposites exist, but only differences of degree'. Instead of opposites, what we really have are 'transitions' (WS 67).

Another illustration of this genealogical sensibility familiar from the previous two works is provided in WS 40, entitled 'The significance of forgetting in moral sensation'. There Nietzsche argues that despite the opprobrium that accompanies any concept of utility, morality began as social utility, which had to struggle against the utility of individuals and make them conform their behaviour to the general interest. This having been, for the most part, achieved, the origins of morality in what is socially useful have been forgotten. (The origins of morality in society's self-preservation are also recounted in WS 44.) Yet another example of the continuation of this thinking comes in WS 43, where Nietzsche puzzles over whether the thinker has a duty towards the truth. The concept of duty appears to be absolute, ahistorical and to compel the subject towards something good. But 'The thinker . . . takes everything as having come into being and everything that has come into being as debatable' (WS 43), making any conventional understanding of duty suspect for him. This short passage poses without resolving how the free spirit stands towards the question of truth and any obligation to pursue it, and can be seen as an early formulation of some of Nietzsche's later ruminations on the will to truth. But for present purposes its insistence that the thinker sees everything historically further testifies to the persistence of this outlook from HAH into WS. WS 189 likewise claims that 'Those who are historically minded [*Dem historischen Kopfe*] can readily succeed in keeping their eyes upon the place of human nature and activity within the totality of time.' Fortier claims that 'historical philosophy is scarcely even mentioned' in WS (2016: 210), taking this to signal a change in focus from HAH. My reading is the opposite; doing philosophy historically remains just as imperative for Nietzsche in this later work as it was in

HAH, even if he talks about it less explicitly or less frequently in WS.[2]

A different example of how Nietzsche's approach does not shun the supposedly darker side of phenomena appears in WS 46, 'Sewers of the soul', which argues that 'The soul, too, must have its appointed sewers, into which it allows its refuse to flow: persons, relationships, social classes for the fatherland . . .' Thus even though the format of the Wanderer's exchange with his Shadow is unprecedented in the previous two works, the content and tone are not so different. While Nietzsche does not shun or deny the supposedly darker dimensions of human existence and experience, they are not in any greater evidence in WS than they were in the previous two texts. This suggests that we receive the dialogue between the Wanderer and his Shadow more as a summary of Nietzsche's stance across these three works than as a bold pronouncement of something new to come in this third text.

Care of the self

One of the things that WS introduces which is different from, but in harmony with, the previous two works is what I call an ethic of care of the self (Abbey 2000: 99–103).[3] Just as the sort of scientific thinking Nietzsche champions in these works claims to content itself with small, unpretentious truths (HAH 3), so in WS 5 he urges readers to pay more careful attention to the closest physical, material and quotidian things instead of feigning a lofty disregard for them. As he complains, we

> do not make the nearest of things, for example eating, dwelling, dressing, social relations, the object of a steady, disinterested and general reflection and reform, but instead,

---

[2] Note that in WS 285, a passage discussed more fully below, Nietzsche uses the phrase 'history of moral sensations' [*Historie der moralischen Empfindungen*] which is a strong echo of the title of HAH's chapter 2 [*Geschichte der moralischen Empfindungen*].

[3] While a number of commentators mention this development, they do not all characterise it using Foucauldian language. See also Ure (2008), Young (2010: 281–5), Fortier (2016: 201–11), Ansell-Pearson (2018: ch. 4).

because this is considered degrading, turn our intellectual and artistic earnestness away from them . . . (WS 5)

In this we see again the role that embodiment plays in Nietzsche's thinking about being human, for many of these matters have to do with how we live in a material way – eating, dwelling, dressing. Such lofty disregard for quotidian matters is not just dishonest but also damaging in his estimation, for these supposedly trivial things have a much greater impact on our health and well-being than we are prepared to recognise. And by not attending to these questions, whenever our bodies and spirits are out of sorts we turn to others for advice – doctors, teachers and pastors. Nietzsche maintains, by contrast, that the best way to care for oneself is with an individualised knowledge, requiring close attunement to the peculiarities of the self and its particular needs and inclinations.

This theme of caring for the self continues in the very next passage as Nietzsche laments that 'the nearest of things are very badly observed by most people and very rarely given much attention' (WS 6). The list of areas of life to suffer from this neglect expands to include how we arrange 'our way of life', how we divide up the day, 'commanding and obeying', 'feeling for nature and art', 'sleeping and thinking' (WS 6). And again he accuses humans of feigning a studied disregard for these matters, having been persuaded by preachers and teachers to turn their minds to higher issues such as religion, the state, service to humanity or science. Nietzsche ends this passage by pointing to Socrates as a counter-example, one who urged people to attend to the closer, human things in their lives rather than matters of the cosmos and the divine.[4] The very next passage looks to Epicurus as someone who also tried to divert people's attention from supposedly higher things on the grounds that disputes about the gods were fruitless and could never be resolved (WS 7).[5]

---

[4] Fortier (2016: 213, 217) comments on the change this signals in Nietzsche's view of Socrates.

[5] Ansell-Pearson (2018) argues that Epicurus is a crucial figure for understanding Nietzsche's middle period writings. Of the three works studied here, WS includes four references to him (see also 192, 227, 295), compared to one in HAH (68) and two in MOM (224, 408).

Both sets of concerns in the passages of WS discussed thus far – exalting the origins and caring for the self – can be read as engaging the theme of the opening chapter of HAH, 'Of first and last things'. Nietzsche is disparaging faith in the first things – i.e. origins – and the supposed light they shed on last ones – in the sense of the latest or more recent things. He is also encouraging readers not to allow their interest in the so-called big, important questions (the first and last things) to obscure a concern with the smaller, more intimate, more tractable ones. Indeed, just a few passages later we find an explicit reference to 'the first and last things' (WS 16) as Nietzsche once again castigates the widespread 'poison of contempt for what is nearest at hand'. He urges readers to 'once again become good neighbors of the nearest things and not gaze beyond them as contemptuously as we have previously done' (WS 16). He advocates that this focus on the nearest things replace that on the supposedly bigger and more important metaphysical and eschatological questions that have occupied humans, such as Why do humans exist? What fate do they have after death? How do they reconcile themselves with God? WS 16 urges that humans can live well without answers to these questions, and that they can do so by focusing on the smaller, more quotidian parts of their lives, just as Socrates and Epicurus encouraged.

Fortier sees this turn to the closest things 'as unique to this book – and to this moment in his [Nietzsche's] life' (2016: 212). As noted above, I see this turn to the care of the self as being in harmony with, and a development of, ideas contained within HAH and MOM rather than a departure from them. This ethic of care of the self attends, as noted, to small, unpretentious truths and requires a forensic examination of the psyche, which are both things highlighted in those earlier works. In chapter 2 of HAH, for example, the passage entitled 'Morality of the mature individual' suggests that people need to become more egoistic, more self-concerned and more attentive to the personal. The other-regarding ethos that has dominated moral thinking has eclipsed the importance of self-regard.

> To make of oneself a whole person, and in all that one does, to keep an eye upon one's own highest welfare – that gets us further than those sympathetic movements and

actions for the sake of others ... we all still suffer from having far too little consideration for what is personal in us; it has been badly developed ... (HAH 95)

In this same vein, HAH's chapter 5 declares that 'Freedom of opinion is like health: both are individual, from neither can a universally valid concept be set up. That which one individual needs for his health is to another a cause of sickness' (HAH 286). This very idea is echoed in Nietzsche's explanation as to why Jesus is a poor physician of the soul: he was 'attached to the notorious layman's faith in a universal medicine ... he sometimes resembles the dentist who wants to cure every pain by pulling the tooth' (WS 83).

But even as WS heralds Socrates as the progenitor of an approach that values these closest things, it does not depict him as being wholly indifferent to matters divine. As Nietzsche notes in WS 72, Socrates did interpret his personal mission of relentless philosophical interrogation of human things within a transcendent framework, feeling himself to be 'a divine missionary'. Nietzsche does his best to leaven the religious dimension of Socrates' mission, surmising that it might be tinged with 'Attic irony and humorous pleasure', and reminding us that Socrates describes it 'without unction: his images of the gadfly and the horse are simple and unpriestly'.[6] Socrates interprets his task as putting the oracle at Delphi's depiction of him as the wisest of men to the test, so it is not a type of piety that commands abject obedience. All these features make Socrates' enterprise 'bold and candid'[7] and 'one of the most subtle compromises between piety and freedom of spirit that has ever been conceived' (WS 72). Nietzsche concludes by remarking that this sort of compromise is not needed today – presumably because free spirits of the present

---

[6] I follow Hollingdale rather than Handwerk in translating *Salbung* as 'unction' because of its religious connotations – these are lacking in Handwerk's 'pomposity'.

[7] Handwerk renders *freimüthige* as 'free-spirited', but given what a specific meaning that has in this context, I prefer to follow Hollingdale and call it 'candid'. Note too that the very next line includes a reference to *Freiheit des Geistes* and so should be translated as 'freedom of spirit' in the way that Handwerk does.

and future will not see themselves as divine missionaries. Indeed, this precondition for free-spirithood is spelled out clearly in WS 182, at least with regard to Christianity. Nietzsche advises that anyone who does not take a critical stance towards that religion should not be counted among the free spirits.

The incompatability of Christianity with free-spirithood is reiterated when WS 86 promotes Socrates as a signpost to the philosophy of the future. He offers a better alternative to the Bible for anyone wanting to advance 'morally and rationally'.[8] This could, of course, seem to be damning him with faint praise, given Nietzsche's critique of Christianity, but as the passage unfolds, its enthusiasm for Socrates heats up. Socrates models 'a capacity to rejoice in life and in one's own self'. His seriousness took 'a cheerful form', while his 'playful wisdom' constitutes 'the best spiritual condition for humans'. This is all complemented by his greater understanding compared to that of Christ (WS 86).[9] This encomium and Nietzsche's general advocacy of Socrates as a philosophical model stands in quite marked contrast to what he had said about Socrates as recently as HAH, for in section 7 there he says that science and philosophy parted company when Socrates and his legatees inquired after the happiness that philosophy could bring. The implication there was that Socrates retarded the growth of knowledge by caring too much about happiness. But in WS Socrates seems to fuse those things and to represent a figure in quest of both happiness and knowledge.

While it is probably an exaggeration to say, as Young does, that for WS 'the aim of philosophy is eudaemonia' (2010: 282), it is certainly striking not just that Nietzsche now makes living well a central concern of philosophy, but that a figure such as Socrates comes to embody this approach, whereas not so long ago he and his influence had been portrayed as an impediment to the

---

[8] Fortier finds significance in the fact that Xenophon's Socrates, rather than Plato's, is endorsed here (2016: 217).
[9] Socrates and Jesus are also paired, tacitly at least, in MOM 94, which depicts both their deaths as suicides rather than judicial murders, in the sense that both figures wanted to die. This makes them models of what Nietzsche describes as rational, voluntary death (WS 185).

development of sound knowledge. I agree with Young that WS sees 'a significant shift in his conception of the nature and purpose of philosophy from that subscribed to by *Human*' (2010: 277). Where I disagree is that the revised conception of philosophy now includes considerations of living well but does not become synonymous with them. Eudaemonia is not philosophy's entire or exclusive aim. Ansell-Pearson also identifies a shift in Nietzsche's conception of philosophy across these works. He reads HAH as negotiating 'the competing claims of the positivist goal of science and eudaimonistic philosophy', and sees Nietzsche as 'aligning himself with the former'. In MOM and WS by contrast, 'he seeks to marry the project of naturalistic demystification with a project of seeking spiritual-physical health and maturity' (Ansell-Pearson 2018: 8; cf. 18). I agree with Ansell-Pearson that by the time we get to WS, Nietzsche is trying to fuse these things into a single philosophy, but where I depart from him, and from Young, is in the characterisation of HAH's view as positivistic. While there clearly are positivist elements in that work, as chapter after chapter of my presentation of the main ideas in HAH indicates, this concern with the relationship between pursuing truth and living well was omnipresent for Nietzsche at this time. As what I dub his 'epistemology-plus' perspective brings out, in addition to the truth value that any approach to knowledge yields, he is persistently thinking about issues related to eudaimonism. He asks what sort of character traits does the pursuit of this form of knowledge require? What will it feel like to pursue and acquire this sort of knowledge? Will a sense of beauty or satisfaction be engendered by this quest? So his more obvious concern with both aspects of philosophy in WS amounts to a reconciliation of, rather than a turn around from, his abiding concerns in HAH.

Free will

With the advent of section 9, Nietzsche switches focus from the unfreedom that people impose upon themselves when they neglect the nearest things (WS 5) to criticising a fake or at least inflated form of freedom, free will. As both HAH and MOM also contain critiques of free will, this is another area of topical continuity across the three texts. The question of free will, bequeathed to Nietzsche by Schopenhauer and the Christian tradition of moral psychology more generally, is one that he chews over across these writings. WS 9 analyses free will as a misinterpretation of those times when a person enjoys a sense of power. The source of this feeling of power varies from individual to individual, but in all cases, feeling strong is mistaken for willing freely and then erroneously transposed from the social-political realm to the metaphysical. WS 10 ventures a slightly different explanation of the idea of free will as a psychological error. It contends that humans take dependency to be an unusual condition and freedom to be their natural element. This assumption gets translated to the will being free. But Nietzsche proposes an alternative explanation according to which dependency and constraint is our usual condition, and what we mistake for free will is simply the absence of any new or additional constraints.

WS 12 also documents the role that the belief in free will plays in stoking humans' sense of their own power, influence, importance and even uniqueness. The belief that outcomes are a matter of choice, that things could have been different had the individual chosen differently, is more than a source of psychological pleasure or displeasure. It also feeds humans' sense of their own species distinction, of their proper place in the cosmos and, of course, for Nietzsche, it feeds their vanity. The belief in free will allows humans to believe that they alone

> are the free entities in a world of unfreedom, the eternal miracle workers, whether they do good or evil, the astonishing exception, the more-than-animal, the almost-god, the meaning of creation . . . the solution to the cosmic riddle, the great master of nature and its despiser, the creature who calls his history world history. (WS 12)

WS 14 also picks up on this theme of human exceptionalism as a form of vanity, albeit without the focus on free will.

These two passages about the psychological payoffs of the belief in free will (WS 10 and 12) are interrupted by one that problematises free will in a different way. Nietzsche argues that the belief that we can isolate facts is wrong. Our experience is instead 'a continual flow . . . a continuous, homogeneous, undivided, indivisible flowing' (WS 11). Similar reflections on the fluid nature of reality as revealed by science appear in WS 14, which cites astronomers on 'the total character of the immense ocean of becoming and passing away' that is the universe. Existing in this protean milieu, any confidence we have that we can separate this from that, name and identify this versus that, and establish causal relationships between things, is false. And just as we saw in Chapter 1 of this introduction and guide, so Nietzsche reiterates here how language conspires in perpetuating this error, for words and concepts separate some things from others and group some things with others, creating the false impression that we are uncovering essences when really we are affixing necessarily arbitrary and misleading labels and classifications. As he warns,

> We are continually misled by words and concepts to think of things as being simpler than they are, separated from one another, indivisible, each one existing in and for itself. A philosophical mythology lies concealed in language, which breaks forth again at every moment, however careful we may otherwise be. (WS 11)

The belief in free will is but one manifestation of this larger set of epistemological errors that we are lured into by language.

The way in which language perpetually aids and abets this misunderstanding of reality is dramatised in the aphorism 'Danger of language for spiritual freedom. – Every word is a prejudice' (WS 55). WS 60 illustrates another way in which words are prejudiced, as Nietzsche reflects on the value judgements with which they are laden. Any attempt to transvalue values, or even to practise the sort of psychology that strives to analyse human behaviour and motivation with some modicum of detachment, has to struggle against the positive or negative connotations that so many words carry. Using the term vanity to illustrate this point, he complains how annoying it is that 'some individual words, which we moralists simply cannot do without, already bear within them a sort of moral censure from ages when the nearest and most natural impulses of humans were made heretical' (WS 60).[10]

In Nietzsche's estimation then, the philosophy of the future faces momentous challenges; it has to come to grips with a recalcitrant Heraclitean reality of constant change and fluidity. The tools it has inherited for doing so are poorly suited to the task, for language reproduces a series of inappropriate assumptions about the nature of reality at the metaphysical level – things can be neatly separated from one another, meaningfully grouped together, etc. – and at the ethical level – words have transmitted value judgements that might no longer be appropriate. In the face of such an amorphous and protean reality, and the need to continually scrutinise one's theoretical tools for their faults, fixed beliefs are out of place. It is no surprise then that WS briefly echoes Nietzsche's earlier broadside against convictions (see Chapter 9 of this introduction and guide) when it declares that 'This thinker needs nobody to contradict him: he suffices for himself in this' (WS 249).

What began as a brief account of Nietzsche's thinking about free will in WS brings out a larger point about these writings, which is how difficult it is to label Nietzsche a positivist in any straightforward way. His depiction of reality as this holistic continuous flow causes trouble for any conventional notion of modern science. For him, genuinely scientific knowledge would have to see and respond to the world in this way, and not try to artificially atomise pieces of information and hypostatise them as enduring facts. But what is also interesting about his depiction of the nature of reality that words, concepts and appeals to atomised facts obscure or falsify is the way it reveals Nietzsche to be positing a metaphysical view of his own. He is here making a strong claim about the nature of reality and how it can best be known. Thus although he has just commended Socrates and Epicurus as role models for turning our minds away from questions concerning ultimate realities, he is unable to avert his

---

[10] I modify Handwerk's translation in two ways: I follow Hollingdale by rendering *eine Art Sittencensur* as 'a form of moral censure' rather than 'censorship', and by rendering *verketzert wurden* as 'made heretical' rather than 'disparaged' so as to retain the religious connotations of that move.

gaze from these things entirely. Instead, Nietzsche's own work continues to reflect on and pose theses about the nature of those realities. It might be the case that Epicurus shows us that 'solving the ultimate theoretical questions is not at all necessary for soothing the disposition' (WS 7), but Nietzsche clearly strives to do more than just soothe his disposition in these writings. So once again we see that his conception of philosophy in WS cannot be restricted to a concern with eudaimonia.

Here my interpretation also departs from that of Ansell-Pearson, who sees Nietzsche as recommending 'an indifference towards faith and supposed knowledge in the domains of metaphysics, morality and religion' (2018: 29; cf. 105). Rather than indifference, what I detect is the attempt to critique erroneous views about metaphysics, religion and morality and to replace them with more reliable ones, or at least to begin that attempt. It is noteworthy here that WS 16 refers to 'what science will finally ascertain about the first and last things', not in order to dispel or mock that possibility, but to insist that while awaiting those findings, one should not continue to think in a traditional way. Awaiting a new set of answers to these questions to replace the answers that religion and metaphysics have traditionally supplied still amounts to thraldom to the belief that answering such questions with certainty is what matters most to human life, while neglecting many of the smaller, human, all too human issues that really do matter in Nietzsche's estimation. But it is pretty clear that he is not recommending the Socratic-Epicurean focus as sufficient, for Nietzsche himself believes that science will continue to uncover truths about the universe that are relevant for how humans perceive and conduct themselves. It will also continue to pierce untrue beliefs about humans, such as the widespread faith in free will. I cannot therefore agree with readers of WS, such as Fortier, who suggest that Nietzsche's very real and express interest in 'the closest things' displaces his interest in history or science in this work (2016: 210–11). Instead as I read it, what I call the ethos of care of the self is articulated and integrated into those continuing concerns.

Nietzsche returns explicitly to this problem of free will in WS 23, but here it is in the context of a cluster of passages about crime and punishment (WS 22–4, 28). This illustrates that his gnawing attention to this question is not simply a philosophical matter: he is intrigued and disturbed by the way in which the belief in free will has penetrated social practices. As the title of WS 23 indicates, he asks whether those who believe in free will are ethically and theoretically entitled to punish wrongdoers. On the face of it the answer is obviously yes – it is precisely those who freely choose to break the rules who most deserve punishment. But Nietzsche mounts an elaborate argument to show that this is wrong, from within the parameters of free will thinking. So here he launches another attack on free will from a different angle, arguing that its role in jurisprudence is inherently contradictory. He picks up on this point in WS 28 with the amusing observation that society punishes someone more heavily if their criminal behaviour is chronic, just as it extends more leniency towards someone who deviates from a hitherto spotless record to commit a crime. He points out that this latter case could make the crime even more culpable precisely because, from the standpoint of free will, the perpetrator has made a radically free choice to act out of character. He concludes from this social practice that punishment is distributed not on the basis of actual guilt and responsibility but on the basis of perceived threat to society, such that the habitual criminal does more damage to the social fabric than does the person who commits a one-off, out-of-character act. In this way, society is effectively punishing (or rewarding) the person's past along with their criminal act, which prompts Nietzsche to wonder why we stop there. Why not go further back into the individual's history and punish all those other forces that might have contributed to the crime – parents, teachers, etc. Once again the doctrine of free will is found to assume that one can neatly isolate facts and deeds, which is, by Nietzsche's estimation, an epistemological and metaphysical error.

But just as an approach to punishment premised on free will is flawed, so is the idea of forgiving someone for their actions. This is the flip side of the same coin. As Nietzsche points out in WS 68, the belief that we can and should forgive someone for their trespasses against us presupposes that they knew what they were doing, made a free and rational choice to do it, and are accountable for their deed. Yet his multi-pronged attack on free will across these works has put that set of assumptions in jeopardy.

Equality

These ruminations on the role that free will thinking plays in jurisprudence are interrupted by some thoughts about the law in general, and its relationship to equality. Nietzsche argues that the law reflects power relations, 'resting upon contracts among equals' (WS 26), and works qua law only so long as those power relationships remain stable. However, 'if one side has become decisively weaker than the other: then subjection enters in and the law ceases to exist'. But the law ceasing to exist need not alter behaviour or outcomes: the newly stronger party can continue to abide by the old agreement on the basis of shrewdness if they do not want to waste the energy of the newly weakened party by igniting some new struggle. It is hard to know exactly what Nietzsche is talking about here and whether these remarks apply to the law as administered by modern states. It could be that he is simply rehearsing a version of his point about the origins of justice from chapter 2 of HAH. As we have seen, he argues there that justice only comes into being when there are adversaries of relatively equal power who realise that continued fighting would damage and then exhaust both, precisely because of the power parity between them. Justice thus originates in power and a calculation by the powerful about what best serves their self-preservation. Any rights accorded to weaker parties by stronger ones exist because the stronger party has some interest in protecting and preserving the weaker (HAH 92, 93). So once again he is trying to show that a lofty good such as justice originates in a pragmatic, power-sharing arrangement that becomes encrusted and anointed over time.

According to WS 29, conditions of equality, when cemented by law in the way that WS 26 describes, can give rise to envy, which is an adverse reaction to any sign of superiority among those who are supposed to be one's equals. Conversely, when anyone falls below the general level, indignation arises. The assumption in both reactions is that equality should trump both fortune and nature. In unequal societies, the same dynamic is played out within ranks, with anyone who distinguishes themselves above their station becoming an object of envy, presumably by their peers (WS 30). WS 31 suggests that envy is likely to be a fairly common phenomenon because equality is artificial and prone to be punctuated by the desire of some to assert their superiority over others. This group of passages about equality, which also includes WS 32, continues one of the important themes of chapter 8 in HAH, but in a much more abstract way than was done there, when Nietzsche reflected more directly about the impact of equality doctrines on modern politics. But his key point remains the same in both sets of reflections: there is nothing natural about human equality. Indeed, much later in WS he communicates this in no uncertain terms, proclaiming that 'the desire for victory and eminence is an unconquerable characteristic of nature, older and more original than any respect for and pleasure in equality' (WS 226). Reprising his argument from his earlier essay, 'Homer's Contest', he describes how the Greek state channelled that desire in a constructive direction with 'gymnastic and musical competition among equals' (WS 226). This allowed the desire for eminence to express itself without any damage to the state. When that competition declined, however, Nietzsche describes the Greek state as falling 'into internal unrest and dissolution' (WS 226).[11]

It is interesting then to see how WS 34, which continues to explore this theme of equality within society, contains an early version of what will become Nietzsche's famous thesis in BGE and GM about master and slave moralities. WS 34 refers to virtues that can be practised within society, such as justice, and compares them with virtues that can harm the wider society – 'for example mercy and leniency toward offenders' (WS 34). The practice of these latter virtues runs against the collective interest in the state being seen to punish wrongdoers in an equal, consistent and predictable way. Things such as mercy and leniency are luxuries that

---

[11] For a translation of, and commentary on, this essay, see http://www.northamerican nietzschesociety.com/uploads/7/3/2/5/73251013/nietzscheana5.pdf (accessed 11 July 2019). WS 29 also rehearses a point from this essay with its distinction between two types of Eris in Homer. Indeed, note 7, page i of Acampora's commentary lists the echoes of this essay in HAH and WS.

only some stable societies can afford and only at some times. They cannot therefore have come about in the usual way – that is, utility crusting into custom over time. Instead they are exceptional, individual virtues – the monarch, for example, has a monopoly on any prerogative to extend mercy. They way in which Nietzsche characterises this type of virtue which could be seen as causing social harm gives us an early formulation of what will become one of his signature claims: the virtues causing social loss

> are therefore virtues among non-equals, devised by the superior individual; they are master virtues, containing the after thought 'I am powerful enough to withstand a perceptible loss; this is proof of my power' – therefore, virtues related to pride. (WS 34)

Having offered further thoughts about equality after WS 26, so in WS 39 Nietzsche supplies some further thoughts about the law. Again he sees it as originating in some sort of temporary, pragmatic settlement between contending parties. Over time its provisional nature gets forgotten and, from being perpetuated in a largely mindless way, it becomes endowed with a significance and permanence it did not originally possess. So once again we see Nietzsche's genealogical sensibility at work, pointing to the difference between how and why things start and how and why they are valued at a later date.

Punishment

In this portion of WS Nietzsche also shines a light on forms of punishment that are meted out outside of, as well as within, the state. His detailed examination of 'Elements of revenge' in WS 33 shows the ambiguity of a single term like revenge [*Rache*] and thus continues the theme of how unreliable language can be for genuine understanding. Sometimes the impulse for revenge can be directed at lifeless objects that have caused hurt in some way; we lash out as if to stop any repeat of the injury. Such retaliation is a form of self-preservation and manifests a fear of what caused the harm – a fear that it might recur. The second sort of revenge is much more other-directed; we devise a targeted way to harm the individual who has harmed us. This type of revenge aims not at self-preservation but at restoring a sort of equilibrium, for the initial attack revealed the assailant's perception that the attacked person was not an object of fear. With this second sort of revenge, the attacked person responds in kind to show that the original attacker is not a source of fear either. Nietzsche points to duels to illustrate this second sort of revenge, based as they are on a high-stakes response to an affront to one's honour that could cause the revenger's death rather than aid his self-preservation.

But there are other variables at play when it comes to whether and how to take revenge. For example, the more the person attacked despises the attacker and his circle, the less likely he is to take the second sort of revenge, as he holds that population in such low regard and does not care what they think of him. No equilibrium is perceived to be in need of restoring. And the more the person who has been harmed loves the attacker, the less likely he is to seek revenge, precisely because he loves the person who harmed him. Although the same term is used for both sorts of reactions, they are very different from one another according to Nietzsche, and often the revenger fails to realise which of the two forms is being undertaken. Part of Nietzsche's aim here is to show that judicial punishment is a form of revenge in both of these senses; society is seeking to preserve itself and deter future injury, and it is seeking to restore its honour after an assault by the criminal. Once again Nietzsche is keen to expose the origins of penal practice in something that would be considered to be base, primitive and, at the very least, un-Christian.

This theme of revenge is taken up again in a later passage, with WS 186 exploring it in the context of society punishing criminals. Nietzsche also speculates there in a highly suggestive but not developed way about the impact that the whole machinery of punishment has on the non-criminals in society. He suggests that it is likely to be more oppressive than elevating for this majority. He writes of 'all higher humanity' mourning when capital punishment is carried out, for, applying a Kantian lens to this, he observes that it sacrifices a human 'as a means to the end of society' (WS 186). The apparatus of punishment thus damages and demeans society while claiming to preserve it. A later rumination on revenge notes that it does not mandate a particular sort of action: even inaction can be construed as a form of revenge. Claiming that one does not intend to avenge some act can itself be seen as a form of revenge (WS 259). So once again Nietzsche elicits the immense subtlety and variety of this seemingly straightforward practice.

Art

Like HAH and MOM, WS includes many reflections on aesthetics. But one way in which this third work's commentaries about art differ notably from those of its two predecessors is that it contains many more reflections on writing style, both prose and poetry. The paragraph deeming Socrates to be better than Jesus as a guide to the future is followed by a very long series of passages about writing style (WS 87–148), which is somewhat ironic given that neither of them left any written record. Nietzsche is clear that writing style matters not just as an end in itself but also for exercising contemporary cultural or political influence; as the passage that introduces this long run of reflections, 'Learning to write well' (WS 87), indicates, writing well is imperative for anyone hoping to shape the future. Whereas in Ancient Athens the accent was on effective speaking because of the small size of the civic community, European society is now too big for that, both geographically and in terms of the expanded citizenry. Nietzsche quickly clarifies that good writing is also intimately connected with good thinking, so he is not recommending a concern with style as a purely aesthetic, superficial or rhetorical matter. He also insists that writing well requires being able to communicate in a manner amenable to translation, again because his audience for the future spills across national boundaries and tongues. Good writing also requires writing in a way that is accessible to those who learn the language as a second (or third) tongue rather than just assuming one's audience inherited this as their first language (WS 87). In WS 110 Nietzsche contends that written communication is not just different from but harder than oral communication. Although both strive to be clear and intelligible, speakers have a much wider repertoire at their disposal than do writers, for the former can employ 'gestures, accents, tones, looks' to express meaning (WS 110).

Nietzsche's ultimate goal in enjoining good writing is thus 'preparing for that still far-distant state of things where their great task falls into the hands of good Europeans: the direction and oversight of the entirety of world-culture' (WS 87). This echoes his position from chapter 8 of HAH which looks forward to the growth of pan-European sentiment, erecting the ideal of 'the good European' (HAH 475). And as we saw in Chapter 10 of this introduction and guide, MOM advises anyone interested in effecting cultural change to pay little heed to national character. The most capable Germans, at least in Nietzsche's estimation, have taken 'the turn toward un-Germanness' (MOM 323). Indeed, as a foil to his vision of the prose style for the good European, WS repeatedly berates German authors for their style (WS 87, 90, 91, 94, 123) – even going so far as to identify weaknesses in Goethe's writing and thinking (WS 214). This critique of Goethe is, however, at odds with another passage where he brackets Goethe from consideration among German authors, for he 'belongs in a higher order of literatures than one constituted by "national literatures"' (WS 125). This again illustrates how good and influential writing transcends national culture. Lessing also figures as something of an exception to Nietzsche's attack on German writing because Lessing had the good sense to school himself in the French tradition (WS 103). The section on 'The treasury of German prose' identifies some other exceptions (WS 109), but for the most part it seems that, for Nietzsche, less is better when it comes to German writing: the less German your writing is, the better will it be.

Because writing well assumes great importance for his wider project of cultural progress, it helps to break the chronology of WS to jump to a much later passage which bears directly upon the ideas contained in WS 87. The title alone of WS 214, 'European books', flags its thematic connection to this discussion of good writing as transcending a national culture. Although the six authors Nietzsche celebrates here are all French, he considers their books to be European, for these writers also 'raise themselves above the changes in national taste and philosophical hues' (WS 214). In this way they presumably model the sort of transnational communication advocated in WS 87. The six French moralists from the seventeenth and eighteenth centuries lauded here include La Rochefoucauld, whom Nietzsche has already praised in HAH as a forerunner of the scientific understanding of the psyche, and Montaigne, who is mentioned admiringly in each of the three works under discussion.[12] Joining their elevated company are four other writers: La Bruyère, Fontenelle, Vauvenargues and Chamfort.

The style of these six authors is said to be marked by 'clarity and elegant precision' (WS 214), which, given the link Nietzsche posits between style and substance, bespeaks clarity and precision of thought. So vast is his admiration for this school of writers that its members not only warrant favourable comparison with the Greeks, but on measures such as wit and style are held to surpass them. But what is perhaps most remarkable about this passage's paean to these six writers is that on two occasions in quick succession Nietzsche admits to finding himself speechless: 'I am at a loss as to how to bring my definition [of their qualities] to an end . . . I am at a loss as to how to conclude my list [of who they have, or rather have not, written for].' Were this a passage from the notebooks, such admissions of loss would be less remarkable, but to publish a passage that twice interrupts itself by saying that it cannot articulate sufficient praise for these writers is certainly noteworthy. And it is especially striking that it appears in the larger context of writing well!

One of WS's reflections on writing resonates with MOM's view that art's future role should be to convey, inspire and perpetuate the best in the human, all too human. WS 88 distinguishes two ways of thinking about good style. One is as the medium for any human mood; the other is as conveying 'a human's most desirable mood'. The passage ends by advocating the second as 'instruction in the best style', for 'it corresponds to the good human being'.

---

[12] See HAH 176 and the concluding passage of MOM (408) where he is one of the six thinkers Nietzsche nominates as his imagined interlocutors. In WS 86 he is paired with Horace as a source for understanding Socrates.

Such a person 'is moved from the depths of his heart, spiritually joyful, bright and sincere, someone who has overcome his passions' (WS 88). A similar idea appears in WS 128 where Nietzsche distinguishes melancholy authors who record what they are suffering from serious ones. Serious ones also record their suffering but communicate how they overcame it and are now 'at rest amid joy' (WS 128). So once again, art that promotes and inspires the best of human qualities, prominent among which is joy, is highly valued by Nietzsche, indicating that the change in his view of art from HAH to MOM has stuck and art is now accorded a role in the future.

And just as MOM offered Ancient Greece as the model for salutary artistic engagements with reality, so here Nietzsche praises this culture for its respect for artistic convention. This contrasts with the modern mania for originality – which is no doubt connected with the cult of genius as discussed in Chapter 4 of this introduction and guide, including the idea that the work of art is created *ex nihilo* from the genius's unique inspiration. Upholding Homer as emblematic of this ancient regard for convention, Nietzsche explains how it enables artists to connect more readily with their audience. This can be a real advantage when a number of artists are vying for public attention. Of course, this regard for convention does not preclude artistic innovation; new styles, which will become conventions in their turn, can still be generated. But the modern preoccupation with originality is largely absent from this culture (WS 122). WS 140 elaborates on this question of how cultural innovation occurs at the same time as engagement with convention. Taking Homer once again as emblematic, Nietzsche argues that the Greek artists both inherited a series of constraints from convention and then went on to forge new constraints for themselves in expressing and expanding their creativity. Their invention was always 'this sort of self-imposed fetter' (WS 140), but they add to the work of art by making the whole process of constraint look easy and welcome rather than oppressive and limiting. Nietzsche's image for this process gives this passage its title, 'Dancing in chains' (WS 140), and as he makes clear just a few passages later, it is not confined to Greek culture. WS 159 nominates Chopin as a more recent artist who danced in fetters 'like the freest and most graceful of spirits'.[13]

WS 159 also mentions Raphael's productive relationship to convention, offering further evidence that this ancient artistic stance can be retrieved. Raphael is also the subject of a longer, earlier discussion, where Nietzsche celebrates him as an artist who 'preserved his honesty' (WS 73). Raphael painted a vision that would speak to those with or without religious faith, and provides the painterly counterpart to the writer Nietzsche admired above whose work conveys both human joy and the artist's own delight in that joy. As Nietzsche describes Raphael's Sistine Madonna, 'This [mother's] face and this gaze radiate joy back upon the viewers' faces; the artist adds his own joy to the joy of the recipient of the art' (WS 73). The fact that Raphael painted religious subjects, worked in a heavily religious context and from religious commissions also speaks to one of the questions posed in the chapter on MOM, whether art from an earlier religious era can have continuing relevance in the future. This example provides further support for the suggestion there that because artworks are not irretrievably tied to the circumstances or meanings of their creation, a religiously or metaphysically inspired artwork could occupy a place in a less or non-religious or metaphysical culture of the future.

And just as this stretch of passages about writing style ends, so one on music begins, with this supplying the theme for WS 149–69. The roll call of recent Western composers includes Bach (WS 149), Handel (WS 150), Haydn (WS 151), Beethoven (WS 152), Mozart (WS 152), Schubert (WS 155), Mendelssohn (WS 157), Chopin (WS 159, 160), Schumann (WS 161), Gluck (WS 164) and Piccinni (WS 164). The point made in Chapters 4 and 10 of this introduction and guide applies here too: Nietzsche's

---

[13] Handwerk's valuable observations on Nietzsche's own style suggest that he might also fit this model of artistic work: his aphoristic form 'honed and rehoned . . . requires a continual exercise in self-restraint that was part of Nietzsche's self-imposed innoculation against Wagnerian enthusiasms and excesses . . . In adopting an aphoristic form borrowed from identifiable predecessors and adapted to his present needs, he made it wholly his own' (2013: 563).

focus rests securely upon a selection of relatively recent composers from the Western tradition. Wagner's name is conspicuous by its absence,[14] which makes WS more like HAH than MOM in this regard, for MOM did mention Wagner explicitly. WS 169 describes a 'we', presumably we free spirits, who are friends of music. Music cannot be a substitute for knowledge (the sun) but it can brighten the nights. So once again we see Nietzsche making a greater accommodation between knowledge and art than was the case in HAH. But music's place in a more enlightened future is secure because its significance has been downgraded. It functions now as nocturnal pleasure and release.

However, the very next passage becomes an extended and critical reflection on the reduced role that art in general plays in modern life. Because so many people are so busy with their work, most lack the leisure to give the arts the serious attention they deserve. Squeezed into the interstices of their busyness, art is often consumed when they are exhausted. All art, great or small, must now present itself as 'recreation or amusing distraction' (WS 170). Artists wanting to succeed within this modern environment have therefore to produce works that will appeal to this audience and so resort to

> narcotics, intoxicants, convulsives, spasms of tears: using these means, they overpower those who are fatigued and bring them to a state of exhausted, overwrought animation, where they are beside themselves with rapture and with fear. (WS 170)

The fact that Nietzsche refers to great art in the form of 'opera, tragedy and music' suggests that Young is right to infer that he is implicitly referring to Wagner here (1992: 85). But he does so in a relatively forgiving way, both by deeming Wagner's art to be great (rather than small) and by implying that the maestro would prefer to create for a different, less distracted, less exhausted audience,

---

[14] Young (1992: 85–7) reads some passages as being implicit critiques of Wagner, however – WS 136, 165, 166, 170.

but that the structure and pace of modern life precludes this. And while Nietzsche expresses gratitude for the fact that artists remain willing to produce for this diminished quota of the audience's attention and energy, he is clear that Wagner's sort of art would not be considered great when 'free, full days of festival and rejoicing' are reintroduced to life (WS 170).

Politics

The second half of WS contains a number of passages in which Nietzsche continues to reflect on conventionally political topics, such as democratisation, nationalism, socialism and war. Returning to the theme of Europe's democratisation in WS 275, he declares this process to be 'irresistible'. Contrasting democracy with revolution, he points out that when 'revolutionary spirits' oppose democracy, they unwittingly advance it by engendering the fear of revolution. Outlining the mechanism for this in WS 292, he explains that in order to compete with the socialists, other political parties have to extend more and more concessions to the voters and promise to represent their interests in parliament, including things such as progressive taxation. Through this process the people gradually become 'omnipotent' (WS 292). Nietzsche seems relatively reconciled to democratisation here, seeing it as one of the things that distinguishes modern Europe from the Middle Ages, and, although his language is vague and hard to follow, he seems to interpret it as laying a foundation that will be protective of the works of higher culture (WS 275).[15] Perhaps in this same vein, WS 289 describes democratic institutions as 'very useful and very boring' because they keep tyrannical desires in check.

However, the very next passage to the one that characterises democratisation as unstoppable also discusses universal suffrage, with Nietzsche pointing out that many people who have been granted voting rights elect not to exercise them. He interprets

---

[15] Drochon interprets this passage to mean that democratisation is paving the way for a new aristocracy (2016: 79, 86).

such non-participation by a significant minority as itself a rejection of democracy (WS 276), which leaves us wondering how irreversible democratisation really is. The combined effect of the next two passages serves as a reminder of how novel, and therefore unpredictable, the current situation was. Democratic politics 'has newly grown up overnight' (WS 277) and 'The press, the machine, the railroad and the telegraph are premises whose millennial conclusion nobody yet has dared to draw' (WS 278). About fifteen passages later, however, Nietzsche diminishes the novelty of democracy by saying that, in its current form, it is just new horses driving on the same streets with the same wheels.[16] He does, however, anticipate that this represents the first rather than the final phase of democratisation, for 'democracy is something still to come' (WS 293).

A quite remarkable passage, 'The means to a genuine peace' (WS 284), reveals once again Nietzsche's distrust of national or state boundaries while also showing a less familiar side in its ruminations on how to attain perpetual peace. He deconstructs the claim that the modern Western state maintains a standing army only for purposes of self-defence and never for conquest. That logic only holds if one's neighbours are potential aggressors, but if they too claim to arm themselves purely for self-defence, then the position is unsustainable. The very mindset that our neighbours might be out to get us one day is itself likely to provoke hostility that might lead to war. Hence Nietzsche's conclusion that 'We must renounce the doctrine of the army as a means of self-defense as fundamentally as we renounce the desire for conquest' (WS 284). Genuine peace can only come into being when militarily strong states abolish their weapons and commit to peaceful intentions and means. WS 279 also expresses reservations about the 'modern military system', seeing it as anachronistic in a modern democratic culture.

---

[16] Drochon decodes this passage in the following way: 'while there is a new political institution – the Reichstag (the new horses) – politics has changed little in the new Reich; Bismarck and the Junkers still rule (the same old wheels of power) behind the parliamentary facade, and continue to implement their nationalist realpolitik (the same old [policy] streets)' (2016: 77).

WS 292 explores what might happen as national boundaries break down, with citizens of other countries being seen less and less as potentially hostile others or enemies. Following in Kant's footsteps, he presciently imagines the formation of 'a European union' [*ein Europäischer Völkerbund*],[17] in which each nation will have the status of a canton. Nationalist memories will gradually wither away, supplanted by 'the domination of a democratic principle that is addicted to novelty and avid for experimentation' (WS 292). This future is also imagined as one without armies, as foreign politics becomes more like domestic politics. We also see a side of the peace-promoting Nietzsche in the earlier passage in WS 187 which compares people who need war with those who don't. War can provide 'a remedy for peoples that have grown feeble and wretched: especially if they want to continue living'. But the desire to continue living and to avoid death is itself a sign of 'the senility of sensation', so war might be a remedy, but that which it cures is problematic in itself. We see this as Nietzsche describes a second group of people who do not need war for regeneration: 'the more fully and ably we live, the more quickly we are ready to give up our lives for a single good sensation. A people that lives and feels in this way has no need of war' (WS 187). It is hard to know exactly how to interpret this passage with its generalisations about peoples and their collective emotions and conditions, but Nietzsche is probably obliquely commenting on the militarism of the Prussian state at this time and suggesting that its apparent need for war is symptomatic of an unhealthy culture. But what he says about a whole people giving up its life is hard to fathom; perhaps he is imagining a society willingly succumbing to some form of invasion or imperialism.

This passage also seems to be analogising whole cultures to individuals, for the collective attitude to war as a way of keeping a society alive at all costs seems to be analogous to the individual's attitude towards death as outlined in WS 185. There Nietzsche defends suicide as a form of voluntary, rational death, saying that just keeping oneself alive at any cost allows irrational nature to triumph. He suggest that it makes more sense to stop the machine

---

[17] Hollingdale translates this as 'league of nations'.

when its work has been completed than to keep it running until it dies – that is, experiences natural, irrational death. Nietzsche interprets the opprobrium towards suicide as a legacy of religion and looks forward to a future morality taking a different, more rational attitude towards death, no matter how immoral that might sound today. The range of images used in this passage about death is instructive. The body is a machine that can be stopped when its required work is done or that can be left running until it wears out. The body is 'the miserable substance of the shell [which] determines how long the kernel' – presumably the personality – should last. The body is 'the stupid jailer' while the personality is 'his noble prisoner' (WS 185). Throughout the passage nature is contrasted with reason as body is to mind (or spirit or personality): natural, irrational death occurs when the body wears out, whereas a rational death would be the individual's choice to end his or her life. This intriguing passage suggests that Nietzsche has not yet found a way to break free of Cartesian dualism as he envisages what he takes to be a superior attitude towards death that he hopes will be possible in the future.

But whatever 'War as remedy' (WS 187) conveys, the important thing is that it does not in any way glorify war nor say that it is necessary. Not all cultures have the sickness for which war is the supposed remedy. Going to war is, instead, a symptom of deeper cultural decay and malaise, and Nietzsche imagines and admires a culture that would decline war. This represents a different position from that outlined in Chapter 8 of this introduction and guide which discusses HAH's reflections on war. There Nietzsche maintained that although war and culture cannot flourish simultaneously, periods of war are necessary preludes and postludes to periods of cultural excellence. His logic was that war channels and discharges the violent passions, and cultural creation 'simply cannot do without passions, vices and acts of malice' (HAH 477). In this change we can read WS as effectively applying the ethic of care of the self to whole societies; there is no one-size-fits-all approach to war, and some societies can forego it.

And just as WS 284 reveals Nietzsche to be both envisaging and predicting a politics beyond nationalism, so WS 285 raises his other political *bête noire*, socialism, although in WS the *bête* is more *grise* than *noire*. I say this because Nietzsche is not dismissing the socialist concern about unjust property relations out of hand: he concurs with the socialists that the 'possession of property' needs to 'instill more confidence and become more moral' (WS 285). Instead, he is casting doubt on the compatibility of the socialists' solutions to this injustice with the human psyche, and thereby casting doubt on the feasibility of those solutions. The first possible solution to the problem of the unjust division of property is to divide all property equally. The problem here is that dividing up existing holdings will create bitterness among those whose property is being redistributed. Additional bitterness will be engendered among the new owners as some will feel that their lot is not of the same quality as those of others. Over time further problems arise with the inheritance of property, as its division or consolidation among future generations institutes a new inequality of holdings. So the idea of an equal distribution of property is fraught with problems and ultimately untenable.

The second proposal is to abolish private property all together, making all property communally owned. But this is also fraught in Nietzsche's estimation. He effectively echoes Aristotle's reply to Plato's suggestion that the philosopher rulers hold all things in common, which is that when something belongs to all in general and nobody in particular, it is not as well taken care of as something privately owned.[18] Nietzsche then invokes Plato directly to claim that if Plato was trying to reduce selfishness by eliminating private property, he had failed to realise that without selfishness, the other key virtues would atrophy. Nietzsche suggests that the socialists are rehearsing this Platonic idea which remains plagued by Plato's poor understanding of the human psyche. Lacking 'any history of moral sensations', Plato turns out to be what Nietzsche describes above as a 'moral fanatic': 'he believed ... in good and evil as in black and white: therefore in a radical difference between good and evil human beings, between good and bad qualities' (WS 285).[19]

---

[18] *The Politics*, Book II, 1261b.
[19] His aside there that this belief in the black and white difference between good and evil was shared by 'all of antiquity' is impossible to reconcile, as far as I can see, with other claims about the ancients. See, for example, MOM 220.

Nietzsche's preferred method for achieving this goal of a more just distribution of property is to open as many avenues as possible 'for working toward a small amount of wealth', while also preventing 'effortless, sudden enrichment'. There should also be blocks on any excessive accumulation of wealth, 'and those who possess too much as well as those who possess nothing' should be considered 'a danger to society' (WS 285). In this way he again channels Aristotle with his emphasis on the mean between two extremes. His counsel here is also consonant with his position in MOM where he warned against ostentatious displays of wealth, supported luxury taxes, and urged that wealth be used in the right way for the right purposes. Nietzsche expresses yet further sympathy with the socialist cause, if not the solution, in the very next passage. Although he spends most of it disputing the idea that we can easily or in fact ever affix a just value to labour because of all the variables that go into it, he concludes that 'The exploitation of the worker was, as we now comprehend, something stupid, an exhaustion of the soil at the expense of the future, an endangering of society' (WS 286). This echoes his point in the previous passage about those who are poor being a danger to society, and this same point is reiterated in WS 293. And in WS 220, while he recognises the immense power that machines unleash, he sympathises with those who operate them for the 'despairing boredom of the soul' this creates.

Etcetera

Two topics that receive less attention in WS than they do in the two predecessor works are gender and religion. Nietzsche offers a long reflection on women and pregnancy in WS 17, but does so primarily to refute Schopenhauer's view that while women would be ashamed to be thought of as engaging in coitus, they parade its sometime outcome, pregnancy, with pride. Nietzsche's main point is to criticise the way Schopenhauer tailors the empirical evidence to fit his metaphysical purpose, but in order to do so Nietzsche ventures a more nuanced phenomenology of women and pregnancy. Rather than generalise as Schopenhauer does, he observes that some young women are embarrassed about their pregnant condition precisely because it does implicate them in coitus. Older, lower-class women are more likely to display their pregnancy with pride as evidence that they are still desired by their husbands. Children are also the theme, tacitly at least, of WS 197, which counsels, in a roundabout way, against free spirits reproducing. But on the whole, issues of gender relations, love, romance and family life get much less attention in WS than they did in the previous two works.

Christianity also gets much less sustained attention in WS compared to the two earlier works. The passage discussed above about Raphael as an honest artist operating in a religious context (WS 73) inaugurates a sequence of passages about religion (WS 74–85). The sequence ends with the section, also discussed above, which recommends Socrates over Jesus as a guide to the future (WS 86). The first of these passages analyses the logic of prayer within Christianity to conclude that prayer should be forbidden. Given religion's belief in an all-powerful, all-knowing and benevolent God, prayer seems out of place if its aim is to change God's mind, or if it assumes that his imperfect creatures know better than he does what is good for them or the world (WS 74). While Christianity should, logically, have repudiated prayer, Nietzsche goes on to playfully list the reasons why it not only permitted but also encouraged it. WS 78 reiterates Nietzsche's claim that Christianity blackens humans in the first place and then sells itself as the remedy. He observes that even though faith in the remedy has 'been shaken to its deepest roots', the picture of humans as sinful persists. His repeated references to humans taking joy in themselves show that part of his project here is to displace that picture.

The critique of pity as a debased form of fellow feeling that was begun in HAH (see Chapter 2 of this introduction and guide) also continues in WS and is, of course, connected with Nietzsche's critique of Christianity as a religion of compassion. Passage 45 condemns those who equate pity with the whole of morality (à la Schopenhauer and Rée) and points out that there is a different and better sort of morality than this instinctive one of 'heart and helpful hands'. The alternative 'morality of reason' understands morality to be 'a continually exercised self-mastery and self-overcoming [*Selbstbeherrschung und Selbstüberwindung*] in both large and the smallest of things' (WS 45).[20] WS 62 also challenges the equation of morality with pity, pointing out that in order for pity to be prized, suffering must be presupposed. So anyone wanting to be moral by this code must will the suffering of others. WS 50 offers a different line of criticism of pity, arguing that as soon as we become an object of pity for someone else, we have lost status in their eyes and our own – we are no longer an object of fear to them. How pity came to be prized is therefore a problem for Nietzsche, for originally the person displaying pity was despised or feared – and perhaps both, for anyone showing compassion to us is placing themselves above us.

The language of self-mastery and self-overcoming which Nietzsche claims as part and parcel of the morality of reason, as opposed to that of pity, appears in some of WS's other passages too. WS 37 speaks out against those who would condemn the passions out of hand. Rather than accept this, Nietzsche sees his task, and that of those who think like him, as being to 'take from the passions their dreadful character and to check them sufficiently to prevent them from becoming devastating torrents'. This seems to require not exterminating or extirpating the passions but recognising and managing them, and even potentially 'transforming [them] into joys' (WS 37).[21] WS 65 provides a more concrete image of what Nietzsche means by mastering the passions when it refers to the desire to master one's temper, jaundice, vengefulness and sensual pleasure. These passions can become torrents[22] that will devastate any other achievements if not mastered first. WS 53 envisages a person who has overcome their passions and who can begin to sow 'the seeds of good spiritual works upon the ground of the vanquished passions'. This serves as a reminder that self-overcoming is not an end in itself but a means to something else – in this case future good works.

---

[20] Ansell-Pearson (2018: 89) suggests that Nietzsche's challenge to the equation of morality with the unegotistic starts with *Dawn*, but it is clearly here in WS. See also page 49 above.
[21] I follow Hollingdale by translating *Freudenschaften* as 'joys' rather than Handwerk's 'delights' to pick up on Nietzsche's many other references to joy. See Ansell-Pearson (2018: ch. 6) on joy's centrality for Nietzsche.
[22] Although Nietzsche uses slightly different terms in both passages – *Wildwassen* in 37; *Wildlbach* in 65 – both can be translated as torrent.

The closing exchange between the Wanderer and his Shadow reiterates the importance of what we are calling here care of the self. The Shadow anticipates being a beneficiary of the Wanderer's attention to 'the things nearest at hand', which again suggests an alliance between the Shadow and embodiment, for the body and its particular needs are closely attended to in this ethic. The idea of the Shadow and all that it stands for only being visible in the light of knowledge is reiterated, which is compatible again with the suggestion above that with Nietzsche's form of philosophy, the supposedly darker side of human existence will be given full exposure. Night falls and the Shadow, necessarily, disappears. It is worth noting the title of Nietzsche's next book, *Daybreak*, published in the year following WS (1881), which suggests that the Shadow will return.

Glossary of Key Terms

Aphorism: HAH inaugurates Nietzsche's use of the aphorism as one of the tools in his stylistic repertoire. His use of short, pithy pronouncements is thought to reflect the impact of Paul Rée on his thinking at this time, although Nietzsche could be emulating other writers of aphorisms such as La Rochefoucauld, Chamfort, Schopenhauer, Pascal and Lichtenberg. Nietzsche not only writes aphorisms but also writes about them and advises how they should, and should not, be interpreted. Of the three works discussed here, MOM contains the greatest number of aphorisms.

Enlightenment: Nietzsche applies this adjective to his own work at this time. Associating the Enlightenment with the growth of scientific knowledge, he situates himself as part of the Enlightenment. HAH had originally included a tribute to Voltaire and a passage from Descartes, but both were removed by Nietzsche from the later edition. His use of the term enlightenment is, however, nuanced and perhaps idiosyncratic. For him enlightenment does not refer just to a specific historical era, but also to a longer, ongoing process that has been present, and either advanced or retarded, across the centuries of Western civilisation. The Renaissance, for example, counts for him as an enlightened phase in Western history because of its great respect for scientific thinking. Nietzsche condemns the Enlightenment's appropriation by the French Revolution, for an enlightened approach to social change advocates moderate and gradual social and political change.

Epistemology-plus: I coin this term to identify a concern that pervades all three works discussed here. Despite Nietzsche's enthusiasm for science, he is also aware of the troubles that can come from scientific knowledge. His assessment of knowledge is never purely epistemological; he also repeatedly attends to the ethical, experiential and aesthetic dimensions of knowing. He asks, in addition to the truth value that any approach may yield, what sort of character traits does pursuing this form of knowledge require and encourage? What will it feel like to seek and acquire this sort of knowledge? Will a sense of beauty or satisfaction be engendered by this quest? While he does endorse the scientific approach as the best path to true knowledge, Nietzsche repeatedly returns to the dilemma of how to live with the knowledge generated by science.

Free will: One of the major errors in the Western philosophical tradition that Nietzsche identifies is its simplistic faith in free will. He associates the belief in free will and the personal accountability to which it gives rise with Schopenhauer, but it is also a central plank of Christianity. From many and varied angles across all three works discussed here, Nietzsche chips away at this belief, and although he succeeds in complicating our understanding of the ingredients of action, it is not clear that he can dispense entirely with any notion of free will.

Free spirits: HAH calls itself a book for free spirits. In an age of democratisation, free spirits represent a new nobility. These figures possess the courage, modesty and humility to follow Nietzsche on the scientific path to knowledge. Independent thinkers who have liberated themselves from the dictates of custom and convention, they eschew convictions and seek rational explanations for social and political practices and arrangements. Free spirits are likely to be solitary figures who cannot be bound or burdened by personal relationships and commitments, yet they can find a sense of fellowship with the wider and larger community of free spirits. Although Nietzsche is vague about the mechanisms, free spirits will play a role in bringing forth a higher culture of the future, but they do not serve this goal as political actors.

Good European: Chapter 8 of HAH contains Nietzsche's first invocation of the good European (HAH 475), an ideal which carries into his later works. Relentlessly critical of nationalism from HAH onwards, Nietzsche looks forward to the growth of pan-European sentiment and to the development of European institutions. Following in Kant's footsteps, for example, he imagines that the democratisation of Europe will eventually see the formation of 'a European union' [*ein Europäischer Völkerbund*] in which each nation will have something approaching the status of a canton (WS 292).

Maxim see **Aphorism**

Metaphysics: Metaphysical philosophies like those of Plato, Kant and Schopenhauer, which posit a fundamental truth and then task philosophy with getting to that underlying truth, are no longer tenable in Nietzsche's view. He wages war on traditional Western metaphysics in these works, and often groups religion, art and metaphysics on one side versus science and history on the other in the battle for true knowledge. But metaphysical doctrines remain seductive to seekers after truth for non-epistemological reasons – they can be alluring, lofty and comforting. Yet despite sounding as if he wants to repudiate all metaphysics, there are moments when Nietzsche's own metaphysical commitments break through his text. At this time he believes that things are in constant flux, that nothing remains identical to itself over time, that no two things are identical, and so on.

Moralists: The three writings studied here reveal the influence of the French moralist tradition on Nietzsche at this time. This group of thinkers wrote in the seventeenth and eighteenth centuries, with the best known among them being La Rochefoucauld and Pascal. Other figures associated with this tradition include Vauvenargues, Chamfort and La Bruyère. They penned aphorisms that reflected close psychological observation of the details of the human psyche. Their approach tended to be deflationary by puncturing humans' self-image and revealing motivations to be different from, and perhaps antithetical to, the way humans prefer to think of themselves.

Positivism: It has become something of a commonplace to call Nietzsche a positivist at this stage of his work, and some of his enthusiastic remarks about reason and science, along with his energetic attacks on religion and metaphysics, can support such a view. However, deeper and wider inspection reveals that this is not a helpful way to characterise these three writings. His own views about the nature of reality (see **Metaphysics**) complicate any positivist faith in observable data or reliance on sensory experience.

Psychology: With the advent of HAH, Nietzsche begins to present himself as a psychologist, and this self-characterisation continues into his later works. Influenced by the **moralist** tradition, he practises psychological observation that aims for perspicuous encounters with the depths and complexity of the human psyche. His findings are often designed to unsettle humans' self-understandings by showing their motivations to be different than what they take them to be. But unlike his moralist predecessors, Nietzsche also insists upon change in the human psyche over time and across cultures. He is particularly concerned by the damage that Christianity has done to the experiences and self-understandings of its followers, for example. Some of his key foci in these three writings are **free will**, egoism and vanity.

Science [*Wissenschaft*]: With the advent of HAH, Nietzsche becomes a strong proponent of a scientific approach to knowledge and wants to put knowledge of topics such as religion, morality, metaphysics, psychology and art on a more scientific footing. But what he means by science is simply a careful, dispassionate quest for gradual, reliable knowledge. Scientific inquiry aims to see the world as it really is, without wishful thinking or the need for meaning imputing false meanings to it. Because of his belief in continuous flux (see **Metaphysics**), a historical approach to matters such as morality and psychology will be more scientific than approaches that neglect or deny change. Scientific inquiry must also eschew convictions and be ready to reconsider and revise what it takes to be true. But while in these writings he does endorse the scientific approach as the best path to true knowledge, Nietzsche does not shy away from the dangers and debilitations that seeking and finding such knowledge might generate (see **Epistemology-plus**).

Guide to Further Reading on *Human, All Too Human*

Ruth Abbey, *Nietzsche's Middle Period*: a study of some of the common themes across the middle period writings.

Ruth Abbey, '*Human, All Too Human*: A Book for Free Spirits': a chapter-length overview of *Human, All Too Human*.

Vinod Acharya, 'Science, Culture, and Philosophy: The Relation between *Human, All Too Human* and Nietzsche's Early Thought': an examination of some of the continuities between *Human, All Too Human* and Nietzsche's previous writings.

Keith Ansell-Pearson, *Nietzsche's Search for Philosophy: On the Middle Writings*: contains a chapter on *Human, All Too Human* and the meaning of science and enlightenment.

Jonathan R. Cohen, *Science, Culture, and Free Spirits: A Study of Nietzsche's Human, All-too-Human*: a close study of the meaning of science in *Human, All Too Human*.

Pepjin Corduwener, 'Between Libertarianism and Authoritarianism: Friedrich Nietzsche's Conception of Democracy in *Human, All Too Human*': a discussion of the understanding of politics in *Human, All Too Human*.

Christine Daigle, 'The Ethical Ideal of the Free Spirit in *Human, All Too Human*' in *Nietzsche's Free Spirit Philosophy*: an account of the ethical ideal of the free spirit in *Human, All Too Human*.

Paolo D'Iorio, *Nietzsche's Journey to Sorrento: Genesis of the Philosophy of the Free Spirit*: a detailed reconstruction of the biographical context of *Human, All Too Human*.

Brendan Donnellan, 'Friedrich Nietzsche and Paul Rée: Cooperation and Conflict': a study of Nietzsche's relationship with Paul Rée and its impact on his thinking.

Guy Elgat, 'Nietzsche's Critique of Pure Altruism – Developing an Argument from *Human, All Too Human*': a critical examination of the idea of psychological egoism in *Human, All Too Human*.

Jeremy Fortier, 'Nietzsche's Political Engagements: On the Relationship between Philosophy and Politics in *The Wanderer and His Shadow*': an exploration of the free spirit ideal and its stance towards political engagement in *The Wanderer and his Shadow*.

Paul Franco, *Nietzsche's Enlightenment: The Free Spirit Trilogy of the Middle Period*: a study of the middle period writings which devotes a chapter to various themes in *Human, All Too Human*, with a focus on the role of culture.

Graeme Garrard, 'Nietzsche For and Against the Enlightenment': an outline of the shift in Nietzsche's attitude towards enlightenment from *Human, All Too Human* to his later writings.

Laurence Lampert, *What a Philosopher Is: Becoming Nietzsche*: includes a chapter on *Human, All Too Human* and Nietzsche's conception of philosophy in that work.

Iain Morrison, 'Nietzsche's Genealogy of Morality in the Human, All Too Human Series': makes the argument that Nietzsche's concept of genealogy begins in *Human, All Too Human*.

Bernard Reginster, 'Nietzsche on Selflessness and the Value of Altruism': investigates the relationship between altruism and egoism, starting with *Human, All Too Human*.

Robin Small, *Nietzsche and Rée: A Star Friendship*: a detailed and highly illuminating account of the intellectual relationship between Nietzsche and Paul Rée.

Michael Ure, *Nietzsche's Therapy: Self Cultivation in the Middle Works*: a study of some of the common themes across the middle period writings with a focus on philosophy as self-cultivation.

Bibliography

Abbey, Ruth. 1999. 'The Roots of *Ressentiment*: Nietzsche on Vanity', *New Nietzsche Studies*, 3.3–4: 47–61.
— 2000. *Nietzsche's Middle Period*. Oxford: Oxford University Press.
— 2012. '*Human, All Too Human*: A Book for Free Spirits', in *A Companion to Friedrich Nietzsche: Life and Works*, ed. Paul Bishop. New York: Camden House, 114–34.
— 2014. 'Lumping It and Liking It: On Reading the Works of Nietzsche's Middle Period', *Warwick Journal of Philosophy*, 26: 131–54.
— 2015. 'Skilled Marksman and Strict Self-Examination: Nietzsche on La Rochefoucauld', in *Nietzsche's Free Spirit Philosophy*, ed. Rebecca Bamford. Lanham, MD: Rowman and Littlefield, 13–32.
— Forthcoming. 'Continuing Questions about Friendship as a Central Moral Value', *Dialogue and Universalism*, 2.
Abbey, Ruth, and Douglas Den Uyl. 2001. 'The Chief Inducement? The Idea of Marriage as Friendship', *Journal of Applied Philosophy*, 18.1: 37–52.
Acampora, Christa Davis. 1996. 'Re/Introducing Homer's Contest: A New Translation with Notes and Commentary', North American Nietzsche Society, http://www.northamericannietzschesociety.com/uploads/7/3/2/5/73251013/nietzscheana5.pdf. Accessed 10 July 2019.
Acharya, Vinod. 2015. 'Science, Culture, and Philosophy: The Relation between *Human, All Too Human* and Nietzsche's Early Thought', *Comparative and Continental Philosophy*, 7.1: 18–28.

Ansell-Pearson, Keith. 1994. *An Introduction to Nietzsche as a Political Thinker*. Cambridge: Cambridge University Press.
— 2018. *Nietzsche's Search for Philosophy: On the Middle Writings*. London: Bloomsbury.
Ansell-Pearson, Keith, and Duncan Large. 2006. *The Nietzsche Reader*. Malden, MA: Blackwell.
Aristotle, *The Politics*, http://classics.mit.edu/Aristotle/politics.html. Accessed 10 July 2019.
Berry, Jessica N. 2015. 'Nietzsche's Scientific Community: Elective Affinities', in *Individual and Community in Nietzsche's Philosophy*, ed. Julian Young. Cambridge: Cambridge University Press, 93–117.
Brinker, Menahem. 2002. 'Nietzsche and the Jews', in *Nietzsche, Godfather of Fascism? On the Uses and Abuses of a Philosophy*, ed. Jacob Golomb and Robert S. Wistrich. Princeton: Princeton University Press, 107–25.
Brobjer, Thomas. 2004. 'Nietzsche's View of the Value of Historical Studies and Methods', *Journal of the History of Ideas*, 65.2: 301–22.
— 2008a. *Nietzsche's Philosophical Context: An Intellectual Biography*. Urbana: University of Illinois Press.
— 2008b. 'Critical Aspects of Nietzsche's Relation to Politics and Democracy', in *Nietzsche, Power and Politics: Rethinking Nietzsche's Legacy for Political Thought*, ed. Herman W. Siemens and Vasti Roodt. Berlin: Walter de Gruyter, 205–30.
Church, Jeffrey. 2019. *Nietzsche's Unfashionable Observations: A Critical Introduction and Guide*. Edinburgh: Edinburgh University Press.
Clark, Maudemarie. 1990. *Nietzsche on Truth and Philosophy*. Cambridge: Cambridge University Press.
Cohen, Jonathan R. 1999. 'Nietzsche's Fling with Positivism', in *Nietzsche, Epistemology, and Philosophy of Science: Nietzsche and the Sciences II*, ed. Babette Babich. Dordrecht: Kluwer, 101–7.
— 2010. *Science, Culture, and Free Spirits: A Study of Nietzsche's Human, All-too-Human*. New York: Humanity Books.
Corduwener, Pepjin. 2013. 'Between Libertarianism and Authoritarianism: Friedrich Nietzsche's Conception of Democracy in Human, All Too Human', *Studies in Social and Political Thought*, 22: 64–77.

Daigle, Christine. 2015. 'The Ethical Ideal of the Free Spirit in *Human, All Too Human*', in *Nietzsche's Free Spirit Philosophy*, ed. Rebecca Bamford. Lanham, MD: Rowman and Littlefield, 33–48.

Detwiler, Bruce. 1990. *Nietzsche and the Politics of Aristocratic Radicalism*. Chicago: University of Chicago Press.

D'Iorio, Paolo. 2016. *Nietzsche's Journey to Sorrento: Genesis of the Philosophy of the Free Spirit*, trans. Sylvia Mae Gorelick. Chicago: University of Chicago Press.

Donnellan, Brendan. 1979. 'Nietzsche and La Rochefoucauld', *The German Quarterly*, 52.3: 303–18.

— 1982. 'Friedrich Nietzsche and Paul Rée: Cooperation and Conflict', *Journal of the History of Ideas*, 43.4: 595–612.

Drochon, Hugo. 2016. *Nietzsche's Great Politics*. Princeton: Princeton University Press.

Elgat, Guy. 2015. 'Nietzsche's Critique of Pure Altruism – Developing an Argument from *Human, All Too Human*', *Inquiry*, 58.3: 308–26.

Feuerbach, Ludwig. 1972 [1841]. *The Essence of Christianity*, trans. Zawar Hanfi, https://www.marxists.org/reference/archive/feuerbach/works/essence/ec01_1.htm. Accessed 10 July 2019.

Fortier, Jeremy. 2016. 'Nietzsche's Political Engagements: On the Relationship between Philosophy and Politics in *The Wanderer and His Shadow*', *The Review of Politics*, 78.2: 201–25.

Franco, Paul. 2011. *Nietzsche's Enlightenment: The Free Spirit Trilogy of the Middle Period*. Chicago: University of Chicago Press.

Garrard, Graeme. 2008. 'Nietzsche For and Against the Enlightenment', *The Review of Politics*, 70.4: 595–608.

Handwerk, Gary. 2013. 'Translator's Afterword', in *Human, All Too Human II and Unpublished Fragments from the Period*, trans. Gary Handwerk. Stanford: Stanford University Press, 555–84.

Harrington, Anne. 1995. 'Unfinished Business: Models of Laterality in the Nineteenth Century', in *Brain Asymmetry*, ed. R. J. Davidson and K. Hugdahl. Cambridge, MA: MIT Press, 3–28.

Hayman, Ronald. 1980. *Nietzsche: A Critical Life*. London: Weidenfeld and Nicolson.

Hill, R. K. 2007. *Nietzsche: A Guide for the Perplexed*. London: Continuum.

Hollingdale, R. J. 1999. *Nietzsche: The Man and his Philosophy*, rev. edn. Cambridge: Cambridge University Press.

Kamenka, Eugene. 1970. *The Philosophy of Ludwig Feuerbach*. London: Routledge & Kegan Paul.

Kant, Immanuel. 2019 [1784]. 'What is Enlightenment?', http://www.columbia.edu/acis/ets/CCREAD/etscc/kant.html. Accessed 10 July 2019.

Lampert, Laurence. 2017. *What a Philosopher Is: Becoming Nietzsche*. Chicago: University of Chicago Press.

Langer, Monika M. 2010. *Nietzsche's Gay Science: Dancing Coherence*. New York: Palgrave Macmillan.

Large, Duncan. 2014. 'Nietzsche's Helmbrecht, Or: How to Philosophize with a Ploughshare', *Studia Nietzscheana*, http://www.nietzschesource.org/SN/large-2014. Accessed 10 July 2019.

Leidecker, Kurt F., ed. 1959. *Nietzsche Unpublished Letters*. New York: Philosophical Library.

Levy, Oscar, ed. 1985. *Friedrich Nietzsche Selected Letters*, trans. A. N. Ludovici. London: Soho Book Company.

Magnus, Bernd, and Kathleen M. Higgins. 1996. 'Nietzsche's Works and their Themes', in *The Cambridge Companion to Nietzsche*, ed. Bernd Magnus and Kathleen M. Higgins. Cambridge: Cambridge University Press, 21–68.

Martin, Nicholas. 2008. '"Aufklärung und kein Ende": The Place of Enlightenment in Friedrich Nietzsche's Thought', *German Life and Letters*, 61: 79–97.

Morrison, Iain. 2003. 'Nietzsche's Genealogy of Morality in the Human, All Too Human Series', *British Journal for the History of Philosophy*, 11: 657–72.

Mullin, Amy. 2000. 'Nietzsche's Free Spirit', *Journal of the History of Philosophy*, 38.3: 383–405.

Nicholson, Carol. 2012. 'Philosophy and the Two-Sided Brain', *Philosophy Now*, https://philosophynow.org/issues/92/Philosophy_And_The_Two-Sided_Brain. Accessed 10 July 2019.

Nietzsche, Friedrich. 1986. *Human, All Too Human*, trans. R. J. Hollingdale. New York: Cambridge University Press.

—— 1994. *On the Genealogy of Morality*, trans. Carol Diethe. Cambridge: Cambridge University Press.

- 1995. *Human, All Too Human I*, trans. Gary Handwerk, in *The Complete Works of Friedrich Nietzsche*. Stanford: Stanford University Press.
- 1999. *The Birth of Tragedy*, trans. Ronald Speirs. Cambridge: Cambridge University Press.
- 2001. *The Gay Science*, trans. Josefine Nauckhoff. Cambridge: Cambridge University Press.
- 2002. *Beyond Good and Evil*, trans. Judith Norman. Cambridge: Cambridge University Press.
- 2005. *The Anti-Christ, Ecce Homo, Twilight of the Idols, and Other Writings*, trans. Judith Norman. Cambridge: Cambridge University Press.
- 2007. *On the Genealogy of Morality*, ed. Keith Ansell-Pearson, trans. Carol Diethe. New York: Cambridge University Press.
- 2011. *Dawn: Thoughts on the Presumptions of Morality*, trans. Brittain Smith, in *The Complete Works of Friedrich Nietzsche*. Stanford: Stanford University Press.
- 2013. *Human, All Too Human II*, trans. Gary Handwerk, in *The Complete Works of Friedrich Nietzsche*. Stanford: Stanford University Press.

Owen, David. 2003. 'The Contest of Enlightenment: An Essay on Critique and Genealogy', *The Journal of Nietzsche Studies*, 25: 35–57.

Rée, Paul. 2003 [1885, 1877]. *Basic Writings*, trans. and ed. Robin Small. Urbana: University of Illinois Press.

Reginster, Bernard. 2000. 'Nietzsche on Selflessness and the Value of Altruism', *History of Philosophy Quarterly*, 17.2: 177–200.

- 2003. 'What is a Free Spirit? Nietzsche on Fanaticism', *Archiv für Geschichte der Philosophie*, 85.1: 51–85.

Rethy, Robert A. 1976. 'The Descartes Motto to the First Edition of *Menschliches All zu Menschliches*', *Nietzsche Studien*, 5: 289–97.

Rousseau, Jean-Jacques. 2002. *The Social Contract and the First and Second Discourses*. New Haven, CT: Yale University Press.

Safranski, Rüdiger. 2002. *Nietzsche: A Philosophical Biography*, trans. Shelley Frish. New York: W.W. Norton.

Salaquarda, Jörg. 1996. 'Nietzsche and the Judaeo-Christian Tradition', in *The Cambridge Companion to Nietzsche*, ed. Bernd

Magnus and Kathleen M. Higgins. Cambridge: Cambridge University Press, 90–118.

Salomé, Lou Andreas. 2001. *Nietzsche*, trans. and ed. Siegfried Mandel. Urbana: University of Illinois Press.

Schacht, Richard. 1996. 'Introduction', in Friedrich Nietzsche, *Human, All Too Human*, trans. R. J. Hollingdale. Cambridge: Cambridge University Press.

Schopenhauer, Arthur. 1851. 'On Women', in *Essays of Schopenhauer*, trans. Mrs Rudolf Dircks, https://ebooks.adelaide.edu.au/s/schopenhauer/arthur/essays/chapter5.html. Accessed 10 July 2019.

Small, Robin. 2005. *Nietzsche and Rée: A Star Friendship*. New York: Oxford University Press.

Stack, George. 1983. *Lange and Nietzsche*. Berlin: Walter de Gruyter.

Taylor, Charles. 1989. *Sources of the Self: The Making of the Modern Identity*. Cambridge, MA: Harvard University Press.

Ure, Michael. 2008. *Nietzsche's Therapy: Self Cultivation in the Middle Works*. Lanham, MD: Rowman and Littlefield.

Vattimo, Gianni. 2000. *Dialogue with Nietzsche*, trans. William McCuaig. New York: Columbia University Press.

Young, Julian. 1992. *Nietzsche's Philosophy of Art*. New York: Cambridge University Press.

— 2006. *Nietzsche's Philosophy of Religion*. New York: Cambridge University Press.

— 2010. *Friedrich Nietzsche: A Philosophical Biography*. New York: Cambridge University Press.

Index

Acharya, Vinod, 3n9, 7n22, 23n6, 229
amour-propre, vi, 18, 99, 101–2, 106, 107, 109
Anaximander, 93
Ancient Greece, 10, 33, 38, 64, 70–1, 74, 77, 78, 92–4, 99n2, 117, 133–4, 142, 145, 172, 173, 178–9, 207, 210, 212, 213
Ansell-Pearson, Keith, 2n7, 3n8, 6, 12n30, 12n31, 13, 20, 54n16, 130n3, 137n12, 140n16, 143n25, 145n28, 148, 195n3, 196n5, 200, 204, 223n20, 223n21, 229
aphorism, 4–5, 18, 45, 46, 99, 100, 174–5, 225, 227; *see also* style
Aristotle, 133, 220, 221
arrogance, 100, 103, 105, 106, 107–8
art, 12, 14n33, 15–17, 19, 20, 24, 25, 31, 61, 67, 68, 69–79, 81, 83, 88–92, 155–6, 158, 161, 163, 171–82, 210, 212–16, 227, 228

Bach, Johann Sebastian, 71, 182, 214
Beethoven, Ludwig von, 71, 77, 173, 182, 214
benevolence, 18, 50–1, 99, 103–8
Berlin, Isaiah, 96
Bernini, Gian Lorenzo, 70
Berry, Jessica, 7n20
Brobjer, Thomas, 3, 4n13, 5–6, 11n29, 12, 34, 40n4, 43n6, 59n2, 148n30
Burckhardt, Jacob, 142n22, 163n8
Byron, Lord, 67, 70, 121

Calderón, Pedro, 179, 182
Chamfort, Sebastien, 4n13, 100, 212, 225, 227
Chopin, Frédéric, 213, 214
Christianity, 7, 8, 17, 25, 28, 39, 53, 58–68, 73, 79, 94, 97, 109, 142, 146, 167–71, 177, 192, 198, 199, 201, 209, 210, 222, 226, 228
Church, Jeff, 59n3
Clark, Maudemarie, 29n10

Cohen, Jonathan, 5n17, 6n18, 14n33, 16, 80, 87n13, 158n4, 229
convictions, 19, 124, 150–5, 162, 170, 191, 203, 226, 228
Corduwener, Pepjin, 106n14, 131n4, 139n14, 229
crime, 204–5, 209

Daigle, Christine, 94n15, 229
Dante, 70
death, 166, 189, 191, 192, 197, 199n9, 218–19
democracy, 18, 129–32, 134, 135, 138–9, 148, 187, 216–18, 226, 227
Descartes, René, 10, 219, 225
Detwiler, Bruce, 148n31
Diderot, Denis, 182
Diethe, Carol, 4n16
dissimulation, 100, 104, 107, 108
Donnellan, Brendan, 43n7, 230
Drochon, Hugo, 130n2, 138n13, 142n22, 145n27, 148n31, 216n15, 217n16

egoism, 17, 37, 41, 47–9, 52, 76, 163–4, 228, 230
Elgat, Guy, 45n9, 49n13, 230
Empedocles, 64, 93
enlightenment, 6–12, 21, 60, 68, 69, 71–2, 77, 84, 94, 142, 143, 152, 154, 155, 159, 171, 173, 177, 179, 188, 215, 225, 229, 230

Epicurus, 12n31, 189, 196, 197, 203, 204
epistemology-plus, 13–14, 17, 19, 21, 25–8, 29, 32, 34, 36, 43, 55, 57, 66, 88, 89, 96, 144, 150, 158n3, 169, 200, 226, 228
equality, 18, 19, 38, 40, 106, 129–36, 139n15, 140, 148, 191, 206–8, 220
Erasmus, 8, 10
eudaemonia, 199–200, 204

Feuerbach, Ludwig, 17, 58, 59–60, 63
Fontenelle, 212
Fortier, Jeremy, 131, 146, 157, 190, 191, 192, 194, 195n3, 196n4, 197, 199n8, 204, 230
Franco, Paul, 3n12, 7n22, 15, 62, 69, 71, 80, 86n12, 87n13, 129n1, 137n12, 145n28, 146n29, 158n4, 191, 230
free spirits, 17–19, 20, 21, 32–3, 54, 56, 77, 79, 80–1, 83–9, 93–5, 111, 123–5, 130, 131, 132, 137, 144, 145, 146, 155, 159–62, 169, 173, 186, 188, 189, 191–2, 193, 194, 198, 199, 215, 222, 226, 229, 230
free will, 17, 19, 37, 43, 53–5, 162, 164, 191, 200–6, 226, 228
French Moralists, the, 17, 44, 46, 47, 99–100, 149, 167, 212, 227, 228

friendship, 50, 68, 99, 100, 107–9, 116, 117, 165–7, 193

Gall, Franz Joseph, 91
Garrard, Graeme, 9n26, 12n30, 230
genealogy, 3, 160, 193–4, 208, 220n19, 230; *see also* history
genius, 17, 69, 71, 73–6, 79, 85, 86–7, 92, 93, 95–6, 100, 140, 154, 181
  cult of, 71, 75–6, 136, 175, 213
  of justice, 154
  of knowledge, 74, 154
Gluck, Christoph Willibald, 214
Goethe, Johann Wolfgang von, 60, 101n5, 172, 173, 179, 182, 189, 211

Handel, George Frideric, 182, 214
Handwerk, Gary, 4n13, 10n27, 14, 20, 47n10, 71, 98, 149, 158n2, 163n8, 176, 214n13
Haydn, Joseph, 214
Hayman, Ronald, 1n2, 14n32, 35, 158n2
Hesiod, 70, 182
history, 4, 5, 8, 10, 11, 16, 21, 23, 24, 25, 27, 30, 34, 36, 37, 39, 40–2, 46, 47, 52, 53, 54, 61n5, 65n11, 69, 75, 76, 78, 79, 97, 99n2, 110, 112, 113, 114, 115, 125, 128, 137, 139, 142, 151, 152, 153, 158, 159, 161, 162, 163, 169, 170, 182, 183, 186, 193, 194, 201, 204, 220, 225, 227, 228; *see also* stadial view of history
Hollingdale, R. J., 2n5, 2n6, 13, 98, 149, 176
Homer, 64, 70, 173, 182, 207, 213
Horace, 212n12

Kamenka, Eugene, 59n2
Kant, Immanuel, 11, 12, 22, 24, 51, 139n15, 209, 218, 227
Kepler, Johannes, 74, 154
Klopstock, Friedrich, 182
Kotzebue, August von, 182

La Bruyère, Jean, 212, 227
La Rochefoucauld, Duc de, 4n13, 44, 45, 46, 51, 52n14, 63, 100, 212, 225, 227
Lampert, Laurence, 15, 21n2, 29n10, 40n5, 56n17, 67n12, 230
Large, Duncan, 13, 185
Lessing, Gotthold, 70, 211
Lichtenberg, Georg, 4n13, 225
Lorraine, Claude, 182
love, 50, 66, 67, 77, 110, 115, 116, 118, 119, 120–7, 163–5, 166, 167, 168, 183, 184, 193, 209, 222

marriage, 2, 18, 110, 111, 112, 115–20, 123–8, 183, 184
Martin, Nicholas, 5n17, 8n24
Mendelssohn, Felix, 214
metaphysics, 6, 12, 14, 16, 17, 21, 22, 25–8, 30, 32, 34, 41, 42, 58, 68, 69, 71, 72, 77, 79, 80, 83, 88–91, 152, 158–9, 162, 172, 204, 227, 228
Meysenbug, Malwida von, 2, 139n15
Michelangelo, 70, 182
Milton, John, 182
miracles, 41, 72, 75, 81, 86, 87, 88, 181, 201
moderation, 9, 70, 77, 143, 144, 152, 154, 159, 160, 171, 173, 175, 187, 225
Montaigne, Michel de, 166, 189, 212
Morrison, Iain, 40n4, 43, 49n13, 230
Mozart, Wolfgang Amadeus, 182, 214
Mullin, Amy, 94n15, 123n12, 125n13
Murillo, Bartolomé Esteban, 70
music, 25, 67, 71, 76, 90, 175, 176, 177, 214, 215

Napoleon, 76, 136, 181n21
nationalism, 1, 3, 139, 140–1, 169, 188, 211, 212, 216, 217–18, 219, 227

Owen, David, 12n30

Palestrina, 71, 182
Parmenides, 93
Pascal, Blaise, 189, 225, 227
Petrarch, Francesco, 8, 10
Piccinni, Niccolo, 214
pity, 19, 51–2, 103, 106, 109, 184, 191, 222–3
Plato, 22, 93, 140n16, 160, 189, 199n8, 220, 227
positivism, 6–7, 13, 31, 200, 203, 227–8
progress, 8, 24, 25, 33, 81, 82, 84, 88, 97, 123, 152, 159, 211
psychology, 3, 5, 17, 20, 36–7, 42–7, 53, 58, 60–1, 65, 99, 100, 128, 167, 169, 197, 201, 212, 220, 227, 228
punishment, 19, 39, 152, 191, 205, 207, 208, 210; *see also* crime
Pyrrho, 4
Pythagoras, 93

Racine, Jean, 179, 182
Raphael, 70, 214, 222
rationality, 8, 10, 51, 66–7, 80, 84, 88, 94, 128, 138, 151, 169–70, 186, 188, 199, 205, 218–19, 222–3, 226–7
Rée, Paul, 2, 3, 4, 5, 17, 18, 24n7, 25, 36, 39, 43–7, 49n13, 58n1, 63, 110, 111,

125–8, 131n5, 157, 222, 225, 230
Reformation, the, 97, 152, 170–1
Reginster, Bernard, 49, 230
religion, 1, 6, 8, 9, 14n33, 16–26, 28, 30, 31, 32, 34, 47, 56, 58–61, 63, 64, 65n11, 66–8, 71, 72, 75, 77, 78, 80, 81, 83, 84, 86, 88–91, 96, 129, 136–9, 140, 143, 151, 152, 158, 167–71, 172, 174, 177, 178, 181, 191, 192, 196, 198, 199, 204, 214, 219, 221, 222, 227, 228; *see also* Christianity
Renaissance, the, 11, 70, 76, 92, 97, 225
revenge, 36, 38, 100, 208–10
revolution, 9, 18, 77, 129, 142–3, 187, 216, 225
Rossini, Gioachino, 182
Rousseau, Jean-Jacques, 9, 18, 99, 101, 111, 143, 144, 189

Safranski, Rüdiger, 42, 68n13, 91
Salaquarda, Jörg, 59n2, 61n6, 65n11
Salomé, Lou, 3
Schacht, Richard, 2
Schiller, Friedrich, 70, 182
Schopenhauer, Arthur, 1, 4n13, 7, 8, 12, 22, 23n4, 25, 39, 45n9, 53, 61n6, 71, 111–13, 128, 162, 163, 164, 177, 189, 201, 221, 222, 225, 226, 227
Schubert, Franz, 214
Schumann, Robert, 214
Shakespeare, William, 70, 182
Simonides, 70
Small, Robin, 5, 6, 24n7, 230
socialism, 18, 95–6, 129, 139–41, 147, 187, 216, 219–21
Socrates, 27, 33, 94, 124, 196, 197–9, 203, 210, 212n12, 222
Solon, 93
Sophocles, 182
Spinoza, Baruch, 74, 142, 154, 189
stadial view of history, 72–3, 78, 97
state, the, 9, 18, 39, 98, 129–30, 136, 138–40, 141, 142, 143, 145, 148, 177, 186, 196, 206, 207, 208, 217, 218
Sterne, Laurence, 173, 182
style, 3–5, 16n34, 47n10, 159, 164, 210–12, 214
suicide, 199n9, 218–19

Theocritus, 182

vanity, 47, 76, 96, 100, 102, 105, 120, 127, 131, 134, 140, 154, 161, 164–5, 167, 185, 186, 192, 201, 202, 228

Vattimo, Gianni, 7
Vauvenargues, Luc, 212, 227
Voltaire, 8–10, 70, 77, 78–9,
   130, 143, 144, 159–60,
   173, 186, 225

Wagner, Cosima, 1, 25, 120n9
Wagner, Richard, 1, 2n4,
   12, 13, 25, 71, 73–4, 76,
   79, 120n9, 175–8, 180,
   181n21, 214n13, 215–16

war, 18, 20, 129, 136,
   144, 146–7, 170, 216,
   217–19
wealth, 135, 187–8, 221

Young, Julian, 1n1, 6, 13,
   14n33, 20, 43n6, 44n8,
   49n13, 59n3, 61, 68,
   79, 94n16, 139n15,
   158, 179n20, 191,
   199–200, 215